FALSE FIXES

SUNY Series, Teacher Empowerment and School Reform
Henry A. Giroux and Peter L. McLaren, Editors

FALSE FIXES

The Cultural Politics of Drugs, Alcohol, and Addictive Relations

DAVID FORBES

State University
of New York
Press

Published by
State University of New York Press, Albany

© 1994   State University of New York

All rights reserved

Production by Susan Geraghty
Marketing by Fran Keneston

Printed in the United States of America

For information, address State University of New York Press,
State University Plaza, Albany, N.Y., 12246

Library of Congress Cataloging-in-Publication Data

Forbes, David, 1949–
       False fixes : the cultural politics of drugs, alcohol, and
addictive relations / David Forbes.
               p.   cm. — (SUNY series. Teacher empowerment and school
reform)
       Includes bibliographical references and index.
       ISBN 0–7914–1995–9 (alk. paper). — ISBN 0–7914–1996–7 (pbk. : alk.
paper)
       1. Substance abuse—Social aspects—United States. 2. Compulsive
behavior—Social aspects—United States. 3. Postmodernism—Social
aspects. 4. Culture. I. Title. II. Series: Teacher empowerment
and school reform.
HV4999.2.F67   1994
362.29'0973—dc20   93–34537
                                                                           CIP

10 9 8 7 6 5 4 3 2 1

The impalpable sustenance of me from all things at all
    hours of the day,
The simple, compact, well-join'd scheme, myself
    disintegrated, every one disintegrated yet part of the
    scheme,
The similitudes of the past and those of the future

Walt Whitman, *Crossing Brooklyn Ferry*

CONTENTS

PROLOGUE

Drug and alcohol abuse and addictive relations are major issues in our time. Every day many Americans must face them in one form or another, from the fear of drug-related crime to the difficulty of living or having grown up with an alcoholic or substance abuser. I wrote this book to try to make sense out of the various theoretical and political cross-currents swirling about these problems.

Of late there has been no shortage of practical solutions from diverse sources aimed at ridding society of substance abuse and addictions. These include the government's war on drugs, school-based drug abuse prevention programs, progressive political strategies, and the twelve-step recovery movement. Yet as a prevention professional, educator, and citizen committed to personal and political change, I have been dissatisfied with these approaches to varying degrees. Each seems to be missing a crucial piece of understanding about the nature of the problem and, at least in the case of the drug war, may do more harm than good.

For this reason I aim to address not only the broad educated readership concerned with the drug issue, but also public policy makers, professionals in substance abuse prevention, education, and public health fields, political progressives, and those in the recovery movement.

POLICY MAKERS

The government has responded to some degree to many Americans' concerns over health and safety issues stemming from both legal and illegal drug use. It has challenged tobacco and alcohol companies for pushing their products on vulnerable sectors of the population and has funded community prevention programs throughout the country. However, its major priority has been to try to reduce the supply and use of illegal drugs and street dealing through interdiction. I join with others critical of the so-called war on drugs led by the federal government and various corporate interests. The attempt to fix the problem of illegal drug use primarily through law enforcement, mandatory drug tests of workers, and the ban on the supply of drugs is a misdirected, harsh, and addictive measure itself which depends on force and hypocrisy. The war on drugs has never asked why so many people in this society need to take drugs in the first place; it only seeks to make the issue go away. It seems that policy makers cannot afford to ask why since the answers might implicate many in power who profit from the traffic in legal and illegal drugs.

MENTAL HEALTH PREVENTION PROFESSIONALS AND EDUCATORS

Drug abuse prevention professionals and educators have helped students and community residents through counseling and teaching individual skills to strengthen their ability to resist drug abuse. Yet this approach is insufficient and does not get at the broader issues. As a professional working within the field of school-based drug abuse prevention for nine years, I have been frustrated with the field's lack of political and cultural analysis of the problem. Although prevention does try to ask why people abuse alcohol and drugs, the answers it gives tend to be inadequate to the complexities of the dilemma. I find most of the approaches tend to rely on a view of the individual and the community rendered obsolete by dramatic changes in the culture of everyday life, changes which affect the nature of work, the family, schooling, and other relations. Despite a stated interest in students' everyday life, the prevention field is racing to catch up with the way the electronic media and other forms of technology have transformed the nature of childhood and the way children and adults now acquire information and interact with each other.

PROGRESSIVES

The Left has criticized state and corporate power for pushing drugs and for deploying the war on drugs as a means of social control of poor and working people. It has provided important political economic analyses of the drug trade and has argued that drug trafficking and addiction are symptomatic of impoverished social conditions. Yet the Left regards drug taking and people's efforts to fight substance abuse as secondary effects of more significant forces, which minimizes the everyday nature of addictive relations and dismisses the progressive elements of the antidrug movement. Such acts are important on their own terms and are part of how people make their own culture. The Left is often unaware or dismissive of addictive patterns and problems within its *own* practices and derisive of people's need to address these issues which they do not frame in traditionally political terms.

RECOVERING ADULTS

The burgeoning twelve-step recovery movement has helped spread awareness about the nature of substance abuse and its impact on family relations and childhood development and has popularized the term *addiction* throughout society. It has offered help to millions of people who are stuck in troubled patterns of behavior. Yet the recovery movement has ignored the cultural politics of everyday life and offers recovery through the twelve steps as an all-encompassing solution to people's troubled relationships. It turns a deaf ear to an analysis of power and control, which the Left and the women's movement have developed around issues such as the nature of work, the family, and gender relations. It does not seek to engage in dialogue or debate around a politics of addiction and control but instead tends to rely on a totalistic approach which abandons critical thinking, an addictive approach itself.

In this book I offer an alternative analysis of the issues of drug and alcohol use, addictive relations, prevention, and recovery from the standpoint of the cultural politics of everyday life. Addictive relations occur when people do not experience themselves and others as being accepted for who they are. Addictive patterns then are characterized by the loss of control to one form of relation and the denial of a full range of experience. When people abuse substances or become addicted to one form of relating, they are trying but failing to meet certain of their needs; these are false fixes. These addictive patterns are natural to a culture which itself values control over the self and others and denies crucial aspects of everyday experience.

Drug and alcohol use are part of American culture. However, for this reason there is no simple fix which can rid America of them, nor should there be. Prevention and recovery approaches which try to eradicate drugs and alcohol or attempt to substitute one form of an all-encompassing idea or relation for another without challenging the addictive political cultural relations themselves are, like drugs, also false fixes.

It follows that in order to prevent the practices of substance abuse and addiction the culture needs to move away from arbitrary power relations of control and denial and toward the accessibility of power and knowledge for all. To an extent this is occurring as the United States is moving from a modernist to a postmodern culture. I argue that it is within the ground of postmodern culture that an effective radical approach to addiction which includes progressive aspects of modernism can and should develop. In postmodern culture technology and new modes of information through the electronic media transform social relations and the nature of knowledge and power. The self now enters into a relation with objects within everyday life through cultural signs in such a way that each interpenetrates the other. Yet the new cultural forms still allow for the addictive processes of control and denial, and addiction takes on different forms.

The task of a radical cultural politics of addictive relations is to explore and contest addictive forms of everyday life and to help create new expressive selves within fluid relations.

The book divides into four parts and an epilogue. The Introduction, "Addictive America," defines the cultural politics of addictive relations. The starting point for this analysis is the current drug trade, the supply and demand of both legal and illegal drugs. I argue that although the Right seized the initiative in the cultural political front with the war on drugs, the failures of the war have led to increased awareness of the broader nature of the problem. The problem lies more with addictive relations than just drugs themselves, and there is growing interest in exploring addictive cultural patterns, prevention, and recovery from addiction within the society as a whole. I show why conservative, liberal, and leftist approaches to addictive relations, as modernist political narratives, are not adequate to the task and suggest the need to look at postmodern everyday culture as the groundwork for a radical cultural politics.

I argue that everyday culture is the ground on which people

make their own history and is a contradictory realm governed by cultural signs. It is this postmodern culture, with its implicit critique of modernist addictive patterns, which allows for the possibility of a cultural politics which challenges addiction and promotes self-expression through fluid forms of relations.

The second part, "Culture," describes everyday culture in terms of its addictive qualities. In Chapter 2, "Tripping through the Ruins," I argue that essential areas of modernist life, work, family, school, and the state have changed radically in recent years. As a result of changes in technology and the spread of the electronic media, a postmodern culture is emerging. Modernist institutions, values, and relations no longer can be relied upon as structures on which to build a foundation for prevention and recovery for youth and adults. In each area the changes affect substance abuse and the attempts to control it.

Chapter 3, "Control and Denial," explores these characteristics of addiction in both modernist and postmodern culture. In modernism, control and denial are manifest through hierarchical structures such as the alcoholic family, the workplace, and other bureaucracies, and through the consumption of commodities considered as missing parts of the self to which the self can become addicted. I describe a play of Sam Shepard, *Curse of the Starving Class,* about an alcoholic family, and also examine the addictive nature of the tabloid comics as holdovers of modernist relations.

I then contrast modernist forms of control and denial with postmodern ones. *Control* now means appropriating signs and information in order to constitute the self anew. *Denial* refers to information which those in power withhold and predefine. The electronic media allow for the interchange of signs in ways which are themselves druglike. Addiction now means a self which is saturated with one fixed sign and which has lost its fluid, relational nature. I explore the phenomenon of the cyborg as a postmodern self which is a changing identity that is neither entirely natural or artificial. The cyborg poses the issue of whether control in postmodern culture can be used to enslave people within addictive relations or can be used as a means to bring together pleasure, knowledge, and power for the purpose of mutual enhancement.

Chapter 4, "Everyday Highs," discusses how activities such as music and sports, touted by antidrug campaigns as alternatives to drugs, are often linked with drugs and can themselves become addictive expressions tranformed through the electronic media.

The media allow for an interchange between fans and performers in such a way that fans have greater control over how they choose to relate to the performers, while the subjectivity of the performers is dispersed within the fans. In the music section I explore the relation between drugs and music and how, for example, music can be used like a drug. In terms of sports I examine the relation between drugs and athletics and as an example discuss the alcoholic system of Billy Martin and George Steinbrenner. I then look at the electronic media themselves and their role in the government- and corporate-sponsored war on drugs. I show how certain corporate interests use the media like a drug in an attempt to control people in a number of ways, including inviting the viewers to identify with the ads.

The third part, "Prevention," focuses on school-based prevention programs aimed at children and adolescents as well as parent and community programs. In Chapter 5, "The Self," I critique the cognitive/affective dichotomy prevalent in education and argue for redefining the concept of *self-development,* which is the primary goal of traditional drug and alcohol abuse prevention. Modernist prevention professionals tend to regard the buildup of an autonomous self, the task of adolescence, as the best safeguard against becoming addicted to drugs or alcohol. I contrast four modernist assumptions about the adolescent development of an autonomous self with the way the self now appears within postmodern culture. These are the need to have solid, stable adults and institutions, the need to govern feelings, the need for self-esteem, and the need to resist peer pressure. In each area I argue that the self now assumes a relational nature through the impact of the electronic media and through the interaction with popular culture. The modernist model of self-development is inadequate and must be reframed in alternative ways of which I provide examples.

Chapter 6, "School-Basing," further describes the goals and strategies of traditional prevention programs, which are based on a medical model that employs the concept of autonomous selves who are at risk of addiction. I argue that most prevention programs aim to change individuals without examining the troublesome relations in which the self is defined. I examine a number of state-of-the-art prevention programs and curricula in some detail in order to underscore their modernist assumptions.

Chapter 7, "(Po)Mo' Better Prevention," makes a case for a prevention approach which challenges addictive relations in both modernist and postmodern cultures. It builds on the implicit critique of modernist addictive relations within postmodern culture, in particular the privileged use of knowledge and power to control others and to restrict self-expression. It employs a relational perspective which makes use of the electronic media and other aspects of popular culture. However, it also draws on modernist processes of critical thought. I describe a number of programs, such as relationship literacy and a classroom project I worked on with young African-American males. I also describe parent and community prevention programs in light of their capacity to enhance power and knowledge for all.

Part 4, "Recovery," consists of Chapter 8, "Adult Children/Inner Child." In the first section I describe my own mixed experience attending some twelve-step meetings as a way to explore some of the contradictory aspects of the recovery movement. I find the movement to be helpful as a critique of everyday relations in which people feel compelled to control others and to deny truthful experiences. But it is limited in developing these themes in a critical way which can affect broader aspects of everyday culture, and also tends to fall into absolute patterns which are themselves addictive. I suggest a way to reconstrue some of the positive elements of the recovery program as part of a broader radical cultural politics which regards recovery from addictive relations as a political and educational process as well.

In the second section I look at the popular metaphor of the inner child as representative of some people's need to heal themselves from troublesome family and childhood relations as well as a positive sign of more direct, expressive ways of being. I consider the inner child image in movies and popular culture and interpret a play and a movie which depict it, Sam Shepard's *Buried Child,* and the 1990 movie *Rainman.*

The Epilogue sketches the contours of a radical cultural politics of addictive relations in postmodern culture.

BUT ENOUGH ABOUT YOU

In postmodern fashion I must state that this book reflects my own limited, partial perspective and is not an attempt to provide one universal viewpoint valid for all. To play with a popular phrase, as an adult chyld [*sic*] of a dysfunctional society I am a recovering white, heterosexual, professional, able-bodied, male baby boomer and New Yorker. By "recovering" I mean I try to be aware of how my privileged and particular identities unwittingly have shaped my thinking and behavior in a society which arbitrarily rewards certain attributes and discriminates against others.

But despite my self-awareness and my efforts to be inclusive, this book will necessarily reflect my own biases and preferences. I have based it on my experiences within the prevention field as well as on my interpretation of popular sources of information. These include that stuffy doyen of American newspapers, the *New York Times*, an establishment organ but useful if read in the right light (high intensity) and to which I remain addicted. I realize this book may not do full justice to the specific ways substance abuse and addictions affect African-Americans, Latinos, Native Americans, women, gays and lesbians, the physically challenged, psychiatric patients, many working-class people, and numerous other groups who must grapple with these issues every day. I also do not address important related topical issues, such as HIV transmission through heroin needles, crack babies, fetal alcohol syndrome, and other problems involving medical treatment.

Rather than serve as a how-to guide or a treatise with one overarching theme, I hope this book can function something akin to a scaffold on which people can come along and hang their own theoretical and practical designs, or something like a bridge which allows others to cross over toward their own destination.

I identify to an extent with Russell Jacoby as a nonacademic intellectual (in *The Last Intellectuals*). Like him, I was neither aided by foundations nor university grants, nor can I thank research assistants, graduate students, or any sort of advanced study center for a year of support.

I can, however, acknowledge a number of people who helped me at various times with this book. I would like to thank my colleagues at the Brooklyn Diocese Drug Abuse Prevention Program for their support, as well as the teachers and parents with whom I have worked. In particular, Julia McEvoy, Nancy Roberts, Judith Schiller-Rabi, Garda Spaulding, Liz Syracuse and Vivian Theurer read various parts at various stages and provided me with helpful feedback. Thanks also to readers A and B.

I send my thanks to all my friends near and far for their love and acceptance while I worked on the book. Jonathan Back, Richard Friesner, Meredith Kassoy, David Wagner, and Donna

Glee Williams helped me with specific suggestions for the text along the way.

I am grateful to Janet Mittman, with whom I shared many ideas, who offered much support, and who taught me a lot in the way of personal and pedagogical knowledge. I am also indebted to Lynn Chancer, who provided me with considerable encouragement, intellectual stimulation, and the title of the book.

To Stanley Aronowitz, the *iskra* (spark) for this project, I am especially thankful. With a few initial words of encouragement, a willingness to go to bat for me when I needed it, and an infinite reservoir of creative and rigorous ideas from which to draw, he gave me the confidence to see the book through.

I am grateful to Henry Giroux and Peter McLaren, whose enthusiasm for this project, along with that of my editor, Priscilla Ross, meant a great deal to me. Giroux and McLaren have been beacons of inspiration since I discovered their writings in the dark days of the Reagan years, and it is an honor to be included in their series. Priscilla Ross guided me through this process with a firm but gentle hand, skilled in handling the writer's ego as well as a manuscript. Her support has been immeasurable.

Finally, I am thankful to my entire family. I feel blessed to have them all around.

I dedicate this book to my parents with love.

PART 1

Introduction

CHAPTER 1

Addictive America

And where will we take our pleasure
when our bodies have been denied?
Richard Fariña, "Children of Darkness"

To say that America is an addictive society is to risk saying nothing by saying too much. After all, to indict an entire nation as ill may be just another standard jeremiad against the consumer-junkie culture, the kind followed by the customary demand for total social transformation. So we live in a commodity society whose citizens crave techno-fixes for everything and who overdose on cars and designer sneakers. Are we then supposed to forsake our hard-earned comforts and return to a simpler world? Just as bad, to declare everyone an addict may be even more psychobabble about people's compulsive, self-indulgent habits in need of the one true cure from the latest self-help regimen. Suppose there are millions of drug abusers, alcoholics, compulsive gamblers, workaholics, love addicts, and other dependent types in the USA. Must everyone then plunge into recovery groups and chant twelve-step slogans?

If we say that the whole society is addicted, or that everyone is addicted to something, then the term *addiction* loses its meaning. Why then insist on the portentous claim that America is an addictive society? What could I be saying that still makes sense?

I am arguing for the need to see addiction as a form of social relations, and to see addictive relations as a form of cultural politics. *Addiction* as I use it here is not a medical term for a disease but refers to certain everyday ways of relating. It is neither a catchword for the consumer culture nor strictly a behavioral label, although the locus of the body as a contested site of addiction is often crucial. Rather, addiction is a troublesome quality of how people try to meet their personal, everyday needs for plea-

3

sure and sociability (culture) and which has to do with power and control (politics).

Addictions are false fixes, poor substitutes for genuine, mutually satisfying relations. They characterize a culture in which people neither affirm others nor are affirmed themselves as valued beings in their own right. As a consequence, in addictive relations people lose their sensuous, fluid nature and the flexibility to maintain connectedness within shifting contexts and become fixed or dependent on one form of expression. These relations are marked by loss of choice and mutuality, with control given over instead to some substance, thing, activity, thought, or other person. In these patterns people need to control themselves and others at the expense of spontaneity or choice. As such they display rigid, all-or-nothing qualities in everyday activities. In order to maintain control, people must deny knowledge of conflicting needs, feelings, or viewpoints. The effort to overcome addictive relations, both in interpersonal terms and on the level of political institutions, and to gain satisfying ones is part of what I mean by "cultural politics."

A key point about addictive relations as cultural politics, then, is that they have both personal and political dimensions. The personal aspect involves the desire for pleasure, power, and security. This effort centers on the right to experience the sensuous nature of the body and the attempt to find satisfying relations other than through substance abuse or compulsive shopping, working, control of others, or other activities which take over a person's life. It also means the effort to overcome denial and to recognize and accept contradictory voices and perspectives which run counter to the one form of expression on which a person has become fixed.

The political side addresses the issue of power within organizations as well as in interpersonal relations. Many addictive relations are marked by the attempt to control others, since the loss of control is what the addict fears most. But the attempt to overcome addiction includes the battle to democratize all forms of everyday life, to give up arbitrary control over others and allow for unspoken voices which have been denied. This includes the fight to access relevant knowledge and power for all in everyday places like the family, the school, the community, and the state and to enjoy self-enhancing everyday relations.

A progressive cultural politics, then, insists on both the right to sensuous pleasure and the necessity of democratic processes which increase power and knowledge for all. It regards compulsive control over the self and others, and the denial of essential knowledge about the self and others, as both personal and political problems which must be contested. It demands a vision of freely determined, fluid, everyday relations in which people give and receive love and are accepted for who they are.

This book is about cultural patterns and not just about drugs, alcohol, and substance abuse. Yet it is necessary to first examine the role of drugs to understand the broader issue. The recent concern with drugs has sparked an intense and divisive political cultural struggle which has implicated traditional patterns of social life. The crisis has mobilized strong responses such as the federal war on drugs and a new antidrug movement across different sectors of society. These responses have exposed deep moral differences within American society over the politics of pleasure and the nature of relations within the family, school, the workplace, the media, and the society at large. I will first argue that drugs, although they appear to be a separate, isolated issue, are part and parcel of the cultural makeup of daily life, and are the historical and conceptual starting point for a study of addictive relations and the elaboration of a progressive cultural politics.

The impetus for the concern over addiction is the current drug crisis, brought about by the marketing of crack cocaine and the ensuing federal war on drugs that began in the 1980s. Cocaine as both powder and crack, a cheap, accessible, and concentrated form, has harmed the lives of many people, ranging from babies of addicted mothers in the inner cities to professionals, athletes, and entertainers. In cities poor people of color have suffered the most from the illegal drug trade. Users go untreated, young men swell the jails, innocent children are killed in gang war crossfire, and community life is decimated by crime as terrorized residents fear venturing outside their homes. Illegal drug use affects disenfranchised people in other significant ways. Heroin users become infected with the HIV virus by sharing contaminated needles, and the virus spreads through sex with partners or through prostitution among some crack and heroin addicts. The drug crisis has affected the entire society as well, not just in terms of the personal anguish of substance abuse across different classes but also through the increased cost of health care, mental health services, productivity loss, and crime. Yet drugs, which include the drug alcohol, are not some foreign plot or domestic anomaly but are an integral part of the social fabric.

DRUGS: THE DANGLING THREAD

We often speak of everyday life as a social fabric, an interwoven texture of relations which gets us through the day. Within that weave the drug problem appears at first like a dangling thread, a glaring annoyance silhouetted against the curtains, a nagging waif orphaned from a favorite sweater. During the day we will catch a headline about a drug bust, watch a news story about crack mothers, read about a controversial drug on the market, or over-hear that a professional athlete was arrested for drunk driving. Meanwhile we may have to deal with an alcoholic family member, wake up from one too many hangovers ourselves, find that one sleeping pill no longer does the trick, start craving the next cup of coffee sooner in the morning, or vow again to quit smok-ing. Because of our need to focus on getting through the day, we seldom are able to take the one step back which might allow us to identify the recurrent patterns in the social fabric. It is not until we begin to pull at the thread that is the drug problem that we discover that the cloth or garment starts unraveling; it is all of a piece, and the problem is conjoined with the weave itelf. In this society we learn to count on drugs of all kinds as substitutes for a lack of power, security, and self-acceptance, and sometimes it leads to abuse. Drugs are part of everyday life, not just the lives of the Others out there, but of ours as well.

Drug abuse and the entire drug economy are not the simple effects of a foreign import, a thinglike evil from beyond which can be eradicated; nor are they some aberrant, cancerlike disease growing within which can be isolated and extracted. Rather, drugs are part of the sinews and marrow of the everyday itself. The terms borrowed from business and applied to the drug trade, *supply* and *demand*, are telling: drugs are commodities like every-thing else. The supply side refers to making and promoting drugs and getting them to people. The demand side refers to people's desire to consume drugs.

Supply Side

The production, promotion, and distribution of drugs, both legal and illegal, follow the same dynamics as the manufacture, adver-tising, and circulation of all profitable commodities in society. Suppliers are not just drug kingpins and henchmen of the Colombian Medellin cartel; pushers are not just shifty-eyed men lurking near schoolyards. Suppliers are business dealers who provide both legal and illegal drugs for profit, and live in rural towns as well as big cities. They include farmers who grow marijuana, which is a major cash crop in some areas.[1] They include church leaders, neighborhood watch captains, children, and the elderly, all of whom drug enforcement agents discovered to be home manufacturers of methamphetamine.[2] They also include government officials who have condoned international drug trafficking which supplies and distributes illegal drugs such as heroin and cocaine from third world countries to inner-city neighborhoods.[3]

The cocaine trade yields huge profits. It is bound up with large-scale legal banking interests which have benefited from the booming drug market.[4] The money from laundering drug profits is worth as much to the world banking system as is the trade in oil, an estimated $300 billion a year. Banks earn significant sums

Reprinted with permission from Robert Grossman,
The Nation, January 1, 1990.

of interest even on one day's holding because of the volume; as electronic money transfers have expanded in speed and volume, drug dealers and some banks can hide vast sums of illegal drug profits.[5] Because so much of mainstream society traffics in drugs, the difference between good and bad drug pushers and between good and bad drugs often becomes blurred. From the business perspective of many Americans, drugs are part of daily life. In urban neighborhoods dealers and drug runners are often children who earn money for the family, and users may be a neighbor, friend, or relative.

Illegal drug producing and trafficking threaten the profits of legal drug producers like the pharmaceutical, tobacco, and liquor industries. The pharmaceutical industry is one of the country's most lucrative businesses.[6] It makes and promotes drugs which promise a quick fix for every pain or problem and help people get back to functioning in the workaday world. Many of the drugs aim to alleviate symptoms of stress which stem from job-related and other everyday problems of living in a competitive, capitalist culture.[7] They include pills for headaches, insomnia, fatigue, backaches, muscular pain, and upset stomach. Prescription pills for ulcers and hypertension, also symptoms of stress, yield sales of $1 billion or more each year. In 1993 the federal government issued a report critical of the pharmaceuticals for charging exhorbitant prices for drugs. The industry countered that the profits go into further research; yet much of the money goes into marketing, and most marketed drugs are just different commercial versions of the same sleeping pill or tranquilizer.[8]

Drug companies affect people's lives in profound ways. They feed on people's anxiety about their attractiveness and competitive edge as marketable commodities themselves. By saturating the media with ads, they promise consumers success through the purchase of deodorants, mouthwash, shampoos, blemish cremes, hair growth chemicals, and cosmetics. Pharmaceuticals also sell drugs to the medical trade to control and adjust difficult groups, for example, Haldol for nursing home residents, Thorazine for psychiatric patients, Methadone for heroin addicts, Ritalin for children diagnosed as hyperactive, and diet pills (amphetamines), Valium, antidepressants, and other psychotropic drugs for functioning outpatients.

As partners with the drug companies, doctors and those in the medical industry promote drugs as a remedy for almost every symptom. They hand out more prescriptions to women than to men, and for this reason many women have problems with addiction to prescription pills such as Valium.[9] Psychiatric residents, mostly poor and working class, are heavily medicated in order to make them more manageable.[10] Elderly people warehoused in nursing homes also are sometimes overmedicated into docility. A series of studies showed that nursing homes short of staff gave antipsychotic drugs to residents not diagnosed as psychotic as a form of "chemical restraint" to manage difficult behavior and without the informed consent of the person or his or her relatives.[11] An executive of the American Psychological Association called the problem of overmedication and mismedication of older people the nation's "other drug problem."[12]

The federal government protects drug companies from illegal competitors and criminalizes drug traffickers in part because they compete with the legal promoters and cut into their profits.[13] The government also helps drug companies generate new markets for legal drugs. For example, when the United States pressured Japan to remove its trade barriers against cigarette imports, cigarette advertisements that target women and the young increased.[14] Since the 1960s the government has subsidized drug companies through Medicaid reimbursements and research grants.[15] During the Reagan/Bush war on drugs the Anti-Drug Abuse Act of Congress appropriated money for pharmaceutical companies to develop drugs which are supposed to block cocaine craving.[16]

The cozy bond between the drug industry and the government, along with the large sum of money to be made in 1989, led to a number of drug companies pleading guilty to bribing Food and Drug Administration (FDA) officials and to producing inadequate generic drugs—cheaper, supposedly equivalent versions of patented, name-brand products. Companies which get their generic form approved first after a drug comes off patent can gain enormous profits.[17] Because pharmaceuticals oversee themselves with limited FDA control, consumers in 1991 questioned the safety of the antidepressant Halcion and silicone breast implants. Abroad, American drug companies push drugs which the government bans as unsafe onto third world markets in Mexico and Malaysia and sell drugs with labels that omit important medical information in other developing countries.[18]

The liquor and cigarette industries are aggressive promoters and suppliers of the drugs alcohol and nicotine. The tobacco busi-

ness is heavily subsidized by the federal government and competes
with illegal drug producers. It has pursued new markets for years.
My father, a World War II veteran, tells how he and many other
men became addicted to cigarettes during the war when the army
gave out free packs. When I worked on a chronic psychiatric ward
in the 1970s nearly all the male patients, already heavily medicated, were addicted to cigarettes, since they were passed out like
candy. The industry has targeted poor and uneducated people of
color who are more likely to suffer stress, has marketed products
geared to them (such as the ill-fated cigarette Uptown), and has
placed more tobacco ads on billboards in black communities and
magazines.[19] It may be no accident that a higher percentage of
African-Americans smoke cigarettes and that their lung cancer rate
has increased four times faster than that of whites in the last thirty
years; with respect to liquor intake, black men have a 70 percent
higher death rate from cirrhosis of the liver than whites.[20] Yet the
drug companies also invest in endeavors important to people of
color. The tobacco industry is a big contributor to the Congressional Black Caucus Foundation and the Congressional Hispanic
Caucus Institute, and Philip Morris and RJR Nabisco donate significant amounts to the Alvin Ailey Dance Company, the National
Urban League, the NAACP, and the United Negro College Fund.[21]

The legal drug companies also target women, children, and
citizens of third world countries. Tobacco companies have aimed
at women with new products like Dakota and at young consumers through an effective cartoon character for Camel cigarettes.[22] Coors beer focused on women in an ad campaign, and
the liquor industry tapped into the youth market by pushing wine
coolers and forty-ounce malt liquor, favored by an increasing
number of inner-city African-American and Latino youth, some
who call it "liquid crack."[23] Wine coolers are popular among
children, who consider them to be like a soft drink and who find
them easy to purchase. Aggressive ad campaigns for malt liquor,
an accessible, cheap, quick, and powerful high, have won over
many teens, who drink it along with smoking marijuana. In the
face of new temperance trends at home, tobacco companies have
expanded into third world countries and have contributed to an
increase in smokers in Asia.[24] American beer companies as well
have developed a thirst for new international markets because of
declining domestic alcohol use and have expanded rapidly into
alcohol markets in developing nations.[25]

In short, the government has tried to restrict the supply side of drugs. Yet it becomes clear why this strategy fails: the government is implicated in the drug trade, and drugs, both legal and illegal, are too profitable a commodity for too many people.

Demand Side

All kinds of people want drugs of all kinds, including alcohol, nicotine, caffeine, prescription pills, and illegal substances. It is important to acknowledge that people take drugs because they perceive the benefits of the drugs and not because they wish to harm themselves. In a competitive society which does not affirm the basic dignity of each person, Americans take drugs to medicate themselves for feelings of insecurity, sorrow, pain, anger, boredom, or just to become numb. But in other cases they do so to relax, escape, play, be sociable, feel powerful, enhance and expand their consciousness, partake in religious rituals, and enrich their experience on sexual, emotional, spiritual, and intellectual levels. Certain drug taking embodies the palpable desire for transcendence, enlightenment, surrender, joy, connectedness, and sensuality. At other times taking drugs is a means to resist and rebel against restrictive and controlling social forces. Those who use drugs are not simply criminal, immoral, or sick people. Poor people of color in the inner city get the most press on the ravages of crack use, but the majority of crack users are white, and users, as well as alcoholics, include people in small towns, suburban youth, women at home, wage earners, doctors, and corporate executives.[26] The fact that some successful people abuse drugs flies in the face of the myth many tell to children that hard work and achievement are rewarding activities in and of themselves and are sufficient substitutes for drug highs. It undermines the belief that it is poverty per se that causes drug abuse.

The experience of the cast of *A Chorus Line* is an apt example. The musical, the longest-running show in Broadway history, was about dancers who audition for a godlike casting director to whom they must disclose their vulnerabilities as a requirement for winning the part. The story is a good metaphor for the individualistic, competitive, and compulsive quest for success for which just a lucky few in this culture are chosen, and which can lead to drug use as a means to deal with the stress. It happens that in real life "A Chorus Line" was a coke line; the choreographer, Michael

Bennett, and many in the cast were heavily involved in drugs, moving from Valium, uppers, and marijuana to cocaine.[27] Others in high-powered jobs, such as corporate executives, top government officials, lawyers, professional athletes, and entertainers who work long hours, feel pressure to make important decisions and to perform in public. Since they cannot afford to feel unsure or show signs of stress, they use coke to stay on top of incommensurate feelings of self-doubt and low self-worth. Then to come down from the pressures, some combine alcohol with Valium, a benzodiazepine tranquilizer. President Reagan's aide, Michael Deaver, Reagan's national security advisor, Robert C. McFarlane, and President Gerald Ford's wife, Betty, all experienced trouble with these two drugs, and many responsible job holders in Washington, D.C., also rely on this mixture.[28]

Others with less glamorous jobs also medicate themselves to help deal with the daily grind. In some cases stimulants such as cocaine and speed can increase workers' productivity and sharpen performance and do not always lead to workplace problems.[29] Before the recent war on drugs some companies were encouraging workers to avail themselves of Darvon, Valium, and speed in order to help them get through the day and increase productivity.[30] In one government study in the early 1980s, supervisors estimated that 15 to 20 percent of their employees were regular marijuana users and reported that the usage did not have a negative effect on job performance.[31] Millions of working people still smoke cigarettes, and alcohol use has a long history of being part of working men's time away from work. When I worked as a union organizer with blue-collar workers, beer drinking was an integral part of the organizing meetings and rallies. Around 10 percent of the work force has an alcohol problem. The high incidence of abuse among railroad workers, for example, stems from isolation and boredom.[32]

Unemployed workers go through a different kind of stress from anxiety over finances, depression from lack of meaningful activity, and low self-esteem from feelings of worthlessness. As a consequence, they show an increase in alcohol intake, cigarette smoking, and drug use.[33] The armed forces, a different kind of reserve army of labor, has had disciplinary problems with military personnel who have abused drugs and alcohol, not only during the Vietnam War but also with soldiers stationed in Europe. A recent exception was the Persian Gulf War, where soldiers were unable to secure alcohol. Yet alcohol abuse in the military does not occur only among the rank and file. At the 1991 Tailhook Association convention in Las Vegas, over one hundred naval officers were implicated in drunken acts of sexual harrasment and assault; a number of them lied to the investigators about the events.[34]

Drug taking can reorganize a person's time and fill the emptiness of a fragmented sense of self and disintegrated community life. Some people feel more whole and connected from drug use and gain a sense of meaning rather than one of disorganization.[35] For example, suburban women on Long Island, New York, who prostitute themselves for crack arrange their lives around the drug; they meet Johns, hang out with friends, and engage in routines of street life.[36] Drugs like cocaine activate and concentrate desire and power in the form of the body, which has become a dislocated source of subjectivity. By invoking quick changes, they may bring one in synch with the emerging cultural trend toward instant identity shifts.

For many teens and adults as well, alcohol and crack serve as substitutes for self-esteem because these and other drugs medicate for painful feelings. Heroin, sometimes called "mother," envelops the user with a feeling of being loved. In some middle-class circles in the early 1990s the antidepressant drug Prozac became a chic drug which its users swore by.[37] Some suburban youth get drunk at keggers to allieviate boredom and anxiety; their parents deny the substance abuse and are relieved that at least their children are not into crack.[38] This occurs despite the fact that alcohol-related accidents like drunk driving are a major cause of deaths among young adults. Many young athletes as well as professionals take dangerous steroids to build up their bodies in order to better compete. A significant number of youth inhale paint and other everyday household substances in order to get high, often because they are bored or in pain.

The compulsive demand for drugs today reflects the consumptive nature of everyday life. The consumer culture itself has druglike qualities. The act of consumption, with its druglike cycle of desire, tolerance, withdrawal, and renewed demand, now exists for its own sake, detached from production and material necessity. The electronic media, like drugs, are capable of generating fantasy, simulation, or denial of experience in an instant. People consume drugs as one more quick, commodified way to solve problems, to ease their pain, to get through the day, or just for their own sake, often inducing the need for a bigger, better product after the high wears off.

In today's culture drug use also can be a way to resist participating in the cycle of productivity and leisure. In the process of capital accumulation, time is an abstract measure of orderly, structured work in which management regards the last hour of the day as the same unit of output as the first, despite the worker's fatigue at the end of the day.[39] But certain drugs affect the sense of past and future as well as the length of an interlude and break up the narrative of capitalist time. Marijuana allows for an elasticity of time in contrast to the kind employers use during work: spent time, time as money. Cocaine highs may reflect the cultural style of the short frames and sudden time shifts which rupture linear narratives. This kind of resistance is not political in the traditional sense but may contribute to disrupting the structure of social control itself.[40]

In sum, the demand for drugs as a means of self-medication and pleasure includes both legal and illegal drugs and is not different in kind from the compulsive pattern of all commodity consumption in this society.

ADDICTION AS CULTURAL POLITICS

I have argued that both legal and illegal drugs are stitched into the everyday social fabric. The drug issue serves as a starting point for the broader concern over everyday addictive relations within a commodified culture. One way people show an addiction is to crave the effect of a drug. They take the drug because it produces the feelings of acceptance, comfort, or power they are not otherwise getting in a quick and easy way. They may then develop an increased tolerance for the effect and need to keep taking it when the feelings diminish. Yet this pattern is not the only social form addiction takes. The substance abuse field points out that addictions are patterns of relating. They are characterized by all-or-nothing thinking, by perfectionism, and by the need to control some thought, thing, or person. The need to control is often manifest by its opposite, feeling out of control and enslaved to one form of expression. Another key characteristic is the denial of salient information, including the person's own needs and feelings and those of others. These addictive patterns are patterns of this culture as a whole.

Culture is the medium in which we grow up and through which we learn to express and meet our everyday personal and social needs; culture also frames the meaning of a problem. In the words of two addiction researchers, "Growing up consists of finding the right substitutes for your thumb"; that is, as most of us grow up we lose our dependency on one fixed form and develop more flexible ways to express pleasure, gain a sense of security, and enhance our sense of personal power.[41] But the way people try to meet these needs reflects back on the larger culture itself through the forms it offers us. In this sense drug abuse and addictions, as substitutes for thumb sucking, are disturbed expressions within this culture through which we attempt to meet our grown-up needs for power, security, and self-expression. Addictive relations then become a cultural problem as a result of our attempt to meet these social needs through drug use and other compulsive behaviors, since we are not meeting them otherwise as we mature.

In American culture people are not valued for their own sake but for their ability to accumulate power in a conspicuous manner within a competitive, controlling hierarchy. Addictions are intelligible in a culture in which many are estranged from mutual, equitable, self-enhancing relations in everyday life. That so many describe their lives as being out of control speaks to the nature of a culture in which control over others and being controlled by others are paramount. An alcoholic, crack addict, workaholic, or person hooked emotionally on another to the point of severe loss of judgment (check the daily tabloids for examples) is native to a culture which promotes total fixes or cures for people's troubles, which promises people complete control over their problems, and which does not affirm the self on its own merits but by what it possesses. A possession becomes like a drug, a cure-all that exists outside yourself which will solve your problem of feeling powerless and unacceptable. A culture in which people become overidentified with things, ideas, patterns of relating, or other people is one without a sense of the fluid, relational nature of the self. It is one which instead attempts to control and define people within certain limited forms of expression and which denies the awareness of other perspectives and frameworks.

Addiction to substances such as alcohol, cigarettes, marijuana, pills, or food; addiction to buying things like clothes or cars; addiction to accumulating money through gambling, exploitation, greed, or crime; addiction to work, or to one absolute idea or fixed belief, such as religious fanaticism or racial supremacy; addiction to other people through dominating, possessing, serving, or fixing them; addiction to yourself, including addiction to rigid patriarchal gender roles—these patterns are troublesome ways of trying to secure a sense of power and control in this culture. Addictive relations reflect the inadequacy of drugs and other commodified activities to stand in for a real sense of acceptance and power. They point to the failure of the culture to provide for more satisfying, expressive forms of personal and political relations. Addictive patterns, of which drug abuse is one, prevail as people attempt to seek pleasure, lessen pain, and gain a sense of power within a culture which uses commodities and commodified activities as druglike things, which depends on the need to control other people and nature, and which denies a full range of experiences and voices. It is a culture which offers false fixes as substitutes for more fluid, fulfilling ways of being which arise through freely established mutual relations.

BEYOND MEDICINE

Still, are not addictions a disease in some biological sense?

The term *addiction* is a metaphor for a set of cultural behaviors, even when drugs are involved. In arguing this point I will return to the way the term refers to substance abuse. For example, although some studies suggest some kind of genetic predisposition as a factor, there is no clear evidence for an inherited genetic basis for the diverse behaviors subsumed under the term *alcoholism*.[42] Nor are there universal biochemical markers for identifying and defining the presence of addiction to substances. Since not all abused drugs lead to physiological signs of tolerance and withdrawal (for example, PCP, solvents, marijuana, and hallucinogens do not), there is no such thing as a pure physical addiction in contrast to a psychological one in every case. Cocaine and crack intake do not lead to addiction in an unavoidable sense.[43] Drug researchers have long argued that it is not the characteristics of the drug but the social setting and individual differences which are the most significant factors in determining whether to use the term *addiction*. Thus *addiction* is no longer a medical term referring to biological processes but a common cultural signifier. Its meaning has opened up so that it no longer can be defined by medical, mental health, legal, or moral authorities alone.

True, there is a physiological language of addiction. In the brain opiate receptor sites receive neurotransmitters such as endorphins, which are opiatelike chemicals produced by the body. Certain drugs bind to the receptor sites, and when a person takes them the body reduces its manufacture of endorphins. When the effect of taking the drug wears off, the receptors "crave" more opiates. Taking more drugs satisfies the receptors but in time causes the body to produce less of its own endorphins; repeated drug taking can result in changes in the enzymes required for neurotransmission. The person may then feel the need to take even more drugs to maintain the equilibrium, the level of neurotransmission that reduces the discomfort from the enzymatic changes. With stimulants like cocaine the process is different than with narcotics like heroin. Cocaine prevents neurotransmitters from being absorbed back into the cells that sent them. The neurotransmitters stay trapped in the gap between cells and keep firing pleasure messages. When the cocaine runs out, the person experiences loss of pleasure and irritability.

But these physiological processes do not happen without fail in the same way with every person who takes a drug or alcohol. Even when they occur, a person must learn to interpret the meaning of the discomfort as a demand for more alcohol or drugs and then act on it as a participant of a culture, not as a biochemical organism displaying a tropism. The neurochemistry of drug and alcohol use is not the body but is itself another discourse.[44] The importance of this point is that it forces us to look at explanations of social behavior such as drug taking as cultural constructs which are open to different readings and so are contestable.

For example, one proponent of the disease model of alcoholism must conflate two different kinds of language, that of purpose and that of the body, as she tries to explain the presumedly inevitable need for an alcoholic to drink. She claims that "the cells of the body dictate that one must drink to survive. . . . The alcoholic's only connection is to his screaming cells, which demand that he think only of them and how he is going to keep them happy."[45]

But do cells scream? Do they dictate to their owner how to behave? Does a person think about his or her cells? Are cells capable of happiness? If biology dictates behavior then how does the spiritual program of Alcoholics Anonymous (AA), which the author endorses as the solution to the disease, manage to speak to the cells and get them to stop screaming? Is AA then the only means in our culture by which someone can stop drinking? It is not accidental that the author must mix psychological metaphors into the language of biology to maintain the disease model. This is because drinking alcohol to the point of intoxication, although a bodily experience, is not a pure physiological phenomenon but a purposive social behavior which occurs within a cultural context that defines the meaning of needs as well as the meaning of a social problem. To put it another way, drug and alcohol addictions can affect the body in adverse ways and may demand medical care. However, the language of medicine and the medical establishment are subsumed within culture; culture is the broader network of contested discourses of relations. The explanation of addiction then is not reducible to the discourse of physiology. Medical language is not an a priori discourse of truth but must depend on the culture as a whole to give it meaning and validity. In an analogous way, biochemical explanation is not a sufficient level of understanding for addictive behavior but must appeal to the cultural context of purpose, that is, the meaning of the drinking or drug taking, to account for cause.

We are back to culture in speaking about addiction. Many social behaviors parallel the same addictive patterns of loss of control and tolerance effect as drug use. Gambling, shopping, repeating destructive relationships, and the need to control others are social acts which along with substance abuse can share the addictive cycle of desire, withdrawal, and tolerance.[46] Besides taking substances, there are an infinite variety of cultural activities, like skydiving, which people have created through history and which happen to stimulate their endorphin production. When a person becomes dependent on performing these activities which have harmful consequences, it is as much a cultural as a biochemical process. Even benign substances such as air and food can be addicting, as can watching televangelists or playing *Dungeons and Dragons*, whereas drugs like narcotics and marijuana have many beneficial aspects just as they have dangerous potentials.[47] The formal diagnosis of "psychoactive substance dependence" in the *Diagnostic and Statistical Manual of Mental Disorders* (DSM III-R) includes meeting at least three of nine criteria, many of which are social acts such as spending a great deal of time getting, using, and recovering from the substance.[48] The most salient issue relating to whether to use the term *addiction* is the way people live their everyday lives, not only with respect to their own emotional needs but in relation to others. Prevention, treatment, and recovery programs in the alcohol and substance abuse fields emphasize these relational issues long before or after the person uses a drug.

The progressive side of extending the medical term *addiction* to social behaviors is that it highlights certain problems as public health issues since medicine is a language of power in this culture. To regard compulsive acts as objective diseases from a public health perspective removes them from the realm of personal or moral failings and places them in the arena of public concern over health and safety, which are presumed universal, scientific, and enlightened values. There are progressive public health professionals who understand the social, political, and economic context of these acts and who try to link personal problems with the need for social change and increased community power. For example, it may be more sensible to consider smoking as nicotine addiction and attribute a high rate of this disease in an inner-city neighborhood to stress-inducing public health factors such as poverty and the saturation of cigarette billboards rather than to indict each individual smoker as morally weak or lazy. In a similar way, when people in twelve-step recovery groups refer to their problems as diseases which are stronger than their individual wills it provides everyone with a common language and allows men and women and people from different classes and backgrounds to talk about their experiences in similar terms.

But even this view of public health which speaks about social acts as unhealthy or diseased has a negative side which prevents it from going far enough as a progressive cultural politics. It cannot break free of the troublesome aspects of the medical model, which relies on the power of experts who lay claim to effecting a treatment or cure for everyone and which assumes there is a neutral, objective, universal way to identify high-risk or addicted people and to define a problem. The public health model as a cultural discourse of power in effect pathologizes more and more social behaviors which must be brought under its hierarchical control.

Medicine and psychotherapy are growth industries. The medical model they follow tends to extinguish the role of agency and exonerate individual and social responsibility by pointing to diseases as a cause. This mystifies the power relations within which the behaviors occur. To call different behaviors "diseases" promotes the view that they are individual or group illnesses which require a kind of technocratic cure, some presumed objective medical treatment, instead of placing these behaviors within contestable cultural relations of power and the denial of necessary knowledge. To define certain acts as healthy within a conservative political climate can result in strengthening those in power; *health* then becomes an ideological term defined by conservative criteria, a standard of proper behavior used to bludgeon those who do not measure up. The twelve-step self-help recovery movement for alcoholics and drug addicts, their family members, and others also speaks of people's problems as diseases. The movement's cure for those who declare themselves sick is to help them recover from always having the illness. But what is absent from the disease language of public health and recovery is an understanding of the defining power relations which require critical dialogue and political action. There is a need for a radical cultural politics of addictive relations.

CULTURE WAR

The Right in this country was the first to seize the issue of addictive relations as cultural politics. In the 1980s and into the 1990s the Right gained the high ground by first grasping the political significance of two cultural issues, the nature of pleasure and control over the body. The Right has attacked the legitimacy of pleasurable acts of sexuality, the enjoyment of music and art, and drug taking, pressing for such measures as tough law enforcement, censorship, and mandatory blood and urine tests for drugs and the HIV virus. It has battled over control of the body, including attacks on gays and lesbians, abortion and reproductive rights of women and young people, certain forms of artistic expression such as performance art, and drug taking as well.

The Right's anxiety over the need to maintain control over the body has intensified in light of the ongoing disappearance of the body itself. The body has become decentered and dispersed. Bodily sensations have become mediated and in some cases replaced by forms of technology such as phone sex, virtual reality, artificial insemination, and the pervasiveness of video images as substitutes for experience. The Right tries to preserve some pure, idealized boundary of the body. It does this by demonizing the bodies of the Other in contrast to those of encapsulated, pristine, white middle-class people in their beleaguered enclaves. Poor people of color and other groups are cast as the Other, the ones who are violent, diseased, or addicted, in contrast to Us, who are trying to stay pure and fend off the homeless, child abusers, gays, persons with AIDS, and drug fiends. But this way of thinking denies everyday experience. It dichotomizes good and bad in an either/or framework and externalizes evil as something beyond one's own body or self. This process of objectifying a trait also occurs with drugs, which are supposed to be foreign, evil entities extrinsic to one's natural self. The myth is that by contrast all other commodities which we consume, such as food laced with chemical preservatives, pesticides, and steroids, and all of one's other acts, are pure and acceptable.[49] This hypocritical perspective is itself characteristic of addictive relations.

The Right has tried to influence two agents of acculturation, the family (for example, through former Vice President Quayle's family values campaign) and the school (in its attack on multiculturalism), because these are sites in which control over children's choices over pleasure and the body are crucial. Here again the politically charged battle against drugs—for example, through Nancy Reagan's "Just Say No" crusade and the school ad campaign of the Partnership for a Drug-Free America, among others—assumes prominence because it involves both pleasure and the body and influences children within the family and school.

The Right's campaign has touched a nerve in American culture because of the legitimate problems of substance abuse. Yet in some ways their cure has been as detrimental as the disease, if not more so. The illegal Latin American cocaine trade galvanized repressive policies both foreign and domestic. During the Reagan/Bush era, government, corporate, and media interests waged a controversial antidrug campaign or war on a number of fronts. The war included law enforcement crackdowns on inner-city residents, which often involved illegal detentions, searches, and evictions. It also included drug testing in the workplace, an effort to toughen schools' policy toward student drug use, an extensive public relations crusade to resist drugs, and an invasion of Panama in 1989 to abduct former ally and head of the country, General Manuel Noriega, and try him for the ostensible charge of drug dealing. In 1993 President Clinton surprised his supporters and continued the Reagan/Bush policy of allocating more money for interdiction over treatment and prevention.

Yet the Right's attempt to control pleasure ironically has opened up space for the awareness of contradictions within the social order and has contributed to the surge of new progressive forces which it has been unable to contain. Voices of disenfranchised groups whose experiences run counter to and threaten the dominant narratives of American culture have begun to speak up. The process by which the Right's repressive strategy of control in fact helps to undermine its own power shows up in the very war over drug abuse and addiction. By pushing the war to its limit, it has in the end laid bare the broader, cultural political problem of addictive relations within everyday life and has opened the way for the possibility of alternatives to the denial of pleasure.

The attempt to solve the drug crisis has exposed the shifting, contradictory nature of American culture itself, a culture whose master narratives of hierarchical control are unraveling. The culture is undermined not just by the social costs of illegal drug use and interdiction but also by the failures of the war on drugs. The remedy itself perpetuates addictive relations in the way it totalizes the problem as a foreign evil which demands a quick fix, a counterdose of control. The failure of this approach has uncovered the broader addictive nature of everyday relations themselves by forcing the growing awareness that demonizing all drug users and using repressive control does not work. The level of public knowledge has grown from a narrow focus on immediate short-term cures for illegal drugs—for example, from the use of law enforcement as a quick fix—to the awareness that substance abuse and addiction in general are long-term, intricate, and extensive patterns of relations within American society that require new approaches.

THE SHIFT IN CONSCIOUSNESS

Public consciousness is expanding in a concentric pattern from a narrow, myopic focus on drugs to a broader vision of addictive relations in at least three ways. First, it is shifting its concern over illegal drugs to concern over everyday legal ones on which the current economy is also dependent. Second, it is turning from interdiction of the supply of drugs through law enforcement to the prevention of the demand for substances and addictive relations throughout society. Third, it is moving from concern over the immediate physical dangers of drugs to the deeper relational problems of substance abuse and the need to recover from these problems which extend to everyday commodified activities.

In all cases the shifts call forth the need to think through an alternative vision of a nonaddictive society. I would like to sketch this argument as a way to introduce these points which I will develop throughout the book. The political nature of this shift is ambiguous; yet I would argue that the implicit crisis in the response to the drug issue provides an opportunity to develop a viable cultural politics.

Everyday Addiction

The first area of change is the everyday nature of substance abuse and addiction. Public action has moved from condemning illegal drug use alone to challenging the promotion, sales, and use of legal substances such as alcohol, nicotine, and pills on an individual and a societal level. Certain governing, corporate, and community interests have formed a new temperance or sobriety movement.[50] This movement has contradictory political trends; whereas some are in line with the conservative, individualistic, and repressive approaches of the Reagan/Bush era, others are progressive and challenge legal and illegal drug promoters on a grassroots level.

The conservative aspect of the new temperance denies that drug use is part of our culture and takes an all-or-nothing approach, itself characteristic of addictive relations. It denies that drug use serves different purposes, views all drug taking as evil, and aims to control people's behavior. By punishing casual users of drugs such as marijuana, the movement militates against people's desire to reorient themselves with the pleasure of their bodies in a way which can be subversive to the work ethic, to normative institutions, and to people in power. The movement also includes government and businesses which mandate testing employees and poor, pregnant, drug-addicted women. Critics have argued with good evidence that such measures are a form of social control which have less to do with health and safety than with intimidating and managing workers and poor women.[51]

On the more progressive side of the new temperance movement a significant number of people have realized the problems
their substance use has caused them and others in terms of health
and happiness. The movement discourages individuals from
excessive drinking and smoking and advocates personal health
and fitness. The surgeon general's office has encouraged Americans to quit smoking and has criticized tobacco corporations for
their cigarette ads. Prompted by the federal government, some
companies furthered the movement by setting up employee assistance programs and fitness centers for their staff and by urging
businesspeople to give up liquor at lunch.[52] Partly as a result of
corporate efforts, drug and alcohol treatment programs have
expanded and have become a new growth industry.

But these health-oriented measures do not occur just from the
top down. Many working-class and middle-class people have
adopted the new temperance values themselves. Some poor and
working people have taken a stand to rid their neighborhoods of
the drug trade. Community and educational leaders have developed drug abuse prevention programs which educate and organize
local citizens to fight substance abuse. They have pressed government agencies to protect citizens against violent drug dealers and
have demanded better housing, schools, health care, and social services as a preventive strategy. Leaders like Jesse Jackson have
mobilized people of color through working in local antidrug projects which challenge dealers in buildings, streets, and parks.[53] Residents have campaigned against cigarette and liquor billboards in
their neighborhoods since tobacco and alcohol companies target
poor and third world communities and saturate them with ads.[54]

Others use more middle-class tactics which stress personal
behavior rather than political economic factors. Some people have
filed lawsuits against tobacco companies over their relative's
deaths, claiming they were caused by smoking.[55] They have
worked for strict antismoking laws across the country which forbid smoking altogether in public places like airplanes, building lob-
bies, and in some office buildings; Minneapolis, Salt Lake City, and
New York have passed comprehensive laws banning public smoking and limiting selling and advertising cigarettes.[56] Some professional football and baseball stadiums, in response to fans' pressure,
have designated so-called family areas which are off-limits to alcohol. Groups like Mothers Against Driving Drunk/Drugged
(MADD) and Youth Educating for Safety (YES, formerly Students

Against Driving Drunk/Drugged, SADD) stress personal responsibility and recruit and educate other parents and students.

The new temperance movement faces significant contradictions which make it uncertain as to the kind of cultural politics it can carry out. It must confront the fact that illegal drugs are an integral part of the everyday economy of millions of disenfranchised citizens for whom there is no longer any viable employment and to whom the movement offers no real alternative. It must also face the fact that legal drugs are profitable industries upon which the economy as a whole depends. To just advocate for the end of drug use and the drug trade then is unrealistic given the way they are bound up with everyday practices. To do so through harsh measures further serves the forces of social control. The movement does not address the way everyday commodified activities take on addictive qualities themselves within a society which is so dominated by drug use. Yet awareness of these growing discrepancies serves as a potential threat to the dominant order. It can inform a progressive political response which challenges the inequitable power relations of everyday life and advocates for a better quality of life for all. The new temperance trend also forces scrutiny of addictive behavior within progressive political movements themselves.

Prevention

Second, as people become more aware of the physical, economic, and emotional consequences of legal drug use and addiction, they have also recognized the ineffectiveness of law enforcement efforts aimed at total interdiction of the sale and use of illegal drugs. They have begun to shift instead to realizing the need for treatment and prevention of all drug abuse, that is, from trying to control the supply side to influencing the demand side. This has meant moving away from reliance on a powerful, quick fix to control an outside evil to examining why so many people here at home need to take drugs and alcohol. This is a more complex and threatening question which allows the possibility of change within the cultural politics of everyday relations.

Why is the problem with drug abuse not about reducing supply through law enforcement?

Strong law enforcement has its place. All honest poor and hardworking people need to be protected from criminals who rob and murder and who in other ways make decent citizens' lives unsafe and squalid. In decimated inner-city areas the first priority of many residents is safety for themselves and their children and protection from drug dealers and cocaine and heroin addicts in their buildings, streets, and parks. Some collaborate with law enforcement officials and pressure local politicians and government agencies to provide them with protective and other municipal services to which they are entitled.

But to try to reduce the drug supply through legal force alone does not and cannot get at the reason why people sell and abuse illegal drugs. In underdeveloped third world countries peasants will continue to grow coca or poppy plants as long as it is profitable; U.S. foreign policy does little to encourage crop conversion and in some cases encourages growers to cultivate illegal cash crops instead of subsistence ones. At home interdiction and the war on drugs has failed to prevent illegal drugs such as cocaine or opium from entering the country anyway, nor could it ever manage to do so because there are too many ways to smuggle it in.[57] Even if it were possible, people can and do manufacture designer drugs in this country in home labs, including heroin and cocaine analogues.[58]

Punitive measures and scare tactics are not an effective means of deterring demand.[59] There is too much money to be made for jail to serve as a deterrent for street pushers and dealers. Selling illegal drugs is a lucrative business for many poor people, and there is always a fresh supply of young males to replace the ones who go to jail. Jailing dealers and users keeps some of them off the streets for a while, but there is also a large amount of drug use in the jails and next to nothing in terms of treatment.[60] It is a crime itself that more money is later spent to house poor young African-American males in jails than on their education, housing, or health care while they are children.

Law enforcement itself is a growth industry, and some people become addicted to control by force as the answer to all problems. Some of the tactics against drug users threaten everyone's civil liberties; safeguards against police excess have eroded within the last decade.[61] Law enforcement is skewed against the poor. It tends to come down hardest on street dealers and users while the white-collar drug dealers can continue to ply their trade. Because of the money to be made, law enforcement itself has become more of an ambiguous endeavor in which the line between good guys and villains often changes, as in the capture and trial of Panama's Manuel Noriega, a former CIA collaborator, or in the arrest of New York City police officers in 1992 for operating a drug ring.

Yet legalizing drugs is not a panacea, nor is it the crux of the issue. Decriminalizing certain drugs is a good idea, and legalizing other drugs might stop some of the murderous turf wars which terrorize some inner-city areas, although opponents argue that traffickers could still undercut the price. But legalization would do nothing to prevent the abuse of drugs by those who can least afford to secure any kind of social or medical support, and may even increase the incidents of abuse by making them more available.[62] Legalization would have to go hand in hand with both making treatment available to all (*treatment* itself is a contestable term, as discussed below) and providing clean needles for heroin users on demand.

Legalizing further shifts the profiteering and drug pushing to tobacco, liquor, and pharmaceutical corporations. As a legal drug, alcohol is implicated in more crimes, and along with cigarettes, more deaths, than are heroin, cocaine, and certainly marijuana. Also, people can get legal prescription pills which are controlled substances on the street as easily as drugs like cocaine and heroin. For someone who is hooked on the feeling of a drug and feels out of control, his or her body does not know the difference between a legal and an illegal drug.

Even drug treatment, although important, is not an effective way to reduce demand. Most treatment is just somewhat successful. Researchers who summarized two long-term studies of the three major treatment methods—outpatient drug-free programs, methadone maintenence, and therapeutic communities—concluded that a majority of abusers fail to benefit from any program.[63] They cite that only about 24 to 28 percent of those treated return to drug-free and crime-free living. Furthermore, the success rate is linked with socioeconomic level; employed, otherwise functioning users have the best chances, followed by blue-collar users, followed in turn by unemployed people with little education, who have the lowest success rate.[64]

Treatment tends to focus on personal responsibility for change and does not tackle the social and political factors which contribute to substance abuse. Traditional drug-free programs tend to take an absolutist, all-or-nothing view on drug abstinence, itself a characteristic of addictive thinking. They endorse the principle of individualistic moral responsibility for deferred pleasure and impulse control. This puts the clients at odds with the everyday culture. For graduates of a treatment program, then, part of the challenge is to get support to remain drug-free once they return to their communities; it is all the more difficult for those returning to adverse circumstances who had little in the first place. Although wealthier graduates have more resources, all must learn to live in a culture which is itself saturated with addictive relations and varying degrees of substance use on an everyday level.

More successful programs designed for inner-city crack and cocaine users are rare and are not a high priority for federal money: for example, the acupuncture clinic at Lincoln Hospital in the South Bronx.[65] They are also more controversial because they advocate the idea of less use rather than total abstinence in line with the reality of life in a drug culture. The acupuncture clinic, along with the Drug Abuse Treatment Program at Montefiore Hospital in the Bronx, does not attempt moral reeducation or preach absolute disavowal but instead practices what the treatment program director calls "harm reduction."[66] The program aims to provide detox for cocaine users and to get people to use less drugs without pressuring them into a long-term recovery program. These treatment programs do not fall prey to an all-or-nothing approach for all users.

Prevention programs try to reduce youthful demand for drug and alcohol use. They aim to teach youth resistance skills, increase their self-esteem so they will feel good without drugs, encourage alternative activities, and target so-called high-risk youth. But they tend to ignore the everyday cultural and power relations in which people operate and do not challenge the broader nature of addictive relations in the school, family, workplace, and community. The ideological tack of prevention programs is individualistic: they work to change people's personal behavior instead of the political nature of addictive relations themselves.

How prevention programs define a high-risk person is itself a contestable cultural phenomenon in which dominant discourses like medicine label the Other as having a problem of potential drug abuse. Health professionals identify so-called high-risk individuals as those who tend to have non-normative attributes in terms of class, family background, and school behavior; prevention professionals then offer them normative social, communication, and so-called life skills as if these were medically determined remedies. But this process is not scientific but ideological. For example, there is no link between some presumed objective personality trait such as addictiveness and a tendency toward addictive behavior such as alcoholism.[67] The dubious label of *addictive personality* presumes the there are verifiable, stable traits of a person across changing cultural and historical contexts. But this model does not allow for the way personality evolves through and within a changing nexus of social relations involving the family, peers, the community, and popular culture. Nor does it acknowledge that changing personalities interpret and act on everyday culture itself and infuse it with subjectivity. It is not that the individual self is unimportant as opposed to cultural forces; that is a false dichotomy. On the contrary, the self has become all the more significant as the site on which cultural meanings are politically shaped and contested. The fact that so many people today fall into the category of high risk and that so many can relate to the feeling of addictive dependency in some form speaks to the need to look at the cultural politics of everyday addictive relations.

The progressive side of demand reduction is that it is a shift away from futile, repressive measures which try to eliminate the supply of drugs. It offers the chance to ask why people need to take drugs in the first place. Still, traditional demand reduction does not address in adequate ways the issue of why people take drugs, what needs they are getting met, and why the usual alternatives are not viable substitutes. It tends toward absolutist, all-or-nothing approaches which are themselves characteristic of addictive rather than fluid relations.

Drug and alcohol abuse prevention and treatment fields reach an impasse whenever they focus just on teaching personal change around drug and alcohol intake. They cannot aim to eliminate the act of substance abuse alone but must prescribe alternative ways of living. That is, they cannot simply get people to avoid drugs or stop taking them without developing an implicit or stated moral and political way of life as a more compelling choice, a way of life which informs their approach. Treating people for their addiction in the fullest sense, then, means contributing to freeing everyday relations from addictive qualities which restrict access to knowledge and power. To think prevention through beyond the usual bromides means to create healthy democratic relations throughout society that would be fulfilling in themselves, that in fact would prevent people from needing to medicate themselves with drugs as bogus substitutes for personal and political power. It is a call for a progressive cultural politics which challenges those everyday relations that offer people false fixes as surrogates for full self-expression.

Recovery

Finally, more people have become aware not only of threats to their physical health from illegal and legal drugs but of disturbed patterns of intimacy bound up with drug abuse. When people become dependent on drugs as quick fixes for stress, pain, insecurity, and anxiety, this dependency can lead to problems of its own. Cocaine and heroin addiction, pill and alcohol abuse, cigarette smoking, and marijuana dependency can affect people's well-being and relationships and prevent them from living their lives in ways they would prefer.

Since the 1980s an increasing number of people have applied the twelve-step or recovery movement based on the principles of Alcoholics Anonymous to a wide range of activities beyond substance abuse. The movement appeals to those who sense there is something not right about the way they were raised and how they live, and it affords them an accessible means to address the discrepancy between troublesome relations and more expressive ways of being. Twelve-step language and principles have become popularized through media talk shows and programs with charismatic professionals like John Bradshaw and through the spread of lucrative recovery literature, paraphernalia, and treatment spas. Groups like Alanon, Adult Children of Alcoholics, and Codependents Anonymous deal with issues of people who have grown up with or who live with an alcoholic or other substance abuser. *Codependency* has become a popular term which in general refers to a person who denies his or her own needs and perspectives for the sake of the addict."[68]

In twelve-step groups people may undergo a process of self-examination of their childhood and family history. They explore how growing up in alcoholic and substance abusing families often contributes to patterns of compulsivity, self-doubt, control of others, all-or-nothing thinking, and denial of their own needs and feelings. For them, groups are a supportive lifeline where they can feel accepted and relearn social skills. From this process more people are beginning to interrogate the way they were raised and the nature of the privatized nuclear family itself, the rules of child-drearing, and how family relations are supposed to occur.

The recovery movement has struck a chord and has helped to popularize the term *addiction* within society as a whole.[69] More Americans realize how they compulsively depend on things (commodities) experienced as entities extrinsic to their nature—that is, as drugs—to fill up a profound sense of personal emptiness and inadequacy. They recognize that everyday activities in this society such as eating, gambling, shopping, working, raising children, and even love and marriage often have a compulsive, addictive quality. In the late 1980s a number of popular and controversial books described women's dependent relationship with men in terms similar to those in the substance abuse field.[70] Addiction language extended into presidential politics when Bill Clinton and Al Gore borrowed concepts and slogans from the recovery movement in their 1992 campaign. They alluded to unhealthy patterns of conflict and suggested alternative ways to negotiate power.

However, the recovery movement is another contradictory political trend. By viewing behavior as disease, it tends to take a simplistic approach to complex problems which does not bother to distinguish differences between people in terms of class, gender, race, or other categories. The self-help movement is militantly apolitical; yet because it refuses to consider the political context of addiction, it opens itself up to being used in the service of reactionary principles. People in recovery can become as addicted to the groups, to a rigid form of repressive, puritanical self-denial, and to all-or-nothing thinking as they can to anything else. Although the twelve-step groups are anonymous, the larger for-profit recovery movement has its share of charlatan gurus, hucksters, pseudo-intellectuals, and hypocritical religious addicts. Yet the practice of recovering from addictive patterns of which one becomes more aware has the potential to inform a progressive cultural politics if it can acknowledge the addictive nature of everyday power relations in capitalist society. The movement can speak to a culture which appears to be reaching the limits of its belief that everything can be known and controlled. Although this growing discontent with dominant cultural norms as such does not compute into radical politics, it poses a profound potential challenge to those in power who depend on them.

THE FAILURE OF MODERNIST POLITICS

The call for a radical cultural politics of addictive relations arises because the three major modernist political traditions—conservative, liberal, and leftist—have failed to provide adequate accounts of this problem and to offer viable alternatives. These approaches until now have provided coherent theories of political emancipation as well as frameworks for linking personal behavior with the broader movement of history. But their relevance has diminished in light of the significant changes ongoing in the culture today. This holds true with respect to analyzing the drug issue and offering good political cultural alternatives to everyday addictive relations. Of course, none of the three has a monolithic approach to the drug issue, and some camps join others, such as some conservatives and leftists on the issue of legalization. But all tend to share modernist premises about the way society operates and how people behave. All three insist on bolstering certain social structures which they consider to be universal, such as the family, the market, the state, or the working class, and which they believe to be in need of reform in order to fulfill their unrealized or thwarted purposes. They depend on the appeal to progress through linear, rational methods which presume sufficient hierarchical control of practice. They tend to map out the movement of history as a narrative and posit a particular trajectory toward some future end result. The respective narratives have universalist or totalizing claims which show up in their approaches to the drug issue. Because of their modernist premises, all three narratives are unable to theorize about the drug issue in effective terms or to contribute to galvanizing progressive political movements.

Conservatives often regard drug abuse as a breakdown in the proper moral order. Those like former First Lady Nancy Reagan and President Reagan's secretary of education and drug czar William Bennett adopted what they termed a "zero-tolerance" stance which condemns all illegal drug use and places casual usage of marijuana on a par with heavy use of crack. Conservatives prefer to shore up the patriarchal nuclear family as a universal form, strengthen the law enforcement arm of the state through surveillance and punishment, and toughen the individualistic moral fiber of all citizens. One conservative tale with a happy ending to the drug crisis might be one in which the unbridled market would allow for individual happiness for all within the limits of a stable social hierarchy which respects God, the country, and family; drug dealers would end up behind bars or self-destruct; and all children would have good upbringing, know their place, and learn that illegal drug use is morally wrong.[71]

Liberals tend to see drug taking as symptomatic of high-risk individuals or of flaws in the system's provision of services. They may promote the teaching of personal skills to enhance social competence and self-esteem.[72] Liberals also favor more government spending for prevention, treatment, and social services for families and youth. Some speak as if existing components of the society, such as corporations, government agencies, churches, families, schools, and unions, were all viable, intact, neutral, and equivalent agents of power, and they work to bring them to together to solve the problem.[73] A liberal narrative might tell of the gradual, incremental progress gained by reforming the weaknesses of the system through education and government intervention, with the result a more workable corporate-welfare state. In this scenario drug abusers would receive therapeutic treatment so they can return as productive members of society, and children would be taught to accumulate personal skills useful in negotiating bureaucracies and achieving career and organizational mobility.[74]

Traditional leftist approaches tend to see a problem like drug abuse as a symptom of larger systemic problems, as the superstructure or epiphenomenon with respect to the base or economic level. One approach favors a simple, all-encompassing conspiracy theory that claims that the capitalist class or white ruling elite encourages drugs in poor neighborhoods as a deliberate way to sedate the residents or even as a form of genocide. Those who are more critical of the impersonal forces of the system as a whole argue for the need to change the social, political, and economic forces which they see in the final analysis as being responsible for the drug problem; they tend to see the war on drugs as a form of state social control.[75] To varying degrees many on the left assume that the drug problem will be entrenched in the system until something like the following narrative occurs: along with their allies, the revolutionary intellectuals, the working class and oppressed nationalities will organize themselves, overthrow state power, and create a genuine society based on human needs, not consumerism.[76] The anticonsumerism corresponds with a puritanical streak among some on the Left who suspect that pleasure itself is a capitalist plot.

In terms of the need for immediate response, the Left has debated the role of the state and the legalization of all drugs. On one end are those who favor war against the criminal element and urge strong federal action in the inner cities, including executing drug dealers.[77] On the other more libertarian side are those who believe that drug taking is neither good nor bad in itself and in some cases may be beneficial; they argue that legalizing all drugs would eliminate many of the problems linked with the crack trade, and drug addiction could then be treated as a health problem. A more nuanced stance by two progressives is that neither criminalization nor legalization alone is an adequate answer to the drug problem. They argue that much of the federal war amounts to a repressive form of social control which cannot catch every dealer and user, and that legalizing drugs alone would do nothing for communities ravaged by drug abuse.[78]

The two rightly propose that progressives can help people define the legitimate needs they are trying to meet through drug use. But they fall back in part on a theory which relies on the base/superstructure model and privileges the knowledge of the revolutionary. The theory suggests that oppressed people who self-destructively take drugs can come to understand themselves in terms of how they take in the oppressor's degrading image of themselves and turn their rage into acts of self-hate (internalized oppression). But in this analysis, like many on the Left, the reasons people give for taking drugs, their feelings and needs, are secondary. Leftists may often attribute people's reasons to other material forces, which they deem the ultimate actual causes and which at first only they understand by virtue of their vanguard status. This kind of totalizing theory does not allow for multiple voices but instead aims to present the one true account or correct line to those who cannot know why they act the way they do. It denies the way the self now develops through multiple narratives. To attribute the real cause of behavior to a privileged analysis also tends to blind the vanguard themselves to their own addictive patterns of relating. It makes it more difficult for them to practice a flexible, nondogmatic form of self-scrutiny.

A crucial failure of all three metanarratives is their attitude toward popular culture. They tend to regard popular culture with contempt (conservative), without criticism and as a natural phenomenon (liberal), or as a derived and less significant superstructure (leftist). That is, these approaches each assume a political standpoint toward everyday culture with respect to the purported real sources of power; in each case popular culture is the lesser, secondary entity. Popular culture, they assume, is not as legitimate as some predetermined social structure, whether it be a divine social order, the free market, the state, class conflict, or genuine human needs. But this perspective restricts understanding of people's everyday efforts to resist, negotiate, and appropriate consumer culture, let alone to create their own cultural meanings. It preempts an adequate analysis of the place of drugs and addictive relations in everyday life by minimizing the importance of everyday culture itself.

Conservatives defend an idealized, pure culture untainted by mass tastes and elevated from the lesser accomplishments of lesser societies. Educators like E. D. Hirsch and William Bennett, as representatives of white, upper-class, male privilege, have attacked popular culture in defense of Eurocentric high culture such as the Great Books curriculum.[79] Conservative groups have campaigned to convince Congress to eliminate cultural grants through the National Endowment of the Arts. Patrick Buchanan charged that the "arts crowd" is "engaged in a cultural struggle to root out the old America of family, faith and flag."[80] Conservative social policy toward drugs is also elitist in many respects. To promote harsh penalties for users in effect targets poor people of color, and some libertarians on the Right who favor legalization without also endorsing the universal availability of social services and health care for those who need it are consigning poor people to a self-destructive path.[81]

Liberals believe that education should prepare most people for productive membership in a state-regulated corporate society; in recent years neoliberals have come to favor the growth of the market rather than the state to solve social problems. Even within state agencies market practices have gained influence. The New York State Division of Substance Abuse Services, before it merged with its counterpart bureau of alcoholism, borrowed business techniques to try to increase the accountability and productivity of prevention and treatment programs.[82] In some cases liberal educators uncritically rely on everyday corporate culture for educational projects; examples are Channel One, a controversial private eduational TV program which shows commercials in school, and Partnership for a Drug-Free America, a volunteer consortium of media, advertising agents, and companies which promotes antidrug ads aimed at kids.[83] Those who foot the bill have say

over which ideas kids access, often ones that favor continued corporate, nondemocratic control over vast spheres of everyday life.

Last, the Left's framework, which insists on a pure, authentic,
folk, working-class, or people's culture delineated from a bourgeois, commercialized, commodified or sold-out one, is no longer
viable. It has been left behind by the complex interplay of technological and cultural forces which now blurs the genuine from the
artificial in far too many cases.[84] Do Bruce Springsteen fans get
real pleasure from listening to a working-class hero or inauthentic
pleasure from a highly marketed product? [85] Is the excitement a
devoted sports fan feels from following a professional ball team
legitimate and part of a populist tradition or is it commercially
induced and co-opted? When blue-collar workers reach for a Bud
after work, are they being manipulated by Anheuser-Busch ads or
are they partaking in a genuine working-class tradition? Or if
they abstain from drinking, are they doing so out of concern for
their health or are they being pressured by the bourgeois fad of
corporate healthism? The answer in all cases may be: to varying
degrees, both. As one critic acknowledges, we are all immersed in
the contradictions of mass culture and cannot just detach ourselves and regard it from some superior, outside standpoint.[86]

But a number of socialists and feminists do not consider popular culture as a contradictory but legitimate sign of people's
efforts to realize themselves on their own terms. Some progressives who address the drug war focus on how and why interest
groups and social movements themselves define a problem. They
argue that each past drug scare or war on drugs had more to do
with political, economic, racial, class, or cultural matters and less
to do with actual drug use or its effects."[87] This approach is useful
in helping people view a number of past movements against
opium, alcohol, and marijuana with scepticism. But it can lapse
into a functionalism which reduces all antidrug efforts, or any
social movement, to disguised symptoms of real concerns which
the social historian determines to be crucial; for example, it
reduces the current antidrug movement to a case of social control
and ignores its progressive aspects.

The social historian sometimes may see popular movements
as misguided reflections of deeper forces which correspond to his
or her ideological theory of how history ought to proceed. For
instance, Barbara Ehrenreich, a socialist-feminist, argues that the
recent drug frenzy is another episode of moral panic which Amer-

icans experience from time to time and which usually conceals a "deeper anxiety."[88] As one example she quotes another leftist feminist scholar, Barbara Epstein, who argues that the "real issue" of the late nineteenth and early twentieth century temperance movement in which women played a prominent role was women's extreme vulnerability within the traditional marriage; because women could not challenge the institution of marriage itself, they displaced their outrage onto alcohol, which became a "condensed symbol" of husbands' irresponsble behavior toward women, instead of directing their anger toward the search for feminist alternatives. Ehrenreich follows suit and suggests that the current "drug frenzy . . . is displaced rage at the consumer culture to which we are all so eagerly addicted," since we cannot challenge the culture's everyday message of unbridled hedonism.[89]

But by reducing peoples' popular anger over alcohol and drugs to a surface phenomenon or displaced symptom, she dismisses those legitimate aspects of peoples' antidrug efforts and their attempts at making their own history, as well as those legitimate expressions of people's desire found in capitalist consumer culture itself. The belief seems to be that people are unaware of their real feelings, are taking a wrong turn, and are failing to follow the true underlying structures of feminist or class historical development, all of which can be learned best from the socialist and feminist historians and theoreticians themselves.

POSTMODERN CULTURE

Traditional conservative, liberal, and leftist narratives of the drug crisis are at sea because they no longer speak to the experience of everyday Americans; they do not tell the story of everyday life. Conservatives and liberals consider the drug problem not as part of everyday life but as an isolated evil that requires a quick fix or a prescriptive regimen to stop its spread. The Left tends to regard the problem as just a symptom of deeper social problems and the everyday efforts of people to deal with it as either part of repressive social control or the result of moral panic. All three fail to acknowledge and address a major shift in American society, the emergence of a postmodern culture which requires its own level of understanding.[90] Postmodern culture challenges the traditional social relations of a modernist, industrial society and its ideas as reflected in conservative, liberal, and leftist theories. In postmodern culture master narratives which promise ultimate Truth are subject to a process of deconstruction which generates multiple meanings. Traditional narratives which tell of guaranteed progress through rationality and technology, and social narratives which place faith in structures such as the goodness of the family, work, and the state, are no longer inviolable but are contested. Everyday life assumes significance as power becomes diffused throughout all relations and everyday people are able to construct and intrepret cultural signs.

Postmodern culture arises as the making of signs dominates the making of material things, and information in the form of signs becomes a commodity of the first order. Cultural signs lose their absolute meaning and become texts with multiple readings. Capitalist culture itself becomes the instrument for producing a postcapitalist world; cultural signs no longer are accountable to a determining materiality but themselves become active agents which create new social forms:

> Detached from the ontological, natural, and moral foundations that give political, social, and juridical institutions their meaning as representations of a prior referent or truth, the expressions of an inherent or already established moral or social order, cultural signs instead are revealed to be the instruments of the creation of new grounds, new meanings, and new institutions.[91]

In postmodern culture everyday social relations are transformed by the new ways in which information is now transmitted. Electronic-mediated communications such as computers and other media contribute to weakening the link between a sign and the material referent it represents (objectivity) as the language they use becomes more self-referential. As a consequence the materiality of the world plays less of a role in everyday life. Words which used to have straitforward, objective referents are removed from corresponding materiality, in what Henri Lefebvre calls "the decline of the referentials."[92]

Declining referents include words like *life, death*, and *parenthood*. Their meanings are now clouded by technological advances in genetic engineering, fertility, and life support systems and often become the subject of legal and political battles. Other referents are dissolving. The term *family* may now mean a pastiche household with children from different marriages or a gay or lesbian couple; or it may be an empty buzzword for a group of people related by law or blood who are supposed to be close but who otherwise have nothing in common. *Shopping* and *banking* may now mean moving symbols around on a modem at home and no longer involve the actual face-to-face exchange of products or cash. In the 1980s *being religious* in some cases ceased to mean attending church and participating in a community of shared values but referred instead to staring transfixed at televangelists and mailing them enormous donations. *Money* itself has come to refer to an arrangement of oxides on a tape stored in the computer department of a bank, exchanged through modems, and manipulated on display screens.[93]

The media communicate information through signs which are part of their own self-referential language. For example, TV advertising is a language of its own which no longer represents objects in everyday life. Car ads show the car as its own species, a self-referential signifier which does not represent the everyday product itself. Ads depict the car in terms which refer back to the fantasy car along with images that signal pleasure. Because ads are no longer representational, they appeal to the subject to identify with the image, unmoored from any material reality; they may even constitute a subject by depending on the viewer to interpret the ad and find his or her place in it, to join in the game which denies that the ad represents a product.[94]

Postmodern culture also changes the nature of the self and its relationship to objects in the world. Self-identity is no longer a fixed, stable core of personality; instead, people construct their various identities at different times and in different relational contexts. Cultural signs become infused with subjectivity and choice, and the self is saturated with an overwhelming array of cultural signs. Since the self consists of a nexus of relations, it comes into existence, if at all, in terms of its shifting connections with other people and objects.[95] People may live as signs themselves, detached from and unaccountable to some community which once defined selfhood by grounding words in a common history and way of life. Subjectivity occurs not through any cumulative, historical development based in stable social relations but in terms of discrete bits of information, analogous to the way information about a person is stored, arranged, and used in a database.

The new mode of information decenters and destabilizes the self by reconstituting the self's own location in the world:

If I can speak directly or by electronic mail to a friend in Paris while sitting in California, if I can witness political and cultural events as they occur across the globe without leaving my home, if a database at a remote location contains my profile and informs government agencies which make decisions that affect my life without any knowledge on my part of these events, if I can shop in my home by using my TV or computer, then where am I and who am I? In these circumstances I cannot consider myself centered in my rational, autonomous subjectivity or bordered by a defined ego, but I am disrupted, subverted and dispersed across social space.[96]

In some cases drug use facilitates the rapid changes in self-presentation which characterize postmodern relations. Drugs like cocaine and Ecstasy can be accessories for designer selves, as are clothing styles. They can enhance a particular self-image, for example, chic, in line with the postmodern approach to everyday life as a crafted performance.

RADICAL POSTMODERN POLITICS OF ADDICTION

The postmodern culture undermines modernist premises such as the viability of one overarching model or metanarrative of scientific truth. It challenges the belief shared by conservatives, liberals, and leftists that the universal idea of progress is guaranteed through the workings of established structures such as the state or through institutional forms of rationality. In this sense it dethrones the white, ruling-class male whose dominant political perspective expressed through the mode of written language has defined objectivity and reason for much of the world. Disenfranchised voices which have existed on the margins now challenge those who attempt to maintain their control over everyday cultural practices; they do so through a variety of visual, bodily, and other nonlinear forms of knowing. As a consequence privileged sectors of society feel threatened by the breakdown of certain social structures and belief systems which were once held to be stable evidence of the truth. Those who benefit from modernist relations attempt to retain their power and control over others. But they face challenges from disempowered groups who seek new ways to develop themselves which are less addictive, that is, less dependent on the absolute faith in one version of the truth and less dependent on arbitrary control and the denial of relevant needs and feelings.

Everyday culture demands that its own palpable, immanent, and densely textured nature be taken on its own terms, in which power is diffused and contested, multiple meanings arise, hierarchies are challenged, outcomes are not guaranteed in advance, and artifice, simulation, and imagination are material forces which can move people in their own right. Postmodern culture can help banish modernist structures through irony, humor, and playfulness. Rather than operate in the dualistic, exclusionary, either-or categories which characterize modernist and addictive relations, it allows for contradictory, inclusive, both-and perspectives of experience.

With the decline of material referents, cultural signs emerge as new abstractions which interpenetrate and constitute everyday life. By making information available and inviting participation, postmodern culture allows people to freely choose communities and networks based on democratic, non-hierarchical relations. A common culture can arise as people develop themselves not through work and political parties alone but by the creative appropriation and elaboration of cultural signs.[97] Antonio Negri argues:

> The "principle accumulation" of capital, as it is described by the classics, broke every natural and social tie and reduced the subject to a mere quantitative entity and a purely numerical existence in the market. On the contrary the abstraction which is formed today is the one that permeates human intercommunicability and which, on this level, constructs the solidity of communitary relations on the new reality of the subjects.[98]

We appear to be living on the border of modern and postmodern culture, at a time when old ways are crumbling and new ones have yet to appear.[99] The clash between the traditional relations and values and the emerging ones occurs on the level of everyday life. Many experience these changes as a chaotic unraveling of the social fabric. To use another metaphor, traditional signposts are more like broken traffic lights swaying in the wind, their random blinking unrelated to the ongoing traffic below. The changes in social patterns create considerable stress for many. Both the use of drugs as a means to medicate for the pain, and the challenge to drug use and addictive relations as outmoded coping patterns, are reflective of the ongoing changes.

A progressive antiaddictive movement and an affirmative postmodern culture share an essential quality: both undermine allegiance to one fixed meaning of a cultural sign. Just as nonaddictive relations mean that people are not yoked to one unchanging form of need in terms of a substance or thought or behavior pattern, so postmodern relations also allow for multiple readings of any one cultural form; a sign is no longer controlled by one meaning. There are other similarities between the two. Both seek to recover from restrictive relations of control over others and the denial of significant and multivaried viewpoints, voices, and interpretations. Both reject the use of binary categories which dichotomizes social life into either-or terms and instead allow for contradictory aspects of experience. And both affirm the creative, fluid, shifting, and unpredictable character of self-expression which occurs within democratic, mutually determined relations.

A radical cultural politics of addictive relations, or a movement of radical recovery,[100] can emerge which goes beyond traditional leftist approaches and which takes into account the shift to postmodern culture. The model of cultural phenomena as contingent on an economic base is no longer adequate; for example, one cannot explain substance abuse as a characteristic of the superstructure ultimately caused by class conflict or poverty. Unequal power relations of class, gender, and race are now mediated by popular culture as dispersed through the electronic media. The Left itself is infused with some of the addictive relational patterns of control and denial found in the larger culture. An alternative strategy begins not with a prescribed narrative or with preexisting structures but with the culture of the everyday itself, including how people actively work to negotiate social life to meet their needs. It is a strategy which accepts the postmodern claims regarding the fragmentary nature of everyday culture, the dispersed, decentered self, and the existence of multiple meanings and readings of reality. But it rejects the relativism and the denial of the possibility of personal and political change which characterizes some sceptical postmodern views.[101] It encourages educators and others to take popular culture on its own terms, to grasp its contradictory dynamics, and to locate and create the spaces within that culture which allow for the transformative possibilities which many seek, the kinds for which addiction is often a substitute. A progressive cultural politics of addictive relations builds on the positive elements of both modernist and postmodern culture. Affirmative aspects of postmodern culture along with progressive modernist tools like critical thought can help form an alternative cultural politics which challenges outmoded addictive forms of power and control in wide-ranging ways and enables us to develop new selves within new relations. With more awareness of addictive relations throughout the culture it no longer can be politics as usual.

NOTES

1. Fenton Johnson, "High in the Hollows," *New York Times Magazine*, Dec. 17, 1989, pp. 30ff.

2. "Speed's Gain in Use Could Rival Crack, Drug Experts Warn," *New York Times*, Nov. 27, 1988, pp. 1, 26.

3. Alfred W. McCoy, *The Politics of Heroin in Southeast Asia: CIA Complicity in the Global Drug Trade*, Westport: Lawrence Hill, 1991; Peter Dale Scott and Jonathan Marshall, *Cocaine Politics: Drugs, Armies, and the CIA in Central America*, Berkeley: University of California Press, 1991.

4. Jefferson Morley, "Contradictions of Cocaine Capitalism," *Nation*, Oct. 2, 1989, pp. 341–47.

5. "Banks to Plead Guilty to Laundering Drug Money," *New York Times*, August 11, 1989, pp. A1, 12; "Banking's Technology Helps Drug Dealers Export Cash," *New York Times*, August 14, 1989, pp. A1, B4; "A Torrent of Dirty Dollars," *Time*, Dec. 18, 1989, pp. 50-56.

6. "Price Revolt Spreading on Prescription Drugs," *New York Times*, Nov. 14, 1989, pp. D1, 6.

7. See "Stress on the Job Cited," *New York Times*, Oct. 23, 1986, p. C7; Diana Ralph, *Work and Madness: The Rise of Community Psychiatry*, Montreal: Black Rose, 1983.

8. "Drug Companies' Profits Finance More Promotion than Research," *New York Times*, Feb. 21, 1993, pp. 1, 26; "U.S. Study of Drug Makers Criticizes 'Excess Profits,'" *New York Times*, Feb. 26, 1993, pp. D1, 2.

9. *Women and Drugs*, National Institute on Drug Abuse (NIDA), Research Issues No. 31, 1983. See also Naomi Wolf, *The Beauty Myth: How Images of Beauty Are Used Against Women*, New York: Anchor Books, 1992, p. 268.

10. Ralph, *op. cit.*; Michael Schneider, *Neurosis and Civilization: A Marxist-Freudian Synthesis*, New York: Seabury, 1975.

11. "Studies Find Drugs Still Overused to Control Nursing Home Elderly," *New York Times*, March 13, 1989, pp. A1, 12; "Wide Medica-

tion Misuse Is Found among Elderly," *New York Times*, Feb. 15, 1989, pp. A1, 17; Robert Spero, "An Interview with Sidney Wolfe," *Progressive*, March, 1993, pp. 32–34.

12. "America's 'Other Drug Problem' Overwhelms Thousands, Experts Say," *AARP Bulletin*, April 1989, p. 1ff.

13. Schneider, *op. cit.*, p. 211.

14. Alexander Cockburn, "Getting Opium to the Masses: The Political Economy of Addiction," *Nation*, Oct. 30, 1989, pp. 482–83.

15. Ralph, *op. cit.*, chapter 5.

16. Charles R. Schuster, Director NIDA, letter, *New York Times*, Feb. 13, 1989; Daniel Patrick Moynihan, "Yes, We Do Need a Methadone Clone," *New York Times*, Feb. 26, 1989.

17. "The Generic Drug Scandal," *New York Times*, Oct. 2, 1989, p. A18.

18. Stephen R. Shalom, "Made in the USA: Deadly Exports," *Z Magazine*, April 1992, pp. 15–19; "Drug Labeling Abroad Is Criticized," *New York Times*, May 21, 1993, p. A18.

19. "An Uproar over Billboards in Poor Areas," *New York Times*, May 1, 1989, p. D10; "A Cigarette Campaign under Fire, *New York Times*, Jan. 12, 1990, p. D4; "Health Chief Assails a Tobacco Producer for Aiming at Blacks," *New York Times*, Jan. 19, 1990, pp. A1, 20; "Are Blacks the Target of Cig Makers?" *New York Daily News*, Dec. 18, 1988, Bus. pp. 1, 4.

20. "An Uproar . . . ," *ibid.*

21. "For Tobacco's Lobbyists, No Nice Days at the Office," *New York Times*, Feb. 25, 1990, p. E4; "Glad to Get Those Gifts," *New York Daily News*, Dec. 18, 1988, p. B5.

22. "New Cigarette Targets Young, White Women," *New Orleans Times-Picayune*, Feb. 18, 1990, p. A6; Mark Green, "Warning: RJR May Endanger Kids' Health," *New York Times*, Mar. 13, 1990, p. A29; Morton Mintz, "Marketing Tobacco to Children," *Nation*, May 6, 1991; "Smoking among Children Is Linked to Cartoon Advertisements," *New York Times*, Dec. 11, 1991, p. D22.

23. "Coors Takes Aim at Women," *Womanfocus Newsletter*, 656 Elmwood Avenue, Buffalo, NY 14222, Summer, 1988, p. 3; Elaine M. Johnson, "Wine Coolers: They're Not a 'Soft' Drink," Rockville, MD: Second National Conference on Alcohol Abuse and Alcoholism, Office for Substance Abuse Prevention (OSAP), U.S. Department of Health and Human Services, Oct. 30–Nov. 2, 1988, flier; "Alcohol Ads Criticized as Appealing to Children," *New York Times*, Nov. 5, 1991, p. A16; "For Minority Youths, 40 Ounces of Trouble," *New York Times*, April 16, 1993, pp. A1, B3.

24. Cockburn, *op. cit.*; Shalom, *op. cit.*; Iris R. Shannon, "World Cigarette Pushers," letter, *New York Times*, Aug. 20, 1989.

25. "Busch Makes Foreign Moves," *New York Times*, Jan. 21, 1991, p. D7; Merrill Singer, "Toward a Political-Economy of Alcoholism—The Missing Link in the Anthropology of Drinking," *Social Science Medicine*, 23(2), 1986, pp. 113–30.

26. "Cocaine: Middle Class High," *Time*, July 6, 1981, pp. 56–63; "Crack, Bane of Inner City, Is Now Gripping Suburbs," *New York Times*, Oct. 1, 1989, pp. 1, 17; Laura M. Markowitz, "Crack: Middle-Class Malady," *Family Therapy Networker*, Nov./Dec. 1990, pp. 40–41; "Drinking Keeps Its Grip on Suburban Teen-Agers," *New York Times*, Oct. 7, 1989, pp. 25, 26; "Poll Finds 40% of Young Doctors Admit Drug Use," *New York Times*, Sept. 25, 1986.

27. "The Line on 'Chorus Line:' Hi-steppin' Drug Abuse?" *New York Daily News*, June 15, 1989, p. 6; Denny Martin Flinn, *What They Did for Love*, New York: Bantam, 1989.

28. "Stress and the Lure of Harmful Remedies, *New York Times*, Oct. 14, 1987, p. B6.

29. Craig Reinarman, Dan Waldorf, and Sheigla B. Murphy, "Cocaine and the Workplace: Empirical Findings and Notes on Scapegoating and Social Control in the Construction of a Public Problem," *Research in Law, Deviance, and Social Control*, 9, 1987, pp. 37–62.

30. Arlie Russell Hochschild, *The Managed Heart: Commercialization of Human Feeling*, Berkeley: University of California Press, 1983, p. 54; also Ralph, *op. cit.*, and Schneider, *op. cit.*

31. "Preventing Drug Abuse in the Workplace," NIDA monograph, Rockville, MD, 1982, pp. 5–6.

32. Douglas Labier, *Modern Madness: The Hidden Link Between Work and Emotional Conflict*, New York: Touchstone, 1989, p. 94.

33. M. Harvey Brenner, *Mental Illness and the Economy*, Cambridge: Harvard University Press, 1973; "Hazards of Unemployment and Hard Economic Times," International Union of Electricians (IUE) Factsheet, n.d.

34. On the Persian Gulf War, see "Some G.I.'s in Gulf Vanquish an Old Foe: Drink or Drugs," *New York Times*, Feb. 18, 1991, pp. A1, 8; on Tailhook, see "Pentagon Report Tells of Aviators' 'Debauchery,'" *New York Times*, April 24, 1993, pp. 1, 9.

35. Benjamin Stein, "The Lure of Drugs: They Organize an Addict's Life," *New York Newsday*, Dec. 4, 1988.

36. "On Streets to Nowhere," *New York Newsday Magazine*, Jan. 21, 1990, pp. 11, 20.

37. Laura M. Markowitz, "Better Living through Chemistry?" *Family Therapy Networker*, May/June 1991, pp. 23–31; see also Peter D. Kramer, *Listening to Prozac: A Psychiatrist Explores Antidepressant Drugs and the Remaking of the Self*, New York: Viking, 1993.

38. "Drinking Keeps Its Grip . . . ," *op. cit.*

39. See Richard Lichtman, "Notes on Accumulation, Time and Aging," *Psychology and Social Theory*, 1, 1981, pp. 69–76.

40. Jean Baudrillard, *In the Shadows of the Silent Majority*, New York: Semiotext(e), 1983, p. 50.

41. Harvey Milkman and Stanley Sunderwirth, *Craving for Ecstasy: The Consciousness of Chemistry and Escape*, Lexington, MA: Lexington, 1987, p. 27.

42. Stanton Peele, *The Meaning of Addiction: Compulsive Experience and Its Interpretation*, Lexington, MA: Lexington, 1985, p. 49; University of California Wellness Letter, 6(9), June 1990.

43. Ernest Drucker, "In Dickens' America," *Family Therapy Networker*, Nov./Dec. 1990, pp. 42–45.

44. Constance Penley and Andrew Ross, "Cyborgs at Large: Interview with Donna Haraway," in Penley and Ross, eds., *Technoculture*, Minneapolis: University of Minnesota Press, 1991, p. 5.

45. Kathleen Fitzgerald, "Philosophical Floundering and (Higher) Power-less Recovery," *Professional Counselor*, March/April 1989, pp. 58–59; also Fitzgerald, *Alcoholism: The Genetic Inheritance*, New York: Doubleday, 1988.

46. "As Addiction Medicine Gains, Experts Debate What It Should Cover," *New York Times*, March 31, 1992, p. C3.

47. Abbie Hoffman, *Steal This Urine Test: Fighting Drug Hysteria in America*, New York: Penguin, 1987, pp. 35, 56; Milkman and Sunderwirth, *op. cit.*

48. "As Addiction Medicine Gains . . . ," *op. cit.* The DSM III-R is the bible for proponents of the medical model of psychopathology and scarcely acknowledges social factors in labeling behavior.

49. On the disappearance of the body, see Celeste Olalquiaga, *Megalopolis: Contemporary Cultural Sensibilities*, Minneapolis: University of Minnesota Press, 1992; on control of the body by protecting social space, see Susan Willis, *A Primer for Daily Life*, New York: Routledge, 1991, chapter 7.

50. "Alcohol on the Rocks," *Newsweek*, Dec. 31, 1984; "The Sobering of America," *Business Week*, Feb. 25, 1985; "America's New Abstinence," *Fortune*, Mar. 18, 1985; "Cocktails 1985: America's New Drinking Habits," *Time*, May 20, 1985; David Wagner, "The New Temperance Movement and Social Control at the Workplace," *Contemporary Drug Problems*, Winter 1987, pp. 539–56; Richard Goldstein, "The New Sobriety: What We Risk When We Just Say No," *Village Voice*, Dec. 30, 1986, pp. 23–28; "A New Temperance Is Taking Root in America," *New York Times*, Mar. 15, 1989, pp. A1, C6.

51. Susan Faludi, *Backlash: The Undeclared War against American Women*, New York: Doubleday, 1992, pp. 427–30; Wagner, "The New Temperance . . . ," *op. cit.* See Craig Reinarman and Harry G. Levine,

"Crack in Context: Politics and Media in the Making of a Drug War," *Contemporary Drug Problems, 16* (4), 1989, pp. 535–77.

52. "More Aid for Addicts on the Job," *New York Times*, Nov. 13, 1989, p. D1; "Assessing the Corporate Fitness Craze," *New York Times*, March 18, 1990, Bus. pp. 1, 6.

53. "Trench Battle Routs Drugs in the Bronx," *New York Times*, Feb. 12, 1991, p. B1.

54. "Billboard Owners Switching, Not Fighting," *New York Times*, April 4, 1990, p. B1; "A Cigarette Campaign under Fire," *New York Times*, Jan. 12, 1990, pp. D1,4. For a discussion on African-American community activists' efforts against the marketing of malt liquor, see "Under Siege: Liquor's Inner-City Pipeline," *New York Times,* Nov. 29, 1992, sect. 3, pp. 1, 6, and "Alcohol Marketing: Continued Vigilance Is Paying Off," *Scope*, Institute on Black Chemical Abuse, Summer 1992 (2616 Nicollet Avenue, Minneapolis, MN 55408). For a discussion of the prevalence of liquor stores in African-American communities see Marvin P. Dawkins, "Policy Issues," in Thomas D. Watts and Roosevelt Wright, Jr., eds., *Black Alcoholism,* Springfield, IL: Charles C. Thomas, 1983, pp. 206–20.

55. "Court Opens Way for Damage Suits Over Cigarettes," *New York Times*, June 25, 1992, pp. A1, B10.

56. "Mixed Response over Campaign to End Smoking," *New York Times*, Oct. 14, 1990, p. 31.

57. "Four Years of Bush's Drug War: New Funds but an Old Strategy," *New York Times*, July 28, 1992, pp. A1, 12; Mark Fraser and Nancy Kohlert, "Substance Abuse and Public Policy," *Social Service Review*, 62(1), March 1988, pp. 103–26.

58. Jack Shafer, "Designer Drugs," *Science*, March 1985, pp. 60ff.

59. Fraser and Kohlert, *op. cit.*

60. "Explosive Drug Use Creating New Underworld in Prisons," *New York Times*, Nov. 27, 1989, p. A15.

61. Dan Baum, "The Drug War on Civil Liberties," *Nation,* June 19, 1992, pp. 886–88.

62. "Legalizing Drugs: Failures Spur Debate," *New York Times,* Nov. 27, 1989, p. A15.

63. Fraser and Kohlert, *op. cit.*

64. Jefferson Morley, "De-Escalating the War," *Family Therapy Networker*, Nov./Dec. 1990, pp. 225–35.

65. *Ibid.*; Drucker, *op. cit.*

66. *Ibid.* The move away from an all-or-nothing approach to changing addictive patterns is gaining ground. See "New Addiction Approach Gets Results," *New York Times,* Sept. 1, 1993, p. C10.

67. University of California Wellness Letter, *op. cit.*

68. Melody Beattie, *Codependent No More* and *Beyond Codepen-*

dency, New York: Harper/Hazelden, 1989; Pia Mellody, *Facing Code-pendence*, New York: Harper and Row, 1989; Ann Wilson Schaef, *Co-dependence: Misunderstood, Mistreated*, Minneapolis: Winston, 1985.

69. Ann Wilson Schaef, *When Society Becomes an Addict*, San Francisco: Harper and Row, 1987.

70. Robin Norwood, *Women Who Love Too Much* and *Letters from Women Who Love Too Much*, New York: Pocket, 1989; Susan Forward and Joan Torres, *Men Who Hate Women and the Women Who Love Them*, New York: Bantam, 1987. For a critique of Norwood, see Faludi, *op. cit.*, pp. 347–56.

71. See Phyllis Schlafly, "Education, the Family, and Traditional Values," in Harvey Holtz, Irwin Marcus, Jim Dougherty, Judy Michaels, and Rick Peduzzi, eds., *Education and the American Dream: Conservatives, Liberals and Radicals Debate the Future of Education*, Granby, MA: Bergin and Garvey, 1989, pp. 21–29.

72. See G. J. Botvin and T. Willis, "Personal and Social Skills Training: Cognitive-Behavioral Approaches to Substance Abuse Prevention," in *Prevention Research: Deterring Drug Abuse among Children and Adolescents*, NIDA Research Monograph, *63*, 1985, pp. 8–49.

73. See Bonnie Benard, "Visions into Reality: Themes of Successful Prevention Programs, *Prevention Forum*, July 1988, pp. 6–11; T. Holtz, "Theoretical Foundations of Prevention," National Development and Research Institutes, Inc. (formerly Narcotic and Drug Research, Inc.), 11 Beach St., New York, n.d.; Charles Rangel, "Businesses Must Do Their Part to Fight Drugs," *New York Times*, Oct. 12, 1990, p. A34.

74. Michael W. Apple, "Curricular Form and the Logic of Technical Control," in Apple and Lois Weis, eds., *Ideology and Practice in Schooling*, Philadelphia: Temple University Press, 1983, pp. 143–65.

75. David Forbes, "Saying No to Ron and Nancy: School-Based Drug Abuse Prevention Programs in the 1980s," *J. Education*, *169*(3), 1987, pp. 80–90; Margit Kellenbenz Epstein and Eugene K. Epstein, "Codependence as Social Narrative," *Readings: A Journal of Reviews and Commentary in Mental Health*, *5*(3), 1990, pp. 4–7.

76. See C. Clark Kissinger, "A Question of Power: How Revolutionary China Got Rid of Drugs," *Revolutionary Worker*, October 10, 1988; Dennis Desmond and Clarence Lusane, "Stopping Bush's Drug War: A Crisis of Race, Class and Global Politics," Washington, DC 20044: Fighting Words, Box 14242, 1990; Clarence Lusane, *Pipe Dream Blues: Racism and the War on Drugs*, Boston: South End Press, 1991.

77. See Mike Davis, *City of Quartz: Excavating the Future in Los Angeles*, New York: Vintage, 1992, chapter 5; Playthell Benjamin, "Down with Crack, *Village Voice*, Sept. 19, 1989, p. 29.

78. Juliet Ucelli and Dennis O'Neil, "The Cost of Drugs: Toward a Progressive Agenda," *Forward Motion*, May, 1990, pp. 2–9.

79. See Stanley Aronowitz and Henry A. Giroux, *Postmodern Education: Politics, Culture, and Social Criticism*, Minneapolis: University of Minnesota Press, 1991, chapter 2.

80. David Levi Strauss, "Culture Wars," *Z Magazine*, Dec. 1990, pp. 39–41.

81. Desmond and Lusane, *op. cit.*, p. 27.

82. Harold S. Williams and Arthur Y. Webb, "The Business Plan vs. the Proposal: Getting Results," Rensselaerville Institute, Rensselaerville, NY, 1988; Memorandum, Arthur Y. Webb, Director, New York State Division of Substance Abuse Services, Feb. 19, 1991.

83. Chris Whittle, "Commercials, Plus Education," *New York Times*, March 1, 1989; "Talking Too Tough on Life's Risks?" *New York Times*, Feb. 16, 1990, p. D1.

84. See Simon Frith, "Picking Up the Pieces," in Simon Frith, ed., *Facing the Music*, New York: Pantheon, 1988, p. 125.

85. See David R. Shumway, "Reading Rock 'n' Roll in the Classroom: A Critical Pedagogy," in Henry A. Giroux and Peter McLaren, eds., *Critical Pedagogy, the State, and Cultural Struggle*, Albany: SUNY Press, 1989.

86. Elayne Rapping, "Girls Just Wanna Have Fun," *Nation*, Aug. 27/Sept. 3, 1990, pp. 206–09.

87. Reinarman, Waldorf, and Murphy, "Cocaine and the Workplace . . . ," *op. cit.*; See also Craig Reinarman, "The Social Construction of an Alcohol Problem: The Case of Mothers against Drunk Drivers and Social Control in the 1980s," *Theory and Society*, 17 (1), 1988, pp. 91–120.

88. Barbara Ehrenreich, "Drug Frenzy: Why the War on Drugs Misses the Real Target," *Utne Reader*, March/April 1989, pp. 76–81.

89. *Ibid.*, p. 79.

90. For examples of educational theorists who address postmodern culture, see Aronowitz and Giroux, *Postmodern Education, op. cit.*; Henry Giroux, *Border Crossings: Cultural Workers and the Politics of Education*, New York: Routledge, 1992; Patti Lather, *Getting Smart: Feminist Research and Pedagogy with/in the Postmodern*, New York: Routledge, 1991; and Linda J. Nicholson, ed., *Feminism/Postmodernism*, New York: Routledge, 1991.

91. Michael Ryan, "Post-Modern Politics," in *Politics and Culture*, Baltimore: John Hopkins, 1989, p. 83.

92. Henri Lefebvre, *Everyday Life in the Modern World*, New York: Harper, 1971, p. 117.

93. Mark Poster, *The Mode of Information: Poststructuralism in Social Context*, Chicago: University of Chicago Press, 1990, pp. 12–13.

94. *Ibid.*, pp. 63–68; Todd Gitlin, "Car Commercials and Miami Vice," in Gitlin, ed., *Watching Television*, New York: Pantheon, 1987, pp. 139–40.

95. Kenneth J. Gergen, *The Saturated Self: Dilemmas of Identity in Contemporary Life*, New York: Basic Books, 1991.

96. Poster, *op. cit.*, pp. 16–17.

97. Paul Willis, *Common Culture*, Boulder: Westview, 1990, p. 159.

98. Antonio Negri, *The Politics of Subversion: A Manifesto for the Twenty-First Century*, Cambridge: Polity, 1989, p. 207.

99. Aronowitz and Giroux, *Postmodern Education*, *op. cit.*; Steven Best and Doublas Kellner, *Postmodern Theory: Critical Interrogations*, New York: Guilford, 1991, chapter 8.

100. Elayne Rapping, "Needed: A Radical Recovery," *Progressive*, Jan. 1993, pp. 32–34.

101. See Pauline Marie Rosenau, *Postmodernism and the Social Sciences: Insights, Inroads, and Intrusions*, Princeton: Princeton University Press, 1992; Aronowitz and Giroux, *Postmodern Education*, *op. cit.*, chapter 3.

PART 2

Culture

CHAPTER 2

Tripping through the Ruins

They firebombed
The dinner table
Taking us completely
By surprise.

We evacuated
Our casualties
From the patio—
Tracers skittering
Across the summer
Sky.

Dad is a memory
We're trying to keep
Alive.

Ron Kolm,
Suburban Ambush

In recent years the United States, along with the rest of the world, has changed in extraordinary ways. Although the Berlin Wall is perhaps the most visible symbol of change, innumerable walls are coming down every day. Disempowered groups whose own experiences run counter to prescribed customs are deconstructing and retelling the official history of social life, for example, the story of Columbus's so-called discovery of America. Citizens subject symbols such as the American flag, once an unambiguous, sacred icon of patriotism, to multifarious readings in museums and in the streets, thereby undercutting the belief that such signs have one true meaning. Other forms of art highlight the unsettling and bizarre nature of daily life which accompanies the loss of stable values. A movie like David Lynch's *Blue Velvet* (1986) parodies the idealized American community by exposing its underbelly. Lynch discloses the disturbing events in one small town only to restore its saccharine veneer in the end and mocks the myth that things never change. Throughout the society various institutions belie their purpose and things are not what they appear to be. The effects can leave people reeling.

In the official account of everyday life, for example, the one alluded to in President Reagan's 1984 campaign, "It's Morning in America," there is a nostalgic harkening back to a mythic industrial-era community where people felt safe and assured. This myth promises people that there is still certainty, structure, and purpose within everyday routines and institutions. Folks live in intact families and in the morning go off to work or school feeling happy. At other times they have just a drink or two, watch TV, attend church, save money in the local bank, and shop in the local stores. Mom cares for the kids but Father Knows Best. The United States is number one, and the government acts in our best interests, even when it has to lie sometimes. These social agents balance one another; their boundaries are firm and they provide stability and continuity. *It's a Wonderful Life.* When things go awry—a divorce, a layoff, a school dropout, a drunken binge, a foreign country that acts out of line—an intervention or two may be required, but things will right themselves and soon get back to the way they should be.

This modernist myth is akin to an alcoholic denial fantasy. It stands in stark contrast to the shifting, nebulous contours of community life today. When politicians and community organizers invoke the word *community,* it still conjures up the powerful image of a sacrosanct entity, an organic unit of home, church, workplace, school, and civic polity shared by people of different stripes. Yet the word *community* itself has become undone, and its meaning is no longer intact. Communities have become dispersed, decentered, and redefined:

> Most Americans no longer live in traditional communities. They live in suburban subdivisions by highways and sprinkled with shopping malls, or in tony condominiums and residential clusters, or in ramshackle apartment buildings and housing projects. Most of them commute to work and socialize on some basis other than geographic proximity. And most people pick up and move to a different neighborhood every five years or so.[1]

Capital is restructuring community life at a rapid pace. The development of the electronic media has created new networks of communities which transcend place-bound ties and allow for new forms of connectedness and power. Yet the same technology also isolates and segments groups; it fragments experience and limits contact with others. As restructuring occurs on a global scale, it carves up urban areas into concentrated cores of financial and professional service providers and peripheral sites of the poor and powerless. The forces which reconfigure the metropolitan land-scape not only affect the society as a whole but damage the tissue of local community life. Proximity no longer guarantees that peo-ple will fulfill neighborly duties and share mutual concerns. Neighbors at best share similar income, but this fact reflects the class-stratified nature of society and does not imply common interest. Traditional means to restore community like grass-roots organizing then become less effective. The overall changes gener-ate new kinds of communities and with them the challenge to develop alternative political strategies that can use the media and other relevant technologies to access power.

Profound changes have occurred within and between some communal social forms such as the workplace, the family, the school, and government. These referents have had a loaded mean-ing in our culture; they often have stood for well-defined entities and stir strong feelings of inviolability. But in recent years they have been emptied of much of their meaning, transformed into fading traces of forms which are no longer solid. Perhaps no other social phenomenon represents the loss of traditional community more than the increase in the number of homeless across the country. The homeless through their social displacement become vanishing bodies, with less market value than commodities or rental property. They are emblematic of the failure of the job economy, the privatized family structure, the educational system, and the state to provide a decent network of support for so many citizens. Some may make just as strong a case for the deaths of AIDS patients as a metaphor for the spiritual decline of a society which does not care about its citizens, as does Tony Kushner in the play, "Angels in America." Others see drug addicts whose bodies are wasting away as the primary symbol of a tattered social fabric.

In all cases the body as an objective referent disappears, social networks of support unravel, and the cornerstones of modernist society give way to a postmodern culture. In the following part I describe the ongoing changes from modernist to postmodern cul-ture, in particular the way technology and the electronic media have transformed modernist relationships within work, the family, the school, and government. I highlight the way the changes articulate with substance use, addictive relations, and the response to the drug crisis.

But the changes themselves reflect the loss of faith in fixed familiar forms. In this sense the move from modernist to postmodern relations is a move away from relations which depend on the addictive processes of control of others and denial of experience through particular hierarchical forms of social life, although the change to postmodern forms does not guarantee less addictive alternatives. The aim is to show that postmodern culture is not an abstract construct but is manifest through real relations. This trip through the postmodern landscape also justifies an alternative approach to prevention which does not rely on modernist concepts and forms but instead acknowledges the changing nature of American culture.

WORK

The rock-solid belief that work in the form of wage labor is self-redemptive, leads to success, and is necessary for the good of society has begun to disintegrate, leaving a skeletal structure on which people still try to stand. Much work, what remains of it, is boring and unnecessary and has become less central to people's consciousness. As the economy shifts from manufacturing to financial and service industries, more people do word processing and meaningless, nonproductive, invisible, and fragmenting tasks. Many service jobs in advertising, insurance, and finance produce endless bytes of data garbage, and retail jobs (for example, standing around in a designer sneakers boutique or frozen yogurt store) serve as a disguised form of unemployment.[2] The move from manufacturing to service jobs has meant fewer jobs for unskilled workers and more low-paying, part-time work with fewer benefits. The criterion for employment is economic growth for its own sake, not social usefulness.

Within this climate corporate interests have squeezed workers to maximize profits. The antidrug movement in part arose from corporate need to regulate the work force in order to stem productivity losses and increased health costs incurred from employee drug and alcohol abuse.[3] Charles Rangel (D-NY), chair of the House Select Committee on Narcotics Abuse and Control, states, "Winning the war against drugs is in the interest of American business," and cites "distinguished business leaders" who have told his committee that America cannot compete in the world market without ridding our work force of drugs.[4] Employers figure that with a shrinking pool of skilled, experienced workers it is more cost effective to rehabilitate users than to fire them; those workers identified through drug testing may then be mandated to attend the company's employee assistance program under the implied threat of losing their jobs.

The Drug-Free Workplace Act of 1988 recommended that all federal and private-sector employees be tested for drugs. Yet use itself, whether of legal or illegal drugs, does not imply work impairment. Many articles on cocaine problems in the workplace contain no hard evidence about impairment that could justify deployment of mandatory testing and surveillance.[5] Advocates for workers, including unions, argue that measures used against workers such as testing and screening are part of a policy of social control.[6] In any case, there are no foolproof tests that determine the presence of illegal drugs because many legal drugs masking as illegal substances show up as false positives. Drug testing itself does nothing to ensure safe workplace conditions and is a way to intimidate working people. To control individuals is part of corporations' tendency to ignore systematic factors such as unsafe and stressful work conditions for which they bear a large responsibility and which increase workers' stress, illness, and medical costs.

In the 1980s American capital further pursued its transnational interests and fled to third world countries. Corporations shut down manufacturing sites in the northeast and Midwest and laid off legions of employees. The identity of many working people had become bound up with the welfare of their corporate employers. As a result, some males in heavy industry and manufacturing, raised to equate self-esteem with earning a wage and believing that their work was valued, lost faith in their ability to get ahead and in the growth of the economy.[7] In industry as well as service sectors many others discovered that they were redundant as a result of huge advances in technology. Farmers raised on self-sufficiency and family ownership saw their farms foreclosed by banks in the 1980s.

Children of workers and farmers no longer expect to find work similar to their parents'. In cities, because of the loss of a manufacturing base, there are no viable jobs for unskilled labor, and hundreds of thousands of marginally skilled and young people go without legal work.[8] The crumbling manufacturing economy has decimated the infrastructure of inner cities, generating despair and poverty, which in turn breed crack, heroin, and alcohol abuse. To fill the void, people operate huge underground economies in which they peddle goods and services off the books.[9] The illegal drug trade is one lucrative sector of the underground and is often the most profitable alternative.

But the war on drugs has created new work for others. The drug trade in turn feeds an army of gainfully employed who work in law enforcement, prisons, drug testing, and securities industries and services. For example, drug companies take in hefty profits from the use of laboratory testing for illegal drugs of workers by employers. One former government bureaucrat assesses the costs facing employers under the federal drug-testing program and describes what the term *work* now means for some people in a service economy: "A[n antidrug] policy has to be written. That's money for lawyers. A minimum of one hour of training for supervisors is required: money for trainers. Urine is collected forensically: money for collectors. Samples are taken in a hurry to a certified laboratory: money for Federal Express. And tests are reviewed by a licensed physician and then reported to the company."[10] Crime does pay for some.

The antidrug movement has generated a new growth industry, drug and alcohol treatment programs, which have gained new clients and increased profits. This has happened in at least three ways.[11] First, the treatment industry has benefited from the states' fiscal crises, which led to more contracting out to voluntary programs. Second, because alcohol and drug problems have been defined as diseases and patients are eligible for health insurance coverage, programs have increased their funds through third party payments. Last, many corporate hospital chains began marketing their own treatment progams or sold chemical dependency units to private companies. Also, the campaign against drunk drivers along with the legal crackdowns against drug users and dealers has bloated the criminal justice system and benefited some lawyers; defending drunken drivers has become a "booming and lucrative legal specialty" and the "fastest growing area of the law."[12]

Because capital controls technology many workers see it not as a liberating force but as their undoing. Capital does not use technology to reduce time and effort spent doing miserable work but rather serves to force working people to defend their life-draining jobs against layoffs as a measure of economic and psychic survival. Unions, as Stanley Aronowitz has argued, instead of fighting for guaranteed income and less work time, try to hold up the creaking scaffold of meaningless work and in essential ways have become insurance companies for their members. But some workers embrace the implied benefits of technology by refusing to work. Absenteeism due to physical, emotional, or drug and alcohol problems is a form of worker resistance on an individual basis, as is some drug and alcohol use itself.[13] In more advanced countries such as the Netherlands and in Scandinavia the rate of absenteeism is very high, and many workers claim disability benefits on the basis of stress from frustration and boredom from work.[14] Others already laid off because of laborsaving technology have learned to accept nonwork time and to turn it to their advantage. Brooklyn longshoremen made redundant by containerization were able to sustain their sense of community and develop personal interests without the benefit of a work-centered existence.[15]

American working people as a whole have been unable to organize themselves around mutual interests. Trade union membership has declined and with it the influence of unions as a political and cultural force in working people's daily lives. Unions imploded under the weight of antilabor acts by the Reagan administration as well as from the corporate practice of strike-breaking through hiring permanent replacement workers. The ground has shifted beneath workplace organizing as a locus of social change, with its use of face-to-face disputes and consensual debates. Mark Poster argues provocatively that "the factory site, with its massed, impoverished workers, no longer presents . . . the opportunity of revolutionary talk. If contestatory language is to emerge today, it must do so in the context of TV ads and databases, of computers and communications satellites. . . . "[16]

Corporate elites are now more vulnerable to economic forces and have had to adjust to changes in work as well. Although they have more resources with which to handle a crisis they share some similar concerns with the rank and file. Over the last decade corporations trimmed middle-management jobs during a shaky economy.[17] An article on the effects of the 1990s recession on white-collar workers suggests that the fitting visual image to replace the breadlines of the 1930s would be men and women alone in their suburban kitchens using their touch-tone phones to tell a computer they are still out of work.[18] Some executives have started to doubt the culture of work altogether, the compulsive need to work and accumulate money. *Workaholism* has become a familiar word among some sectors of the upper echelons.[19] One management consultant helps executives examine their "addictive-compulsive behaviors" and obsessive need to control others.[20] Many feel trapped within their careers and have sacrificed emotional needs for their work. A survey by a national drug treatment service found that corporate executives and other high-paid professionals use twice as much cocaine as those who make less.[21]

Working and middle-class people have been unable to stay abreast of inflation, and the number of working people with incomes below the poverty level has grown since the late 1970s.[22] As real wages declined and the quality of life leveled off, many of the postwar baby boomers were forced to realize that their prospects for steady material gain were not guaranteed by work.[23] More women have sought work outside the home sometimes just to try to stay even with living costs. Many of them, raised to assume the role of primary childcaretaker, now find themselves as both breadwinner and parent unassisted by men and by society at large. The workplace has yet to even deal with the need for childcare, flex-time, job sharing, paternity leave, and other ways to accommodate the needs of working mothers and parents. Many parents work two jobs at odd hours and are unable to spend leisure time together or develop any sense of family life.

In short, there are few adequate jobs for people; much work itself is unnecessary, unfulfilling, and barely sustaining; the increasing technological nature of work relies on self-referential language and has less to do with actual materials; and the work ethic has become less satisfying for people across different classes. The norms and values which hold everyday work life together grow more irrational.

FAMILY

The sanctity of the family as extolled by the Right has a pious stink which will not go away. It is as if the corpse is rotting before people's eyes, yet they look under the bed for the source of decay.

For many the privatized, nuclear family has been unable to deliver the goods its ideology proposes: to serve as a place where you receive nurturance and unconditional acceptance, experience a sense of stability and security, and learn healthy and appropriate social skills and moral values. The Right has captured people's legitimate yearning for these things and packaged and sold them in the form of the patriarchal family: strong dad, nurturant mom, well-adjusted kids. But to restrict care to the family impoverishes the rest of society: "As a bastion against a bleak society [the family] has made that society bleak. It is indeed a major agency for caring, but in monopolizing care it has made it harder to undertake other forms of care. . . . Caring, sharing and loving would be more widespread if the family did not claim them for its own."[24]

Some feminists have argued that the patriarchal nuclear family is a Procrustean bed which cannot accommodate many men, women, children, gays and lesbians, and other singles for whom the family is restrictive and life draining.[25] So-called singles are never quite considered to be bona fide adults until they marry.[26] Gays and lesbians by and large remain stigmatized outcasts who have been subjected to more open hostility since the Reagan era. Yet their increasing visibility and militance around gay rights in the military and elsewhere, the demand for more AIDS research funding, and the support for teaching tolerance and condom distribution in the New York City schools have challenged traditional gender roles forged within the patriarchal family and have shaken up the society as a whole. The adult children of alcoholics movement which emerged in the 1980s has dealt another blow to the idealized family. It has shed light on how alcoholic and other troubled privatized families wreak havoc on children's development.[27] Alcohol abuse is often implicated in child and spousal abuse as well as in incest.

Many families are unable to stay together. During the 1980s divorce became the norm in many areas, and the intact nuclear family now represents a minority of households. Yet those headed by single women, though numerous, are still considered deviant and suffer from systematic lack of material, financial, and social support.[28] Many women spend much of their lives alone caring for children and for indigent or sick relatives at home.

Childhood is dangerous for many, especially for poor black males.[29] In some inner-city areas children who deal drugs have turned family structure upside down as they assume the role of family breadwinner. In other families crack abuse has depleted the financial and emotional resources of grandmothers, aunts, and other relatives who were part of the support system for the children. Throughout the country children have become runaways or throwaways, leaving or forced to leave impossible circumstances.[30] Many homeless children are incest victims and come from substance-abusing families. Some create satellite families on the streets or join gangs, which sociologist Terry Williams sees as representing "new family structures, new values. They're organized resistance."[31] But much of the disaffection and terrorism of youth gangs in the United States and Britain is based not on rebellion or avowal of some positive class subculture, which would still involve participation, but on despair.[32]

The family is a crucible where people's deepest emotional needs are forged. But the ways these needs were met a few years ago, if they ever were, are not adequate for the way life is today. For many who seek or live with marriage partners, the ideology of the past, to adapt Marx's phrase, "weighs like a nightmare on the brain of the living." In my personal and professional experience I find that women who have begun to demand equality of partnership from men discover many men to be threatened, emotionally withdrawn, or otherwise abusive, and to lack the social skills needed in interactive work and childrearing.[33] Some women learn to be attracted to the very qualities in a man which later become a problem in a relationship or marriage, qualities which were better suited for an earlier, industrial society: strong, rational, decisive, in control, able to provide for others. Many men first look for women who can do the affective work necessary to help them regulate their moods, sustain a relationship, maintain a social network, and raise children. But often they are later overwhelmed or angered by a woman's assertion of needs and expression of her own feelings or by her presumed lack of rationality and other male-identified traits.

The boundary between the supposedly peaceful, privatized family as sanctuary and the hostile outside world has begun to blur. The electronic media have brought alternative ideas into the home from the outside. One effect is that more women and children can now label the emotional and physical terrorism they have experienced behind closed doors and are more aware of their legal and psychological rights. The state now intervenes in more active ways in cases of domestic violence and child physical and sexual abuse. (However, intervention itself is troublesome when it tends to violate the personal rights and dignities of its clients, which often happens with the poorer ones; just as often the state fails to protect women and children or provide a decent alternative for youth through the foster care system.) Because of technology fewer males need to perform manual labor and more women are freed from the cycle of childrearing. The electronic media help break down the barriers between public (male) spheres and domestic (female) ones: "Men are now able to 'hunt' for information at home computers and women can breastfeed children while doing business on the telephone."[34]

In the changing family the father is no longer the center of control and reason, and the mother is no longer just the self-sacrificing nurturer. The breakdown in this division of labor between male authority and female caretaking loosens rigid gender roles and allows for contrary feelings and more fluid ways of being. Some people are finding alternative, often contradictory ways of relating to partners and children which are neither strictly feminist nor traditional.[35]

But many parents are overwhelmed with changes in their personal lives and fail to renegotiate the outmoded boundaries between themselves and their children. The parents become needy themselves, and their children, to use an apt bit of mental health jargon, become parentified. Television has helped blur the border between childhood and adulthood. Unlike printed media, which can filter out certain information, TV shows expose children to private adult contexts where adults may express uncertainty, childlike behavior, and secret ruses in order to show children they know best. Meyrowitz refers to the secret of secrecy, that once adults could keep secrets from children and also keep their secret keeping secret:

> As television blurs the dividing line between adults' backstage behaviors and their onstage roles, many child-like behaviors emerge into the new, public adult role. Television's exposure of the "staging of adulthood"—with its secret-keeping and the secret of secrecy—undermines both traditional childhood naivete *and* the all-knowing, confident adult role and fosters the movement toward a "middle region," uni-age behavioral style.[36]

The changing boundaries between adults and children are a problem for many, but there is no going back. The more parents try to wrap themselves in the iron-clad rules of traditional patterns of childrearing, that is, child control, the tighter the chains become: don't express your feelings, don't question authority, don't betray the family, be nice, be overresponsible. In many families women are battered and trapped, children are harmed in emotional, physical, and sexual ways, and men are confused, threatened, and angry to the point of violence. Families are working harder to maintain a sense of status in a competitive, hierarchical society with fewer paths to achieve it. The desperate attempt by parents to ensure a future of middle-class propriety in the face of the demise of familiar values leads to anguish and ennui for many youth.[37] Upholding the modernist family carries a high cost.

SCHOOLS

Schools face a crisis of purpose and meaning. Critics of education have written from conservative, liberal, and radical perspectives about the need for school reform.[38] All recognize that schooling today does not meet the needs of children or of society and is a disgrace in many ways. Academic standards based on tests have declined, and American students rank below those of other industrialized countries. Crime, violence, vandalism, teen pregnancies, suicide, and high dropout rates characterize many schools. Drug use is symptomatic of the boredom or stress that students experience. The 1990 annual federal government survey of high school seniors, a measure of middle-class behaviors, reported that cocaine use continued to decline but that alcohol and cigarette consumption remained high.[39]

The problems with schools reflect the problems of the society as a whole. School funding ranks below that of other major industrial countries, and there is little commitment to children's health care and well-being.[40] But mainstream educators, politicians, and corporate and media heads rail against lower standards and assume that the problems are a matter of quantitative adjustments, without looking at how the purpose of education has changed. At best, some want to upgrade the teaching profession and encourage top college students to pursue teaching careers (the Teach for America Program) without a commitment to an increase in salary.

Schools no longer serve to train a future work force because there are few available jobs. Yet many schools continue to act as if industrial era factory and clerical jobs still exist, as if the diverse school population of African-Americans, Latinos, Caribbean immigrants, and disaffected white youth will be absorbed into a viable manufacturing economy as did earlier generations. A growing number of radical cultural educators who promote critical pedagogy and the study of popular culture have handed down a trenchant indictment of schools: they tend to instill arbitrary social control through petty rules, rote learning, and the teaching of facts devoid of value and historical context; they operate within dense, rigid bureaucracies which seldom make use of the cultural capital of teachers and students; and they rely on formal learning imposed from the top down instead of starting with children's knowledge generated from their own experience which can be validated and held up for critical scrutiny.[41] One critic describes schools as repositories for youthful consumers of "economically generated waste" where children passively absorb curricular products and materials.[42] Students are unfulfilled, bored, and anxious. There is no useful place for them in society other than school, which cultivates these feelings of discontent, which in turn help to transform them into restless consumers in search of ever more satisfying products and services.

But the consumptive nature of childhood creates a crisis for youth and society at large. As youth partake in the consumer society, the age-appropriate boundaries of childhood and adolescence dissolve. Children now absorb considerable information from popular culture to which adults alone were once privy. Children are less innocent and more like adults by virtue of easy access to movies, videos, tapes, computers, modems, cable TV, and pay telephone services. These modes of information short-circuit the age-based course of social knowledge which children once learned through printed material and instead present sophisticated knowledge all at once. The immediacy of popular culture in children's lives has made school knowledge more irrelevant and has undermined the legitimacy of the values taught by school authorities.

> Through electronic media, young children are witnesses to "facts" that contradict social myths and ideals in school. Children see politicians disgraced, police officers and teachers on strike for higher pay, parents accused of battering their children.

Through television news and entertainment, children learn too much about the nature of "real" life to believe the ideals their teachers try to teach them.[43]

In light of what children learn elsewhere, the absurdity of arbitrary school adult authority becomes more apparent. For example, shows on television during the fall 1990 season—"Parenthood," "Ferris Bueller," "Hull High," "Uncle Buck," and "Parker Lewis Can't Lose"—reflect the subversive attitude many students hold toward the meaninglessness of school and the lack of legitimate authority of many teachers and principals, who are shown up to be clowns or fools.[44] Some critics lament youth's loss of innocence and the loss of authority to the power of television.[45] But this nostalgic view denies the reality of popular culture in the lives of children. Schools would do better to study television and help students analyze both its manipulative and liberating aspects. Most schools fail to provide for the social needs of children today, to help protect them against violence, AIDS, drug abuse, teen pregnancy, and child abuse, and to offer them viable skills for the future. To that extent they remain in cultural bankruptcy.

THE STATE

The brief era of the American empire is in decline. Despite the 1991 Persian Gulf War victory, Americans have not forgotten the failure of intervening in Vietnam as President Bush had hoped they would and have become even more sceptical of the Gulf War's moral basis over time. The empire continues to face global and domestic challenges to its rule. Japan and Germany, two countries it helped rebuild, have become powers in their own right. Oil-rich nations have asserted their economic strength in America's face; in some cases extremists have held Americans hostage, carried out terrorist attacks (the *Achille Lauro* and Pan Am flight 103), and have drawn the military into quagmires in Lebanon and the Persian Gulf. The collapse of the Communist regimes in Eastern Europe failed to yield a peace dividend at home and underscored the state's inability to tackle domestic ills such as racism, AIDS, homelessness, a savings and loan swindle, and infrastructure maintenance.

The state as a site of authority itself has become delegitimated and decentered. The European Economic Community that minimizes borders, the regional movements for autonomy in Eastern Europe, and the breakup of the Soviet Union have helped weaken the power of the centralized state worldwide. Transnational corporations without allegiance to any country have become superpowers in their own right and generate global economic inequities. Nation states are supposed to manage these disparities. But this task is immune from political debate, and the state, as it takes in less revenue, adopts the policy of austerity and forfeits the idea that politics can lead to a better world.[46] As the state's fiscal crisis worsens, the government sells off its services, even its name, to the private sector. In an effort to raise money, the Federal Archives allowed Philip Morris, the tobacco corporation, to cosponsor an exhibit on the anniversary of the Bill of Rights.[47]

Working and middle-class people have become more alienated from government and politics in recent years.[48] The executive branch grew in corruption as it became less accountable, as evidenced first by the Watergate scandal and later by Iran-Contragate and other Reagan-era scandals. A bare majority bothered to vote in the 1988 presidential election, and an anti-incumbent sentiment emerged in 1990. Throughout the 1980s the Right drew on citizens' distrust of government and led tax revolts on both state and federal levels. One of President Reagan's goals was to get government off people's backs. He deregulated industries and cut back taxes, moves which benefited corporations and the wealthy and ushered in a period of considerable greed. George Bush continued to reduce the state's commitment toward human welfare and encouraged private voluntarism ("a thousand points of light").

The bloc of labor, liberals, African-Americans, and others formed during the New Deal relied on the state, in particular under the Democrats, for social reform. But the alliance dissolved, and neither the state nor the Democrats, beginning with President Carter's budget cutbacks for social spending, serve as guarantors of civil rights, occupational health and safety, subsidized housing, health care, or food benefits for homeless, poor, and working people. In urban centers state-oriented agencies—such as the Democratic party clubhouse, which once served as a community center where citizens could engage in local power brokering and gossip—play less of a role in everyday life. On the Left the Leninist strategy of seizing state force has given way to diverse centers of protest, social movements which do not demand state power but in some cases accommodate themselves to it.[49]

Whereas the central authority of the state has decreased at home and abroad, its power seems to be dispersed everywhere. Former actor President Reagan embodied this paradox. He advocated weakening government but spread the idea through the strong power of the executive. He did this in part by infusing every household with the flickering cathode glow of his mythic vision of America. Reagan was everywhere and nowhere. He made up stories, fumbled with facts, and dozed during meetings. But his paternal image held the country in a druglike trance while he read his lines with charm, all the while dismantling the government. His gestures often were more important than any substantive actions, and his performance and image as president were as significant as the fact that he was president.[50] George Bush may have won his term because he presented an on-screen image more like Reagan than did his opponent.[51] Bush later managed to make himself disappear as a person of substance. One columnist termed him the "Incredible Shrinking President" because he shunned responsibility for his tax hike and failed to demonstrate domestic leadership, and Gary Trudeau's comic strip *Doonesbury* portrayed both Bush and Dan Quayle as invisible.[52]

The electronic media help undermine politicians' authority. Television subverts the mystique of power when it exposes the personal idiosyncrasies of leaders beneath the harsh glare of floodlights. The media have held politicians to a hyperstandard of morality through the relentless exposure of their personal lives; examples are 1988 Democratic presidential candidate Senator Gary Hart's infidelities, defense secretary candidate John Tower's drinking problem, and candidate Bill Clinton's marital problems. Through repetitive assaults the media saturate citizens with images and soundbites of politicians which strip their words of meaning and force. During the 1992 New Hampshire Republican presidential primary, challenger Patrick Buchanan ran a TV ad which played back President Bush's 1988 broken pledge, "Read my lips. No New Taxes." One journalist described a new twist to the cycle of viewer interest, then bordom and disgust, with watching a commercial over and over:

> At some point, maybe around the 50th showing, for some viewers the sound bite begins to acquire a surreal fascination, as if it is disclosing something deep inside Mr. Bush. As he jabs his finger into the air and screeches again, with each commercial he

begins to seem more and more desperate, more and more absurd. For these dedicated television viewers, it has been difficult to take the President seriously ever since.[53]

Through technology and the media the state dismantles itself and disperses its power over its citizens within more areas of life. Michel Foucault argues that power today is imposed less through brute force and more by the constant monitoring of everyday life that adjusts behavior to the norms. Privacy disappears and people learn to participate in the surveillance process as they discipline and monitor themselves through database technologies. Mark Poster argues:

> Social security cards, drivers' licenses, credit cards, library cards and the like—the individual must apply for them, have them ready at all times, use them continuously. Each transaction is recorded, encoded and added to the databases. Individuals themselves in many cases fill out the form; they are at once the source of information and the recorder of the information.[54]

As the perceived Communist menace has vanished and the government can do less in the face of domestic problems, terrorism, global insurgency, and competition, it fabricates enemies abroad and at home to shore up its legitimacy. Drugs become concentrated evil; the bad guys are Latin American suppliers and inner-city drug pushers and users against whom the government wages a war on drugs. Much of the war, the repressive use of state force and propaganda, is a way to counter the weakened legitimacy of the state. The war, of course, has failed to reduce the drug supply, help drug addicts, or restore a sense of safety within urban areas.[55] In some neighborhoods in New York City residents feel that the drug dealers have a free hand and that the arms of the state, that is, politicians and the criminal justice system (the police, courts, prisons), are more powerless in the face of rampant crime than in the past.[56]

On a broader level the war mentality limits debate about the necessity, tactics, and purpose of a war in the first place.[57] It prevents public scrutiny of drug policies which affect supply and demand, for example, a Latin American policy which leads *campesinos* to produce coca as a cash crop and a social policy of neglect which contributes to drug demand at home. Instead the government wages war on pleasure by defining all drugs as dangerous and casts sex and rock and roll in the same light. The government tries to restore some its power by increasing surveillance over its citizens through drug testing, restricting birth control and abortion information to teens and women, and censoring rock lyrics.[58]

The war mentality posits absolute evil in some foreign substance or subversive group while those on the side of the state assume the role of good guys. Yet this strategy is no longer effective because the government cannot control information about what it does. Media exposure of the hypocrisy, pious absolutism, and lawbreaking of some politicians and law enforcers themselves contributes to a climate of moral ambiguity with respect to the war on drugs and police work itself. Other media images show that control of others through legal force can become an addiction as well. Movies with Sylvester Stallone, Arnold Schwarzenegger, and Steven Seagal justified such a high level of violence in the service of the law that the line between right and wrong grew hazy. In movies like *To Live and Die in LA* (1985) and *Rush* (1992) police officers succumbed to corruption and crossed over the ambiguous line of the law in order to get the dealers. They sometimes became addicted themselves, as did the drug agent played by Don Johnson in a series of episodes of the TV show "Miami Vice." *Rush* shows the results of addictive behavior on both sides of the law; the undercover cops become addicted after following the orders of the obsessed, fundamentalist police chief to set up a dealer through illegal means.

The state's tough enforcement of drug laws has not stopped the violence which plagues many inner-city neighborhoods. It may even strengthen the violent code of behavior which some urban teenage males adopt. One researcher argues that "it is now a rite of passage that you must go to prison on at least a misdemeanor. What you see on the street is the ethics of a maximum-security prison."[59]

In sum, the state suffers from a legitimation crisis. Citizenship disappears as traditional politics is no longer a viable activity which engages the imagination and efforts of the populace. State law enforcement is less a clear-cut case of right over wrong as it is an ambiguous activity which more people now question. The electronic media have undermined and transformed politics, and politics becomes the effort to secure everyday life itself.

SUMMARY

Our trip through the postmodern landscape shows how modernist community dissolves into a fragmented hyperspace of floating signs. The changes represent a loss of stable relations for better and worse. The electronic media and other technologies unmoor adherence to reified, addictive forms which depend on a certain kind of control over others and the denial of contradictory experiences. Drug and alcohol use per se are part of these forms. The hypocrisy of the conservative's war against drug and alcohol consumption is that it does not admit the link between substance abuse and addictive patterns and these traditional forms which conservatives try to idealize and uphold. To cling to forms which have outlived their purpose is itself an addictive process which attempts to reify changing relations. The progressive side of the battle against drugs and alcohol argues that certain modernist forms are outmoded. Yet it must acknowledge that the legitimate elements of modernist institutions need to reappear within new social contexts. This changing landscape forms the backdrop for an understanding of everyday addictive relations and the efforts toward prevention of and recovery from those relations within an emerging postmodern culture.

NOTES

1. Robert B. Reich, "Secession of the Successful," *New York Times Magazine*, Jan 20, 1991, p. 17.

2. See Daniel A. Foss and Ralph Larkin, *Beyond Revolution: A New Theory of Social Movements*, South Hadley, MA: Bergin and Garvey, 1986, pp. 149–58; Stanley Aronowitz, "Why Work?" *Social Text*, 12, 1985, pp. 19–42.

3. See Keith Dixon, "The Coercion of Labor by Mental Health Professionals," *Social Policy*, 14(4), 1984, pp. 47–54; Peggy Mann, "The Hidden Scourge of Drugs in the Workplace," *Readers Digest* reprint, Feb. 1984; "More Aid for Addicts on the Job," *New York Times*, Nov. 13, 1989, p. D1; Diana Ralph, *Work and Madness: The Rise of Community Psychiatry*, Montreal: Black Rose, 1983; David Wagner, "The New Temperance Movement and Social Control at the Workplace," *Contemporary Drug Problems*, Winter 1987, pp. 539–56.

4. Letter, "Businesses Must Do Their Part to Fight Drugs," *New York Times*, Oct. 12, 1990, p. A34.

5. Royer F. Cook, "Drug Use among Working Adults: Prevalence Rates and Estimation Methods," in Steven W. Gust, Ph.D. and J. Michael Walsh, Ph.D, eds., *Drugs in the Workplace: Research and Evaluation Data*, Rockville, MD: NIDA Monograph 91, 1989; Craig Reinarman, Dan Waldorf, and Sheigla B. Murphy, "Cocaine and the Workplace: Empirical Findings and Notes on Scapegoating and Social Control in the Construction of a Public Problem," *Research in Law, Deviance, and Social Control, 9*, 1987, pp. 37–62; "Testing Employees for Drugs," *New York Times*, April 12, 1992, p. F27.

6. Reinarman et al., *ibid.*; Wagner, *op. cit.*; "Worker Drug Test Provoking Debate," *New York Times*, May 3, 1986, pp. 1, 32; "Testing Employees . . . ," *ibid.*

7. "Hard Work Can't Stop Hard Times," *New York Times*, Nov. 25, 1990, pp. A1, 30.

8. "Youths Lacking Special Skills Find Jobs Leading Nowhere," *New York Times*, Sept 14, 1990, p. B1.

9. "On the Sidewalks, Business Is Booming," *New York Times*, Sept. 24, 1990, p. B1.

10. "Booming Business: Drug Use Tests," *New York Times*, Jan. 3, 1990, p. D2; see also "Boom in Drug Tests Expected," *New York Times*, Sept. 8, 1986, pp. D1, 21.

11. Craig Reinarman, "The Social Construction of an Alcohol Problem: The Case of Mothers against Drunk Drivers and Social Control in the 1980s," *Theory and Society, 17* (1), 1988, pp. 91–120.

12. "Lawyers Are Finding Ways to Circumvent Stricter Statutes against Drunken Driving," *Wall Street Journal*, Nov. 2, 1984, p. 33.

13. Douglas Labier, *Modern Madness: The Hidden Link between Work and Emotional Conflict*, New York: Touchstone, 1989, p. 35; Ralph, *op. cit.*

14. "The Dutch Forget the Work Ethic and Call In Sick," *New York Times*, Oct. 6, 1990, p. 5.

15. William DiFazio, *Longshoremen: Community and Resistance on the Brooklyn Waterfront*, Hadley, MA: Bergin and Garvey, 1985.

16. Mark Poster, *The Mode of Information: Poststructuralism and Social Context*, Chicago: University of Chicago Press, 1990, p. 80.

17. "Jobless Executives Get Solace and Aid in Support Groups," *New York Times*, Sept. 24, 1990, p. A1.

18. "Economic Trend for 90's: Fear," *New York Times*, Nov. 5, 1991, p. B1.

19. Bryan E. Robinson, *Work Addiction: Hidden Legacies of Adult Children*, Deerfield: Health Communications, 1989; Stephen Rothman, "Working Ourselves to Death," *Focus*, Feb./Mar. 1990, pp. 16ff.; Diane

Fassel, *Working Ourselves to Death: The High Cost of Workaholism and the Rewards of Recovery*, San Francisco: HarperCollins, 1990.

20. "A Spiritual Healer for the Workplace," *New York Times*, June 10, 1990.

21. Labier, *op. cit.*

22. "Hard Work Can't Stop Hard Times," *op. cit.*

23. Barbara Ehrenreich, *Fear of Falling: The Inner Life of the Middle Class*, New York: Harper, 1990; Katherine S. Newman, *Falling from Grace: The Experience of Downward Mobility in the American Middle Class*, New York: Vintage, 1988.

24. Michelle Barrett and Mary McIntosh, *The Anti-Social Family*, London: Verso, 1982, p. 80.

25. Barrie Thorne and Marilyn Yalom, eds., *Rethinking the Family: Some Feminist Questions*, New York: Longman, 1982; Lynne Segal, ed., *What Is to Be Done about the Family: Crises in the Eighties*, New York: Penguin, 1983.

26. "Society Looks Askance at the Family of One," *New York Times*, Feb. 28, 1991.

27. "Alcohol and the Family," *Newsweek*, Jan. 18, 1988, pp. 62–68.

28. Ruth Sidel, *Women and Children Last: The Plight of Poor Women in Affluent America*, New York: Viking, 1986.

29. "Childhood Is Not Safe, Congress Study Warns," *New York Times*, Oct. 2, 1989.

30. "Strife in Families Swells Tide of Homeless Youths," *New York Times*, Feb. 5, 1990, pp. A1, B8; Sandy Carter, "Children of Crisis," *Z Magazine*, January, 1991, pp. 33–36.

31. Interview, *New York Newsday*, Nov. 1, 1990, p. 84.

32. Aronowitz, *op. cit.*, p. 36.

33. See Pamela M. Fishman, "Interaction: The Work Women Do," in Rachel Kahn-Hut, Arlene Kaplan Daniels, and Richard Colvard, eds., *Women and Work: Problems and Perspectives*, New York: Oxford University Press, 1982.

34. Joshua Meyrowitz, *No Sense of Place: The Impact of Electronic Media on Social Behavior*, New York: Oxford University Press, 1985, p. 224.

35. See Judith Stacey, *Brave New Families: Stories of Domestic Upheaval in Late Twentieth Century America*, New York: Basic Books, 1990.

36. Meyrowitz, *op. cit.*, p. 249.

37. Ralph W. Larkin, *Suburban Youth in Cultural Crisis*, New York: Oxford University Press, 1979.

38. Stanley Aronowitz and Henry Giroux, *Education under Siege: The Conservative, Liberal and Radical Debate over Schooling*, South

Hadley, MA: Bergin and Garvey, 1985; Harvey Holtz, Irwin Marcus, Jim Dougherty, Judy Michaels, and Rick Peduzzi, eds., *Education and the American Dream: Conservatives, Liberals and Radicals Debate the Future of Education*, Granby, MA: Bergin and Garvey, 1989.

39. "Drop in Youths' Cocaine Use May Reflect Societal Shift," *New York Times*, Jan. 25, 1991.

40. "Survey of 9 Million Pupils Finds Lag in Education," *New York Times*, Sept. 27, 1990, p. A19.

41. See Stanley Aronowitz and Henry A. Giroux, *Education under Siege, op. cit.*; Stanley Aronowitz and Henry A. Giroux, *Postmodern Education*, Minneapolis: University of Minnesota Press, 1991; Robert B. Everhart, *Reading, Writing and Resistance: Adolescence and Labor in a Junior High School*, Boston: Routledge and Kegan Paul, 1983; Paolo Freire and Ira Shor, *A Pedagogy for Liberation*, South Hadley, MA: Bergin and Garvey, 1987; Henry A. Giroux, ed., *Postmodernism, Feminism, and Cultural Politics: Redrawing the Boundaries of Educational Criticism*, Albany: SUNY Press, 1991; Henry A. Giroux and Peter McLaren, eds., *Critical Pedagogy, the State, and Cultural Struggle*, Albany: SUNY Press, 1989; Henry A. Giroux and Roger Simon, eds., *Popular Culture, Schooling, and Everyday Life*, Granby, MA: Bergin and Garvey, 1989; Peter McLaren, *Life in Schools*, New York: Longman, 1988; Ira Shor, ed., *Freire for the Classroom*, Portsmouth, NH: Heinemann, 1987; David W. Livingstone, *Critical Pedagogy and Cultural Power*, South Hadley, MA: Bergin and Garvey, 1987.

42. Larkin, *op. cit.*, p. 216.

43. Meyrowitz, *op. cit.*, p. 255.

44. John J. O'Connor, "TV Sitcoms Do Little for the Education Crisis," *New York Times*, Sept. 13, 1990, p. C25.

45. David Elkind, *All Grown Up and No Place to Go: Teenagers in Crisis*, Reading, MA: Addison-Wesley, 1984, pp. 99ff.; O'Connor, *ibid.*

46. Stanley Aronowitz, "Postmodernism and Politics," in Andre Ross, ed., *Universal Abandon? The Politics of Postmodernism*, Minneapolis: University of Minnesota Press, 1988, pp. 47–48.

47. "Agency Is Assailed on Deal with a Cigarette Company," *New York Times*, Nov. 10, 1989, p. A20.

48. "Alienation from Government Grows, Poll Finds," *New York Times*, Sept. 19, 1990, p. A26.

49. Aronowitz, "Postmodernism and Politics," *op. cit.*, pp. 54–55.

50. See Meyrowitz, *op. cit.*, p. 303.

51. Douglas Kellner, *Television and the Crisis of Democracy*, Boulder: Westview, 1990.

52. Martin Schram, *New York Newsday*, Nov. 1, 1990, p. 84.

53. "TV Viewers Get to See the Candidates, and See the Candidates," *New York Times*, Feb. 16, 1992, p. 26.

54. Poster, *op. cit.*, p. 93.

55. "A Losing Battle," *Time*, Dec. 3, 1990, pp. 44–48; Anthony Lewis, "The Czar's New Clothes," *New York Times*, Dec. 14, 1989, p. A39.

56. "An Everyday Officer's War for Neighborhood Quality," *New York Times*, Jan. 21, 1991, pp. B1, 2.

57. Lynn Chancer and David Forbes, "From Here to Panama: Face it, We're Addicted to Lies," *Village Voice*, Jan. 23, 1990, pp. 31–32; Barbara Ehrenreich, "Sounds of Silence," *Savvy Woman*, June, 1990, pp. 51–53.

58. T. G. Carpenter, "The New Anti-Youth Movement," *Nation*, Jan. 19, 1985; Richard Goldstein, "The New Sobriety: What We Risk When We Just Say No," *Village Voice*, Dec. 30, 1986, pp. 23–28; Reinarman, "The Social Construction . . . ," *op. cit.*

59. Jerome Miller of the National Center on Institutions and Alternatives, quoted in "The Deadliest Year Yet," *Time*, Jan. 13, 1992, p. 18.

CHAPTER 3

Control and Denial

You see control can never be a means to any practical end. . . .
It can never be a means to anything but more control. . . .
Like junk . . .

William S. Burroughs, *Naked Lunch*

Looking for an angry fix
Allen Ginsberg, *Howl*

Although they are in decline modernist forms of everyday life still abound while postmodern relations are emerging. We appear to be living on the border of both cultures. The alcohol abuse field has analyzed troublesome relations in terms of the addictive qualities of control and denial. I extend this analysis here to illuminate American culture in personal and political terms by describing both modernist and postmodern culture with respect to these addictive features.

THE MODERNIST ADDICTIVE CULTURE

The decaying modernist industrial culture, organized around the purpose of production for profit, is grounded in the workplace, the family, the school, and the state. Each of these cornerstones of modernist life is structured as a hierarchy; hierarchical relations control people so that they behave only in certain ways and deny the expression of various voices and viewpoints which run counter to the dominant forms of power. At work the owners, not workers, decide what is to be produced, how, and by whom; in the family it is dad, not mom, who is the head of the household; at school students do as they're told by the teacher, who determines what counts as knowledge; and at the top if the president, as leader of privileged white males everywhere, says something is best for everyone in the country, it must be so. In that modernist culture people depend on hierarchical means of gaining approval and self-acceptance as a person: if you produce the correct response and deny your own feelings and opinions, you could please the boss, your dad, your husband, the teacher, or the president and win legitimacy. A person's performance rather than his or her intrinsic worth often is what earns validation from an outside source. Because it is a competitive hierarchy, only a few can succeed.

That hierarchical culture of control and denial in which certain feelings and needs are unacceptable and in which self-worth and approval are contingent on acceptable performance, or productivity, is addictive. The drug which characterizes that culture is alcohol. To the extent that our culture still relies on modernist, hierarchical institutions, it will generate the need for alcohol with its attendant, addictive patterns of interpersonal relations.[1] What does alcohol abuse have to do with everyday modernist life? Alcohol abuse is not simply some biochemical process; rather, it is bound up with distinct forms of social relations.

The alcohol abuse field describes two key characteristics of an alcoholic and members of an alcoholic system to be control and denial. *Control* refers to the compulsive need to manage unacceptable things about yourself and the need to govern the feelings and behaviors of significant others; as a characteristic of addictive behavior it goes hand in hand with its opposite, feeling out of control. *Denial* is another term for dishonesty and estrangement from yourself and others. It means avoiding awareness of important needs and feelings as well as certain things about yourself, including having a drinking problem that you cannot completely control. When people are in denial, they are cut off from what others see about them. In their social estrangement they may regard other people as Others, people with whom they have no recognizable qualities in common.

Alcoholic addictive relations are prototypical of modernist culture. When people cannot experience themselves as whole lovable beings without performing for an extrinsic source of approval, then they may continue to seek something transformative beyond them which will complete their life and make them acceptable. The compulsive craving to get filled up, to overcome a personal deficit by relying on an extrinsic thing or person as savior, is an addictive process. In this society what is acceptable for many is to use a drug, alcohol, as a means to deal with lack of self-worth, insecurity, and other undesirable feelings. One out of four families has alcohol-abusing members; some children from abusing families are at later risk of abusing alcohol and other drugs themselves as adults.

Alcohol is still the number one drug of choice and sets the standard for the cultural norm of medicating yourself for unacceptable feelings. The message that many children and people learn is that when you do not feel accepted for who you are, which is often the case, you can use alcohol, or some other drug, to heal that feeling. Hollywood movies will often have a film character get drunk in order to signal when he or she feels pain or loss of self-worth. For example, the 1992–93 season films *A Few Good Men*, *A River Runs Through It*, *Unforgiven*, *Passion Fish*, *Scent of a Woman*, and *Indecent Proposal* all rely on this technique. Yet this device is so common, as is the portrayal of unacknowledged alcoholic characters, that movie critics seldom mention it.[2] This denial itself contributes to the way drinking as a survival tool becomes part of the unspoken relations of everyday life.

In fact, the relational patterns within the alcoholic family system fit the experience of many people from nonalcoholic but otherwise similar family systems as well, that is, those people who suffer from everyday modernist hierarchical relations. In many families children's own needs and feelings are not validated but are denied in favor of the parents'. The boundaries that mark the child as a person in his or her own right are not respected; parents invest in children as private property, as extensions of themselves or projections of their own unfulfilled needs. Children who grow up without a solid sense of themselves in turn often spend their own adulthood trying to please and/or control others in compulsive ways.

Alcohol abuse reflects the hierarchical culture of control and denial on a personal scale in two major ways. First, an abuser, often but not limited to the husband and father, drinks as a way to deal with the fundamental lack of self-acceptance he or she feels, having failed to receive unconditional acceptance within his or her own life. Many people use alcohol and other drugs to reparent themselves, to try to fill up the sense of loss and emptiness, to make up for a missing sense of being nurtured, comforted, and loved. The drug medicates for feelings of low self-worth, anger, and social anxiety. Alcohol abuse also serves as a source of relief from having to live in a hierarchical, controlling, denying culture which makes many people feel ashamed about their own feelings and locks them into restrictive gender roles which are determined by the need to gain outside approval, such as always-in-control-don't-show-emotions dad, or I-must-deny-my-own-needs-for-the-sake-of-the-other mom.

Often the person has cut off his or her feelings as a means of self-protection. Sometimes it is only when the person is drunk that he or she feels really alive, feels allowed to be himself or herself and to speak about unacceptable things or express forbidden feelings, including sexual ones. Other times the pain of living is so powerful that people drink to become numb, to cut off feelings. In either case the drinking can then take on a life of its own as the person continues to drink in order to avoid the pain of withdrawal itself. Because the society looks down upon loss of control from drunkenness as shameful behavior, the person often denies the drinking problem and develops elaborate rationalizations to sustain this way of coping which has now become part of his or her life.

The second way alcohol abuse reflects the culture of control and denial in personal terms is through the alcoholic family system, which can take on its own defensive characteristics and perpetuate the addictive patterns. An alcoholic can be a source of embarrassment and a family secret for the abuser and the family members. The family develops its own set of norms to control itself on the outside and denies feelings and experiences as a means of self-protection. The traditional role of the wife and mother coincides with the enabling spouse, or codependent, who denies her own needs and feelings for the sake of the drinker and the family. The codependent may learn that the most important way to survive is to please others.

In an alcoholic family system members may have no fundamental acceptance of themselves or of each other; instead there is shame.[3] There is a need to control the self and others. Certain feelings which contradict the behavior of the alcoholic, or the official version of the family, must be denied and remain unspoken. Nonalcoholic family members, instead of directly giving and receiving mutual respect and acceptance, may learn ways to survive and gain approval in convoluted, compensatory ways through pleasing, avoiding, deceiving, manipulating, or entertaining the one in power.[4] There may be extreme distance between family members, or its opposite, enmeshment and disrespect for personal boundaries, including incest, all of which reflect problems with intimacy.

Professionals who work with children of alcoholics identify a number of functional roles which the children often assume in order to survive the family system: hero, scapegoat, mascot (clown), and lost child. Each role may serve to draw fire away from the drinker and is often symptomatic of a system in which certain events and feelings must not be discussed. The funny and poignant movie *Parenthood* (1990) provides a classic portrait of adult children of an alcoholic family. The four grown children of the Jason Robards alcoholic character play out the four roles to varying degrees and in varying combinations. Steve Martin's character is anxious and plays the clown and hero; Diane Wiest's is depressed and lost; Tom Hulce's, the father's hero, is in fact a manipulator and gambler who is scapegoated by others; and Rick Moranis, the control freak son-in-law, wants his daughter to be perfect while his compulsive wife is a closet junk food junkie. The patterns affect the next generation of children as well.

In many cases an alcoholic family system works to maintain the drinking pattern because it is preferable to having to face their other problems with a sober family member. Although not all children of alcoholics suffer, many as adults find it difficult to trust others and experience confusion over boundaries, suffer fear of abandonment, and exhibit extreme dependence. A number who live with the ache of emptiness from a nonvalidated self go on to abuse alcohol and/or other substances themselves as a means to fill the void. Another painful legacy of some families with an alcoholic or alcohol-abusing parent is fetal alcohol syndrome, which affects the physical and educational development of the child.

Members of substance-abusing families may learn particular survival skills and then transfer them to other hierarchical relationships at work, at school, and in their own families.[5] But other agencies are also similar to the alcoholic family to the extent that people control others or themselves to perform the correct way and deny certain needs and feelings.[6] For some successful managerial and professional people, splitting themselves in two through drinking is a means of coping with the anxieties and pressures of competitive success. Drinking can function to maintain the executive's sense of competence while guarding against fail-

"Dammit! I resent being treated as if I were sober!"

© 1991 by John Callahan. Reprinted with permission.

ure: if the person fails, it can be attributed to the drinking; if the person succeeds, it can be seen to have occurred despite the handicap.[7] Some workplaces operate like alcoholic systems without the alcohol, ones in which the boss, like an alcoholic parent, is obsessed with control, is unpredictable, denies his or her own incompetence, and spills his or her personal problems all over the worksite without respect for boundaries. Because they are dependent on approval, some workers expend emotional energy to avoid the boss's moods, cover for, or take care of his or her needs, and then deny the events and their own feelings. Similar patterns occur in other systems such as schools, government agencies, and political groups where secret power struggles, deceit, and denial take place in order to maintain the structure of the organization. Although many such families and systems avoid any conflict at all, others appear to be addicted to conflict because it is a familiar way to stay engaged. When people learn more effective ways to resolve conflict, they sometimes dread the aftermath of the emotional void, which they often do not address; the conflict or its avoidance fulfilled a purpose.

The Left, which represents the oppressed, is sometimes no different than other addictive, hierarchical groups and has its share of control freaks, self-denying workaholics, and rigid, obsessive people who see things in black-and-white terms. An example of an alcoholic system on the Left was the Democratic Workers Party, a Leninist sect which flourished in the United States in the 1970s and 1980s.[8] Party members granted their leader, Marlene Dixon, unlimited power in the organization. According to ex-members, Dixon was an alcoholic who established rigid rules to maintain control of the party ideology and membership, such as the use of harsh criticism of members and the reliance on an inner circle of power which restricted access to her and kept her alcoholism a secret. The reasons that some members stayed in the party despite the abuse is similar to those of enabling members of an alcoholic family: people did not trust their own perceptions when they felt something was wrong but always doubted themselves, feeling that their "incorrect attitudes" and lack of political knowledge could only be corrected by further loyalty to the party leadership. The leadership constantly reinforced this lack of self-esteem, while members were increasingly isolated from nonmembers. In 1985 the party expelled Dixon and disbanded itself. In hindsight the demise of this group was part of the challenge to all Leninist systems, with their lack of democracy, authoritarian leadership, and cult of personality, which occurred in Eastern Europe a few years later.

But so-called democratic groups are not exempt from some of these patterns. With hindsight I also can see how, as a member of various ad hoc organizations, I contributed to another kind of denial common to some groups which claim to be democratic collectives: there often was a power hierarchy, but the group did not acknowledge it because it was not supposed to exist, which led to some convoluted and self-defeating behaviors in order to maintain the status quo. Another kind of denial in leftist organizations and families, also similar to alcoholic family systems, is around members' own needs and problems. A common assumption is that you are not supposed to talk about your personal pain or troubles because there are always other people who are a lot worse off than you, the ones you should be trying to help. The question which seems not to occur to members of this kind of system is, why would someone want to join a movement in which people ignore their own personal needs and deny themselves pleasure?

On a larger scale, in this country President Reagan acted in many ways like a different kind of alcoholic parent who presides over a family willing to collude in his delusions for the sake of security. He denied the existence of enormous social problems and assured everyone that everything was all right; he literally turned a deaf ear to questions, blacked out at meetings, made up stories, failed to remember crucial statements and events, and deceived the public during the Iran-Contra scandal. Reagan's and Bush's militaristic interventions at home and abroad in Granada, Panama, and the Persian Gulf are examples of the need to try to control others' behavior by force. Their successes also depended on denying some of the failures and casualties which occurred through restricting information. There is a seductive appeal to this and any paternalistic system of control and denial, a promise held out that your own personal needs and desires for security and pleasure can be guaranteed from without.

Alcoholics often experience delusions, fantasies, and magical thinking, what those in recovery sometimes refer to as "stinkin' thinkin'": for example, if they only had x, some mystifiying, unattainable thing invested with magical properties, everything in their life would be fine. In the modernist culture, consumption, the other side of production, also reflects this mystifying distance or alienation between the person and his or her needs and desires. Marxism, as a modernist theory, offers an appropriate critique of the addictive nature of modernist consumption from the standpoint of those who purport to speak for authentic working-class interests, that is, those who aim to show the mystified producers their own real needs. From this perspective working people, because they are not validated as fully developing persons living within a competitive hierarchy, will try in compulsive ways to make up for what they lack by purchasing and consuming goods and services which they themselves produce, things which they may believe to be magical antidotes to feelings of misery and inadequacy. They are alienated from, or in denial about, their own nature, power, and needs.

Like drug-induced delusions, modernist ads imbue commodities with qualities which promise more than the product or service itself, such as status, popularity, sex appeal, sophistication, wisdom, excitement, or equanimity, qualities which people feel they are missing without these things. People are alienated from a part of themselves; their sense of fulfillment and wholeness then emanates from outside, from the consumer items themselves. Ads induce a process of consumption, which is akin to the process of addiction: the extrinsic item provides these qualities just long enough, that is, superficially, so that the next act of consuming can be done as soon as possible, while the consumer still denies that the thing is not all it is packaged to appear. Advertising and packaging induce the feeling of desire (craving) which attaches the missing qualities to the object. After buying the commodity and playing, using, or wearing it for a time (tolerance), the person may feel it is not enough, the item does not live up to the initial feeling of craving. The person may feel he or she is missing something again (withdrawal) and pursue bigger, better, newer, improved things in the hopes of satisfaction. A commodity promises promising itself[9]; because in the end you are not validated intrinsically but only by what you consume, you develop addictivelike withdrawal symptoms and the compulsive need to consume more.

In the modernist culture in which producers are estranged from their own needs it follows that they are susceptible to succumbing to glamorously packaged legal drugs such as alcohol and nicotine, which are posited as missing parts of a person's identity. Tobacco consumption has long been linked with the image of the tough masculinity required of an industrial society. For example, pipe smokers are men like Popeye the sailorman and controlled, ultrarational types like Sherlock Holmes and brainy professors. Cigar smokers are the likes of Al Capone, the gangster, successful fathers of neonates, and capitalist financiers. Cigarette smokers are any one of a number of tough guys ranging from those played by Humphrey Bogart to the cowboy Marlboro Man. But in postindustrial society the roles of men are changing and tobacco consumption has decreased; the tobacco industry is on the defensive.[10] As the society has changed, the industry has tried to target other markets, such as working-class women (for example, the cigarette Dakota) and poor and disenfranshised people at home and abroad, such as African-Americans and people in third world countries that are still industrializing.[11] Yet many people also are addicted to consuming itself (shopping) and chasing after money by gambling in the stock market, state-run lotteries, and casinos, and through sports betting.[12]

EVERYBODY'S GOT A HUNGRY HEART
(BRUCE SPRINGSTEEN)

Food addictions are a problem for millions of people who live in a society which depends on overconsumption. While much of the world starves, many Americans often eat too much and suffer from heart disease, obesity, and compulsive overeating, since food is plentiful and food consumption is big business. Feminists describe the emotional underpinning of compulsive eating and how many women use food as a means to medicate for emotional starvation.[13] The other side of the coin is addictive eating disorders such as anorexia and bulimia, in which the person is obsessed with controlling her body image. These tend to occur in developed countries, often among middle- and upper-class girls and women who experience considerable family pressure and have little self-confidence.[14] Girls and women learn that their success often depends on their looks, and many are unhappy with their body image, which they contrast to professional models and movie stars. Addiction to a slender body image is also linked to addictive substance abuse, including diet pills. One researcher said that almost all the adolescent girls he surveyed who reported daily smoking said they used smoking to try to control their weight.[15]

The pain of emotional hunger, lovelessness, and spiritual malaise characterizes a society in which many do not lack material needs. There is no definitive way to compare this grief with the kind which comes from starvation or physical deprivation along some objective hierarchy of oppression; they are incommensurate. This anguish is part and parcel of the American culture and must be taken on its own terms, just as seriously as the kind which people experience in some third world countries. One critic of adult children of alcoholics (ACOAs) self-help groups, Wendy Kaminer, is disturbed by John Bradshaw's comparison of ACOAs with survivors of concentration camps, both of whom he believes share posttraumatic stress symptoms.[16] Kaminer contrasts ACOAs with Cambodian victims of the Khmer Rouge who have their own support groups in the United States, and concludes that the people in twelve-step groups have relatively trivial problems. Although it is reckless to equate all sufferings in an exaggerated manner and deny differences, it is also foolish to minimize or downgrade someone else's pain because it does not measure up to some absolute or even relative standard. Cambodians and other immigrants themselves do not come to the United States just so that they and their children can exist without torture and pain, nor solely for material comforts. They want to develop their many-sided selves and have fulfilling, mutually satisfying relations; that is, they want to partake in American culture as middle-class

Americans. But it turns out that once they join others and establish a certain standard of living, they and many others are still dissatisfied. The contours of American culture mark the realm of struggle, and other structures and needs which consider emotional pain as secondary cannot be imposed from without. The political way through must occur in ways that make sense to this culture with all its contradictory tendencies. What it also requires is an understanding of how the privileges and problems of our culture are linked with, but not reducible to, the political and economic exploitation of third world countries.

Within modernist culture modernist theory can represent to people the source of their problems. For example, Marxist theory offers the label of *working class* to those who experience powerlessness; it can point to the factory and plant as sites which produce unequal class relations. Machinery as forces of production once embodied a dynamic sense of progress toward the future. But Frederic Jameson argues that "the technology of our own moment [the computer, the television set] no longer possesses this same capacity for representation. . . ."[17] To a certain extent hierarchical relations of power have become dispersed, mediated, and transformed through complex electronic networks of communications which erase direct social representations of personal problems. Many working people who are unhappy now live in a culture in which the network of power is opaque. As modernism dies, it leaves a trail of walking wounded in its wake. Power relations no longer easily yield to a rational understanding which could map personal pain, including alcoholism, as a symptom of unjust social arrangements.

Sam Shepard's play, *Curse of the Starving Class*,[18] is about an alcoholic family, as are many of his plays, but it is also an All-American family, the kind that can be found across all parts of the American landscape. The family has food: "We're not part of the starving class!" the daughter, Emma, yells into the refrigerator in one scene; but they are emotionally hungry, people cursed with an emotional starvation which mirrors the paradoxical emptiness of the commodity wasteland in which they live. The play deals with a working-class family which faces considerable problems and displays many of the dynamics of an alcoholic system: social isolation, symptom maintenance, cyclical mood swings, male violence and domination, the struggle between fathers and sons, and the attempt to live out a prescribed role as if nothing is wrong. It is useful to describe it in some detail here because it typifies the kind of pain which many people experience every day from living within an invisible, inchoate hierarchy of power. The title is ironic on a number of levels; not the least is that the starving class is no longer literally starving, nor is it any longer able to rise up together as a class. But it still appears cursed because it has yet to discover a new way to respond to cultural forces which allow for the possibility of nourishing relations.

Early on in the play the father, Weston, an alcoholic, arrives home furious at the family; he claims they've left the upkeep of the house all to him. When drunk he is capable of kicking down the front door and terrorizing his wife, Ella, and teenage children, Wesley and Emma. Weston is uninterested in keeping the house and dismisses his son's idea of working the land. He owes people money and wants to sell the house and escape to avoid his creditors. All the while Ella has proceeded with her own plans to sell the house from under her husband and abandon him because she is fed up with his drinking. Ella reminds Weston that self-destructiveness, one of the forms of the curse, runs in his family. Weston himself tells Wesley that he was infected with a poisonous outlook by his own father who, in the midst of being with his family, remained apart from them.

In the last act Weston is sober and performs a complete turnabout. He is now cheerful, patient, and optimistic and decides to keep the land in order to grow avocadoes. He admits to Wesley that he neglected the chores and left them up to him but claims he is providing for the family now. But it is too late to succeed at the role of breadwinner; Wesley confronts his father with the fact that he had borrowed money from people when drunk and they are after him for it. Weston replies that he could sell the piece of land he bought in the desert, but his son tells him that the agent, the same one who is arranging the land sale with Ella, had ripped him off. Wesley, meanwhile, literally takes on his father's alcoholic persona. He retrieves Weston's filthy, discarded clothes and wears them. In carrying on the symptom or curse within the family system, he expresses the dazed, defeated, and alienated self his father had tried to deny and uses it as an attempt to stay loyal to his father. He ravenously begins to eat all the food in sight.

Weston's manic optimism quickly turns to despair. He explains that he always figured on the future getting better:

I figured that's why everyone wants you to buy things. Buy refrigerators. Buy cars, houses, lots, invest. They wouldn't be so generous if they didn't figure you had it comin' in. So I went along with it. Why not borrow if you know it's coming in. Why not make a touch here and there. They all want you to borrow anyhow. Banks, car lots, investors. The whole thing's geared to invisible money.[19]

Other family members also tell how invisible forces infect them with a sense of emptiness and despair. In the midst of Ella's attempts to change her life she becomes despondent, sensing a curse which is ever present and which they pass down after inheriting themselves. Wesley describes the problems in their lives in terms of impersonal, invisible forces which surround them. He objects to his mother selling the land to the agent, whom he calls a "zombie," and envisions a deadened, petrified commodity landscape spawned by unbridled development and populated by half-dead people: "There'll be steel girders spanning acres of land. Cement pilings. Prefab walls. Zombie architecture, owned by invisible zombies, built by zombies for the use and convenience of all other zombies."[20]

Emma, as the youngest and as the daughter, is on the bottom of the family hierarchy. She too has the curse in the double sense, her first period, which marks her initiation along the blood line into the restrictive, female adult role set out for her. Emma fantasizes about escaping, gets into trouble, and in the end does run away. Before she does she advises her brother to see beyond people who "look you in the eyes. You gotta' look behind them. See what they're standing in front of. What they're hiding. Everybody's hiding, Wes. Everybody. Nobody looks like what they are."[21]

Within the restrictive class milieu there is only a certain amount of love and acceptance available to feed all family members; everyone is hungry. The disturbed, repetitive patterns are symptomatic of their loveless condition, which gets passed down through the form of the isolated, privatized, alcoholic family. Members are caught between the idea of the family as a place for affection, security, and rootedness and the reality that it cannot meet their needs within a broader, unnamed, mystified system of relations.

In this play Shepard stands on the border of modernism and postmodernism. He presents a modernist, social determinist view of his characters, who must face the postmodern world of crumbling families, the logic of invisible money, and declining material referents. His characters are class-bound, not allowed to cast their subjectivity beyond their assigned positions and act on the world with any success. Instead they are condemned to live out recycled patterns of despair as a function of their social condition, unable to access any of the postmodern, invisible modes of power which could link them up with others. Yet they are stuck in their relations without even the modernist hope of a rational way out either through psychotherapy or class struggle; in this sense they are postmodern because they are beyond the reach of traditional family therapy or working-class politics. In a poignant way they typify those who dwell in a liminal realm where modernist hope has died but the promise of new and better relations has yet to be born. The alcoholic, addictive nature of the family system in which they starve is inseparable from the set of cultural relations which define their lives.

COMICS

A reader can find a full-color picture of addictive modernist relations in one everyday place, the syndicated comics in the daily and Sunday tabloids. Certain comic strips continue to reflect sexist gender hierarchies which are inseparable from the alcoholic quality of relations. For example, *Hagar the Horrible* and *Andy Capp* naturalize male inebriation and the quarrelsome but long-suffering or enabling wife. The characters are stereotypically working class and sexist: the men are gruff, aggressive, and bumbling and are often dependent on the women to get through the day, while the women put up with the men's foibles, including drunkenness. Alcohol and sexist roles show up in other hierarchical comic strips which are holdovers from the forties and fifties, such as *Beetle Bailey,* the army private, and the *Lockhorns,* a miserable marriage, in which the husband is often holding a glass of booze as he excoriates his wife. The wife is the one who goes on compulsive shoping sprees, as does *Blondie.* The addictive or codependent quality of controlling other people is a recurrent theme in two strips involving women, *Cathy* and *Momma.* Cathy and her boyfriend, Irving, are addicted to their relationship: each tests the other, tries to break up but cannot, and often tries to control the other through obsessive thinking and convoluted, deceptive strategies which usually result in the opposite of what was intended. In *Momma* the mother is often in a power struggle with her children, using convoluted arguments and guilt trips when trying to find out everything they do and with whom they go out. One piece of the humor in *Cathy* which sometimes falls flat and ends up as a painful deprecation of women is her transparent attempts to deny her insecurities about her looks, attractiveness, and food and weight obsessions. Other strips like *Family Circus* deny much of social reality by continuing to represent an ideological view of wholesome white, middle-class family life.

It may not be accidental that these depictions of declining modernist culture appear in a mode of information which itself is in decline, the tabloid. In New York in 1990, the *Post* almost went bankrupt, and in the same year a bitter strike over the fate of the *Daily News* began which almost led to that paper's bankruptcy. The *News* has had its own addictive appeal as a commodity, relying on sin, sex, and sensationalism served up under blaring headlines and in graphic photos; but it spoke in the clear, direct prose of the everyday to an industrial working-class readership. That readership diminished as more people became service providers, left their connections with urban neighborhoods as they moved to the suburbs, and began to get their news from watching TV.[22] The *News* management challenged the unions on some featherbedding practices in the face of new technology; workers were again forced to defend jobs that may be less useful than in the past, as management followed the union-busting strategy of replacing strikers with scabs, a strategy which was used to break strikes throughout the 1980s. Although newspapers in other cities are financially secure, there are fewer readers, and the papers face competition from computer networks and help-wanted data banks.[23] In the alcoholic culture of the tabloid comics lies a confluence of modernist trends which seems capable of disappearing at any moment.

POSTMODERN ADDICTIVE CULTURE

The modernist culture, in its death throes but still thrashing about, faces challenges from many places in everyday life. Power itself is being dispersed and depersonalized within an emerging culture of signs which redistributes control and redefines denial. Instead of performing to gain acceptance through personal hierarchical forms of control, people in postmodern culture seek to realize themselves through a culture of signs which radically reconstrues the nature of subjective needs and desires themselves. It is no longer a question of effecting a true self or of meeting intrinsic needs in some pure realm like the family, or leisure time, or some presumed authentic working-class or ethnic culture which stands apart from false outside needs such as capitalist consumer items. People's social, psychic, and erotic needs are now constituted in part through those signs of everyday life which hold out the promise of self-expression through discursive interplay with new technologies as well as with ads, music videos, movies, TV shows, computers, and popular music. The business of the day is less the producing of materials and more the defining of images of needs and desires. Hollywood and Madison Avenue create such palpable images and bring them to life. They have been aided by advances in electronic media such as split screen and remote control television, cable TV, miniature TVs, videos, walkmen [sic], cassette players, compact disc players, laser discs, Qsound, personal computers, simulated programs, virtual reality, modems, electronic mail, telemarketing, fax machines, telephone conversation services, and electronic billboards, all of which personalize the sybaritic sensations of desire. In modernist culture sex is relegated to the private realm of the public/private dichotomy. But in postmodern culture sexuality is dispersed through an array of cultural signs, and everyday objects become eroticized with subjective sensuality. Postmodern culture enables people to become cultural producers who appropriate and interpret signs and communicate within new, shifting, and recombining communal configurations.[24]

The postmodern consumer culture depends on control and denial as well, hallmarks of an addictive culture, but in qualitatively different ways than the modernist culture with its emphasis on performance and personal approval. *Control* by those with power now means those who manipulate information, such as owners of corporate television. The governmental and corporate network of power is diffused and decentered by people who discipline and control themselves every time they plug into the database, and it is those in power who have access to the data. But control on certain levels is also exerted by computer hackers who network with each other nationwide, desktop publishers, people who make and distribute videos and musical tapes, artists who work as "cultural jammers" who subvert the corporate media, and even couch potatoes who zap past the commercials and select channels.[25]

Denial as an addictive quality in this new arrangement of power refers to the information that is not conveyed; those who determine what counts as categories of data select salient information and omit that which is not. For example, surveillance of people not only restricts access to the information about them to a privileged few but relies on databases which use digitally encoded information. Digital encoding arranges information in limited categories, a process which incurs a loss of data. Database language in effect constitutes new subjects by defining a person according to categories which those in control preselect and arbitrarily relate to each other. Corporate media news denies full coverage by excluding alternative critical perspectives on crucial issues and by encoding news in good-bad, black-white categories. It determines that news consists of selected, superficial highlights or soundbites which reinforce the perspective of the dominant power structure without allowing for contradictory information or analysis by disenfranchised voices or opposing political groups.[26] But again, the same technology of electronic media allows for democratizing knowledge by making information available to everyone and challenging denial. Jean-Francois Lyotard argues that the public should have free access to the memory and data banks.[27]

In postmodern culture the need to overcome feelings of personal inadequacy and the need for self-fulfillment and personal power are induced and then slaked through the exchange of signs of information, much of it transmitted through the electronic media. In modernist culture self-realization occurs when you consume or possess a product which is a predetermined need and which stands outside yourself. But in postmodern culture subjectivity becomes defined by identifying with images and sensations of mass culture themselves so that appearance or style can in fact constitute identity. Signs from mass culture define the parameters of personal desire, but individuals can deliberately appropriate signs; the signs themselves become imbued with subjectivity, which becomes dispersed and embodied within the signs. Kenneth Gergen similarly refers to the "saturated self" in postmodern culture, in which the self has become populated with images and voices chosen from the vast network of everyday experiences made possible by changes in technology.[28] He shows that people come to reflect their social surroundings, which in turn, because they are relational, incorporate personal consciousness.

In the modernist version people are subject to manipulation by ads to become dependent on external commodities, for example, gasoline. In contrast, postmodern ads, such as those for Amoco and Sunoco high-octane gas, show gasoline consumption to be a transcendental or exquisitely luxurious experience in which the image of personal pleasure is at one with using the gasoline. Many new ads are parodies of modernist ads; they wink at the viewer and invite one to share in the irony, to join in the game that denies that the ads represent something genuine. (In fact, high-octane gas, for example, does not improve engine performance and is sheer image.) When signs for commodities embody desire and are infused with subjectivity in this way, they allow for the possibility of judgment and choice. The ads depend on the viewers to interpret them and to invest them with their subjectivity.

One consequence of the conflating of mass-produced signs and subjectivity is that one no longer can take a privileged (hierarchical) position and claim that a person has false consciousness or is denying his or her true identity, needs, or feelings. People construct their selves as narratives. They create new social forms and rituals which they base on commodified relations but which are not reducible to them. For example, black and Latino gays who "vogue," that is, adopt the poses of fashion models and the clothing from commercial houses of design, consciously select and appropriate a commodified, glamorous self-image and in effect reconstitute themselves in a new way.[29] Of course, none would say they are in actuality glamorous models. But neither can one say with authority that these are in reality just poor, exploited, and oppressed people manipulated by corporations and who are denying their sad existence.

In this sense denial, or alienation, must be redefined. In the end it can only be agreed upon by the participants themselves, through self-realization and/or through democratic dialogue with others in which information is reconstituted. This contrasts with reliance on the normative canons of social acceptability as predefined within the hierarchical power structure of government bureaucrats, mental health professionals, and academics. It also opposes reliance on the claims of conservative elitists or leftist vanguards. The implications for substance abuse prevention (and treatment) are considerable: it means that new, nonhierarchical relations using new modes of information are necessary. Every cultural sign can be contested and reappropriated; there is no longer any one overarching authoritative interpretation which controls the sign, and the liberating elements of a sign must be sorted out from those restrictive ones within specific contexts.

To crave and consume commodities is not just a compulsive act by which corporations manipulate consumers but can be a way to realize personal desire. To purchase and consume things provides a sense of power and control and a means to express longings for passion and fulfillment.[30] Even when people play the lottery or bet on teams or in casinos against the house odds, they assert the validity of their own knowledge and abilities over the power of the experts.[31]

Similarly, to take drugs is not simply a matter of consuming chemicals which affect the body in a predetermined way. This is a modernist viewpoint which deems a drug to have universal, standard properties such as addictiveness. Instead, drugs are culturally constructed signs which people interpret and use in more than one fixed way and to which they assign various meanings. For people who feel inadequate and disorganized, drugs can organize their lives and give them a sense of confidence, wholeness, and direction. Alcohol, for example, can be a personal badge of status or acceptability (wine experts, connoisseurs of scotch) as well as a badge of shame.

Cocaine may be the prototypical postmodern drug because in this culture it enhances a personal sense of self-esteem, power, and control. A culture's drug of choice reflects its ability to meet people's needs; in the United States some people across all classes use cocaine, a stimulant, to medicate for their low sense of personal efficacy and lack of self-worth. The common denominator is the desire to feel powerful, and what happens on the street in the inner city often parallels what happens on The Street, or Wall Street. Those Wall Street scam artists and dreamers obsessed with power trips and get-rich-quick schemes may also need a hit to get through the day, as do their counterparts in the inner city. In the 1980s cocaine became equated with the glamorous lifestyle of the Wall Street Masters of the Universe, typified by the rush of feelings of power, confidence, and ability gained from ruthless competition, high risk taking, and quick, intoxicating, money-making deals and takeovers. Similarly for some inner-city youth dealing cocaine is the fastest means to gain power and status within the context of their lives.[32] The two streets sometimes come together. In the drug-plagued New York City neighborhood of Washington Heights a significant number of customers are from the wealthier New Jersey suburbs across the George Washington Bridge.

For some crack users the surge of power experienced from the drug becomes something to live for when there is little else. In one study researchers found no evidence that crack is instantly addictive or violence inducing, and that the percentage of users who get in trouble with crack is about the same as with other drugs; but the minority of users who do get in trouble exhibit less control over their intake than the problem users of other drugs.[33] The researchers found that these crack abusers are susceptible to "environmental triggers"; some said they even felt the uncontrollable urge to use when they saw President Bush hold up a bag of crack in a televised speech on the war on drugs. From their perspective what was most salient about the image was the bag, not what the President said.

First, this example reveals that Bush of course intended viewers to interpret his speech in the exact opposite way. For someone else equally susceptible to the trigger of the image of authority, to watch an image of the president of the world's most powerful country condemn a drug might be a convincing argument for abstaining. In some other country, such as Iran during the days of the revered Ayatollah, for example, this might be more likely to occur. The Entertainment Industries Council, a nonprofit group, tries to achieve this reverse trigger effect here in the United States through antidrug spots which use celebrities from TV and Hollywood.[34] The significance of this example is that it shifts the argument about addiction away from deterministic models of chemicals and biology and onto the ground of cultural signs, the meanings of which are not predetermined but which people must interpret and find salient in order to have an effect. The use of various popular political and media figures also raises the issue of when signs are addictive and manipulative and when they enhance subjectivity and critical choice.

Second, even when a user interprets an environmental trigger which sets off a craving, it is not an iron law of nature that the craving must then lead to consuming the drug, since this requires the social act of finding a dealer and buying crack. In the same study the crack abusing women easily got the drug from dealers, whom they could see and find everywhere, which makes it appear that craving must lead to consumption. But this is as much a statement about the social milieu in which the women live as it is about compulsive behavior. The study raises the issue of the need for new nonhierarchical relations in which people create and interpret powerful cultural signs which present alternative visions of how personal life could be.

The transformation of image and the immediacy with which people transport themselves to realize their needs and desires in postmodern culture is akin to taking a drug. The changes produce new identities and can provide instant pleasure, alleviate symptoms, and reduce pain. When people use the electronic media, the changes are instantaneous. Electronic media works like a drug rushing through the bloodstream: they directly affect the senses and passively produce the desired effect, bypassing cognitive processes such as deliberate thinking or practice. The way a viewer identifies with the characters who are suddenly transported into another dimension within the hyperreality of TV ads is akin to drug highs. The quick jumpcuts in music video frames and TV ads parallel the quick rush experienced from cocaine. Listening to a rock song with a hook (a catchy riff or set of words which sticks in your mind) which is played many times over the radio makes you feel compelled to buy it, in order to control the sensation of listening to it as a mood enhancer or mood regulator. The dissociative experience of listening to your own choice of music through a walkman [sic] while trying to escape from some unpleasant urban scene is like being stoned. What is arguable or contested in each instance is the degree to which the user is critically controlling the experience and/or is being manipulated by the corporate media.

Not only the form but the content of the images of desire found in ads, TV shows, and other entertainment is infused with addictive qualities. For example, the TV series with the highest ratings for many years was "Cheers," a well-written, funny show which took place within the confines of a bar.[35] Modernist culture contained neutral, informal public spaces apart from family and the workplace such as taverns where people could socialize and recognize and share common problems; but these spaces are disappearing.[36] Here the media reappropriated a fading modernist institution, the neighborhood corner bar. The theme song helped explain the show's popularity by praising a place "where everybody knows your name" and where you can be accepted. The show appealed to people's nostalgia for a lost sense of community, and the bar functioned as an electronic equivalent of an alcoholic fantasy community. The place was never smoky or smelly, the patrons rarely had to work, were seldom grossly inebriated, and conducted much of their personal life there. In a postmodern age of AIDS, feminism, and twelve-step programs the show allowed for promiscuity, male chauvinism, and heavy drinking as if nothing had changed.

Besides the camaraderie the centerpiece of the show for a number of years was the relationship between Sam (Ted Danson), the bartender and a recovering alcoholic, and Diane (Shelly Long), a waitress. Their interplay was often characteristic of people raised in substance-abusing families and typical of drug-related behavior itself. They were both ambivalent about each other but were addicted to their pattern of relating, falling into uncontrollable passion one moment, hurting and rejecting each other the next. Both were so afraid of rejection that they performed elaborate power plays and deceptions so that neither one would be the first to be rejected by the other. Diane manipulated herself as a maddeningly desirable but unobtainable object by intellectualizing everything while Sam maintained his own power by distancing himself as a sex-addicted stud who went out with other women. Although the show lost some of its chemistry when Kirstie Alley (Rebeccah) replaced Shelly Long, some of the same power patterns between the two leads continued. One NBC programming executive said that even if Ted Danson were to leave, "We think we could just keep the show going with the other people in the bar. We think the bar itself is one of the stars on 'Cheers'."[37] Despite this insight, Danson's departure in 1993 did close the show because he served to maintain the dynamics of the alcoholic ensemble or system. Each episode, like a bout of drinking, ended with a sudden blackout. The enormous media hype for the final blackout was a last call for a passing way of life; Rebeccah got married, Norm, the barfly, got a job, and Diane and Sam, who had joined a support group for his sex addiction the week before, rejected each other for one last time.

CYBORGS, DRUGS, AND CONTROL

In postmodern culture the body as an objective referent is vanishing. Technology changes the dualist relationship between the machine and the body such that each interpenetrates the other. This occurs not only through advances like genetic engineering, body replacement parts, plastic surgery, and breast and penile implants, but in the ways microelectronic technology becomes an everyday extension of the human body, such as with laptop computers and mobile phones. Machines themselves, like talking computers and talking cars, assume human characteristics; military strategy, with its smart bombs used in the Persian Gulf War, relies on the control of information through technology.

The cyborg, a cybernetic organism which is both technological and biological, may best signify this melding of artifice and nature. The cyborg is both a metaphor and an actuality. It is, in Donna Haraway's terms, a matter of both (science) fiction and lived experience in which the modernist dualisms such as mind and body, public and private, men and women, self and other, and organism and machine are all in question:

> High-tech culture challenges these dualisms in intriguing ways. It is not clear who makes and who is made in the relation between human and machine. It is not clear what is mind and what body in machines that resolve into coding practices. . . . Biological organisms have become biotic systems, communications devices like others. There is no fundamental, ontological separation in our formal knowledge of machine and organism, of technical and organic.[38]

The popular science fiction movie *Terminator 2* demonstrates some spectacular cyborg images through the cinematic technique of morphing, which joins images of organism and machine. Another kind of cyborg image is in Michael Jackson's video for the song "Black or White," which morphs images of multicultural people of different ages and dissolves the border between one presumed natural identity of self with an other.

Haraway's own versions of cyborgs are postmodern socialist-feminists. They reject the totalistic, controlling, male-identified hierarchies and theories of identity based on supposedly natural distinctions. They favor instead partial, contradictory, and open-

ended constructions of personal and collective selves. Her proto-
types include women of color who self-consciously construct
themselves from fragmented, marginal, and illegitimate identities
rather than accept naturalized, essentialist, and inferior ones
assigned to them by Western culture. Haraway sees the cyborg as
emerging from within the new network of "the informatics of
domination," the new technology of information control, and
argues for the need for feminists to seize this new ground of
power for their own purposes.

The cyborg is a powerful referent for what it says about the
body and drugs and about the dual-edged nature of control, an
addictive quality which gets played out through the cyborg and
the network of technology. First, the fact that the body is denatu-
ralized and becomes a more contested, adaptable site for pleasure,
including machines as extensions of the body, means that there is
no longer a concept of a pure, natural, drug-free body which can
stand apart from bad outside influences such as drugs. Not only
can people consciously change the nature of their bodies through
drugs, technology, and machines, but industrial chemicals in the
air, water, and food, and possibly electromagnetic waves may all
affect emotional and physical states as well as alter genetic material. The change in the traditional boundaries of the body and
nature itself calls for contested meanings of what is healthy or
legitimate pleasure through drug taking and other self-altering
behaviors. Pleasure, such as drug taking and sex, is necessarily a
political question because it can no longer be read off from some
innocent state of nature, which itself has become artifactual.

Second, because postmodern culture has redefined the addictive nature of control, the cyborg, as a postmodern signifier,
evokes the political contest over technological control in a dramatic way. Donna Haraway's call for a cyborg world in which
people are not afraid of partial identities and contradictory viewpoints enhanced through technologies stands in contrast with the
more male-defined informatics of domination, a technological
grid of corporate and military control which restricts information
and regulates peoples' lives. This conflict shows up in cyberpunk,
a genre closely aligned with science fiction and represented by its
best-known writer, William Gibson, author of *Neuromancer*.[39]

In *Neuromancer* Gibson's world is not so much a picture of
some distant future as it is a metaphorical representation of the present.[40] References to direct, natural sensory feelings or perceptions

do not occur, and all characters' experience is mediated by designer drugs like endorphin analogs, or by machines, in particular the computer. The computer has dissolved the boundary between natural and artificial experience through cyberspace, "a graphic representation of data abstracted from the banks of every computer in the human system."[41] To master computer cyberspace through direct brain-computer interface allows for both the possibility of dehumanized control and a means to undermine domination by others.

Cyberspace travel is a neurological rush analogous to drug taking, with the accompanying issue of whether the experience constitutes addictive loss of control or a means to enhance power and pleasure. In *Neuromancer* the protagonist, Case, is an alienated console cowboy, a data thief adept at working cyberspace and opening up fields of information, who was caught stealing from his bosses, who then removed his power to access cyberspace. The drug metaphor is evident in the book. Case drinks when he is in pain, and has fallen into the "prison of his own flesh."[42] But when he enters the matrix of cyberspace, he leaves his body behind in a rush of exultation and operates on an "almost permanent adrenaline high."[43] Like drug taking, traveling through the matrix has its pleasures; it extends consciousness beyond the body and enhances the power of knowledge by manipulating information. But just as drug misuse can lead to an overdose or a bad trip, cyberspace travel also has its dangers, in this case, "ice" (intrusion countermeasures electronics). Ice protects the data and can permanently incapacitate the trespasser if stumbled upon.

Peter Fitting interprets Gibson's technological future partly as a "masculinist" one in which feelings have disappeared, one that hooks everyone into a global market of consumer desires controlled by corporations; but he also suggests that it is compatible with Haraway's feminist call for technology as a means of subverting the power network of corporate and military command and of accessing information for democratic and pleasurable purposes.[44] Manipulating information through cyberspace is a druglike high which disturbs traditional views of the self; the boundaries of the body are now both intruded upon and enhanced by interacting with knowledge.[45] As with taking a drug, the relation between the self and the so-called objective world of facts is now realigned, with each one interpenetrating the other.

Does this postmodern self abuse the druglike pleasure of everyday cyberspace, modern technology, and get addicted to information and to controlling others in the modernist way? Or can knowledge, pleasure, and control come together in a postmodern, democratic, feminist culture and enhance new selves in new relations?

NOTES

1. See Ann Wilson Schaef, *When Society Becomes an Addict*, New York: Harper and Row, 1987.

2. For a discussion of how women alcoholic characters in film use their bodies to gain power and subvert social rules, see Melinda Kanner, "Drinking Themselves to Life, or the Body in the Bottle: Filmic Negotiations in the Construction of the Alcoholic Female Body," in Catherine B. Burroughs and Jeffrey David Ehrenreich, eds., *Reading the Social Body*, Iowa City: University of Iowa Press, 1993, pp. 156–184.

3. John Bradshaw, *Bradshaw on: The Family*, Deerfield Beach: Health Communications, 1988; Charles L. Whitfield, *Healing the Child Within*, Deerfield Beach: Health Communications, 1987.

4. Ellen R. Morehouse and Claire M. Scola, "Children of Alcoholics: Meeting the Needs of the Young Children of Alcoholics in the School Setting," National Association for Children of Alcoholics, n.d.

5. Patricia A. Pape, "Family Business: ACOAs Often Try to Recreate Their Families in the Workplace," *Focus*, Feb./Mar. 1990, pp. 22ff.

6. Ann Wilson Schaef and Diane Fassel, *Addictive Organizations: Why We Overwork, Cover Up, Pick Up the Pieces, Please the Boss, and Perpetuate Sick Organizations*, San Francisco: Harper, 1990; Batya Weinbaum, *Pictures of Patriarchy*, Boston: South End Press, 1983.

7. "The Strange Agony of Success," *New York Times*, Aug. 24, 1986, pp. F1, 12, 13.

8. Peter Siegel, Nancy Strohl, Laura Ingram, David Roche, and Jean Taylor, "Leninism as Cult: The Democratic Workers Party," *Socialist Review*, 96, 1987, pp. 58–85.

9. Michael Schneider, *Neurosis and Civilization: A Marxist/Freudian Synthesis*, New York: Seabury, 1975, p. 223.

10. "Tobacco Industry Counterattacks," *New York Times*, Nov. 23, 1988, Bus. pp. 1, 41; "For Tobacco's Lobbyists, No Nice Days at the Office," *New York Times*, Feb. 25, 1990, p. E4.

11. "For Tobacco's Lobbyists . . . ," *ibid.*; "New Cigarette Targets Young, White Women," *New Orleans Times-Picayune*, Feb. 18, 1990, p. A6; "A Cigarette Campaign under Fire," *New York Times*, Jan. 12, 1990, pp. D1, 4; Alexander Cockburn, "Getting Opium to the Masses: The Political Economy of Addiction," *Nation*, Oct. 30, 1989, pp. 482–83.

12. Fred E. Waddell, "Compulsive Spending Addiction," *Profes-*

sional Counselor, May/June 1989, pp. 48–51; "The Strange Agony . . .," *op. cit.*; Jay B. Rohrlich, "Wall Street's Money Junkies," *New York Times*, May 7, 1987; "Has the Growth of Legal Gambling Made Society the Loser in the Long Run?" *New York Times*, May 31, 1989, p. A18; "Hospital Leads Patients to Where All Bets Are Off," *New York Times*, Jan. 22, 1989, pp. 31, 18; "Bloodless Instant Replays," *New York Times*, Nov. 14, 1989; Malcom Moran, "How a Game Can Reveal a Problem," *New York Times*, Jan. 23, 1990, p. B1.

13. Kim Chernin, *The Hungry Self: Women, Eating, and Identity*, New York: Harper and Row, 1986; Susie Orbach, *Fat Is a Feminist Issue*, New York: Berkley, 1982.

14. Marilyn Lawrence, *The Anorexic Experience*, London: Women's Press, 1984; Susie Orbach, *Hunger Strike: The Anorectic's Struggle as a Metaphor for Our Age*, New York: Avon, 1988; Naomi Wolf, *The Beauty Myth: How Images of Beauty Are Used Against Women*, New York: Anchor Books, 1992.

15. "Why Children Smoke (and Why They Won't Listen)," *New York Times*, Feb. 6, 1992, p. C12.

16. Wendy Kaminer, *I'm Dysfunctional, You're Dysfunctional: The Recovery Movement and Other Self-Help Fashions*, Reading, MA: Addison-Wesley, 1992, pp. 80–85; John Bradshaw, *Bradshaw On: The Family, op. cit.*, pp. 92–93.

17. Frederic Jameson, *Postmodernism, or, the Cultural Logic of Late Capitalism*, Durham: Duke University Press, 1992, p. 36.

18. Sam Shepard, *Seven Plays*, New York: Bantam, 1984.

19. *Ibid.*, pp. 193–94.

20. *Ibid.*, p. 163.

21. *Ibid.*, p. 197.

22. "As City Shifted, News Lost Its Punch," *New York Times*, Oct. 31, 1990, p. B2.

23. "Rethinking Newspapers," *New York Times*, Jan. 6, 1991, pp. F1,6.

24. Paul Willis, *Common Culture*, Boulder: Westview, 1990. On the transcendental qualities of the technology of popular culture, see Frank Owen and Carlo McCormick, "Out of Your Head," *Rock & Roll Quarterly, Village Voice*, Fall 1991, pp. 7–9.

25. "The Merry Pranksters and the Art of the Hoax," *New York Times*, Dec. 23, 1990, pp. H1, 36; Stuart Ewen, *All-Consuming Images: The Politics of Style in Contemporary Culture*, New York: Basic Books, 1988.

26. Daniel C. Hallin, "Network News: We Keep America on Top of the World," in Todd Gitlin, ed., *Watching Television*, New York: Pantheon, 1986, pp. 9–41; see also Susan Douglas, "Chameleon in the White House," *Progressive*, July 1993, p. 17.

27. Francois Lyotard, *The Postmodern Condition: A Report on*

Knowledge, trans. Geoff Bennington and Brian Massumi, Minneapolis: University of Minnesota Press, 1984, p. 67.

28. Kenneth Gergen, *The Saturated Self: Dilemmas of Identity in Contemporary Life*, New York: Basic Books, 1991.

29. As shown in the movie *Paris Is Burning* (1990).

30. Judith Williamson, *Consuming Passions: The Dynamics of Popular Culture*, London: Marion Boyars, 1987, pp. 12–13.

31. Cary Goodman, *Choosing Sides: Playground and Street Life on the Lower East Side*, New York: Schocken, 1979, pp. 167–68.

32. Terry Williams, *The Cocaine Kids: The Inside Story of a Teenage Drug Ring*, Reading, MA: Addison-Wesley, 1989.

33. Sheigla Murphy and Marsha Rosenbaum, letter, "Myths about Crack," *New York Times*, Feb. 8, 1990.

34. "Can the Rich and Famous Talk America out of Drugs?" *New York Times*, Nov. 12, 1989, p. E5.

35. "Nothing Succeeds like Old TV Shows," *New York Times*, Dec. 24, 1990, pp. 11, 19.

36. Ray Oldenburg, *The Great Good Place: Cafes, Coffee Shops, Community Centers, Beauty Parlors, General Stores, Bars, Hangouts and How They Get You through the Day*, New York: Paragon, 1989; "Old Standby, the Corner Bar, Falling Victim to New Values," *New York Times*, Nov. 18, 1989, p. A1.

37. "Nothing Succeeds . . . ," *op. cit.*, p. 37.

38. Donna Haraway, "A Manifesto for Cyborgs: Science, Technology, and Socialist Feminism in the 1980's," *Socialist Review 80*,1985, p. 97. See Donna Haraway, "A Manifesto for Cyborgs: Science, Technology, and Socialist Feminism," in Linda J. Nicholson, ed., *Feminism/Postmodernism*, New York: Routledge, 1991, pp. 190–233, and Donna Haraway, *Simians Cyborgs, and Women: The Reinvention of Nature*, New York: Routledge, 1990.

39. William Gibson, *Neuromancer*, New York: Ace, 1984.

40. Peter Fitting, "The Lessons of Cyberpunk," in Constance Penley and Andrew Ross, eds., *Technoculture*, Minneapolis: University of Minnesota Press, 1991, pp. 295–315; Pam Rosenthal, "Jacked In: Fordism, Cyberpunk, Marxism," *Socialist Review, 91* (1), 1991, pp. 79–103.

41. Gibson, *op. cit.*, p. 51.

42. *Ibid.*, p. 6.

43. *Ibid.*, p. 5.

44. Fitting, *op. cit.*; see also Andrew Ross, *Strange Weather: Culture, Science, and Technology in the Age of Limits*, New York: Verso, 1991. For a discussion of whether information technology will be controlled in the name of public interest or corporate profit, see the July 12, 1993, *Nation*.

45. Rosenthal, *op. cit.*

CHAPTER 4

Everyday Highs

BODIES ELECTRIC: MUSIC AND SPORTS

In postmodern culture the electronic media affect pleasurable activities to the extent that they can become either self-enhancing or addictive. I first examine music and sports and then the corporate media in terms of their use of popular culture to wage the war on drugs. In all cases postmodern culture has realigned everyday forms of cultural expression in such a way that they can either create more fluid, mutually satisfying relations or increase control over others and deny them access to information. These processes occur within a new ground in which the self and the sign are able to absorb and transform one another through the electronic media.

Two important areas of everyday life are popular music and sports. These cultural forms are visceral, bodily activities which evoke strong feelings of sensuality and the yearning for transcendence. Because of these qualities, drug abuse prevention programs often suggest participation in music and sports as alternatives to drug use. Yet postmodern culture has provided the means to transform these interests into all-consuming passions which are capable of inducing the addictive qualities of control and denial themselves. A newspaper ad by the Partnership for a Drug-Free America is telling in the way it refers to drugs, sports, and music as habits: "Kids need something better to do than drugs. Like sports. Dance. Or music. Because good things can be habit-forming, too. So get them into a good habit. Today. Or they may get into a very bad one."[1]

But the idea that sports and music are inherently healthy alternatives to addiction is a myth. There is no guarantee that these or any other habits will not become compulsive, addictive behaviors themselves. Not only are popular music and sports sponsored by drug and alcohol companies, but their form and content today exhibit characteristics which generate addictive patterns. They have been transformed into cultural signs which people use to control their own experience and/or that of others in ways that may be self-enhancing but also enslaving. In postmodern culture people's selves can become saturated with images and meanings from corporatized music and sports through the electronic media. These activities in turn can become imbued with the subjectivity of the fans. But when the self becomes overidentified with and overdependent on one form of life, it loses its relational aspect and becomes a fixed, rigid entity. Everyday cultural activities have been transformed by the electronic media and can either enhance self-expression or induce addictive relations.

Addictive Music

> *I'm Your Pusher*
> Ice T

Popular music is a powerful form of expression which evokes strong feelings pro and con. Conservatives attack rock and roll as a subversive and rebellious influence on children.[2] Some have tried to blame music for certain problems, such as teenage suicide (heavy metal), drug use (rock), and violence (rap) while they excuse the failures of adults and societal institutions and displace them onto music. Some progressives complain, however, that rock has lost much of its power as a force of resistance and has become co-opted by the establishment. TV ads have bought up the rights to many oldies, and the songs from people's youths are now identified with commercial products.[3] Both perspectives assume rock to be some pure essence which either corrupts people or is corrupted itself. But it makes more sense to consider rock as a contradictory form which can move and influence people one way or another as well as serve as little more than a banal, safe expression of watered-down tastes, among other things. Racist and anti-Semitic skinheads enjoy their own brand of hate rock (called Oi!) as much as other groups, which shows that rock is not intrinsically progressive.[4]

However, one thing which the debate demonstrates is that, in postmodern culture, to consume popular music and art has become a passionate, personal means of expression for millions of people. The conflict over censorship for federal funding for the arts led by conservative Senator Jesse Helms, the 1990 trial over the Robert Mapplethorpe exhibit in Cincinnati, and the obscenity trial for selling the music of 2 Live Crew, a rap group, are nothing less than political struggles over peoples' right to personally identify with popular cultural forms of desire.[5]

The electronic media have expanded the boundaries of subjective pleasure in terms of experiencing music. They dissolve the boundaries between musicians and the fans; the musicians and their music become imbued with subjectivity, and the fans become more musical. This allows for greater control for both the corporate music business and the fans. Recent advances in electronic reproduction, such as Qsound, have made it possible to experience music in the realm of a druglike hyperreality; an overall sound can be created which would not be apparent to an audience listening to the same music performed live. Other technologies allow the listener to manipulate the sound of the same recording to simulate different listening spaces, such as a church, concert hall, outdoor concert, or club. The popular karaoke bars allow anyone to sing his or her favorite songs along with a professional sound track. Even with walkmen [*sic*] and other more accessible equipment, music listeners can envelop themselves, as if they were stoned, to such a degree that the boundary between one's self and the source of the sound becomes blurred.

Through the accessibility of the media, fans can personally identify with music and rock stars and incorporate their style into their own image, while the stars themselves take on subjective qualities. Many youth identify commercial rap, heavy metal, punk, and pop music with their own distinct personal styles and outlooks, such as through caps, t-shirts, and other fashions. With electronic advances fans and musicians can now choose to piece together those disparate elements of various styles which appeal to them. For example, hip hop allows the disc jockey to control the music by sampling different sounds from various records and incorporate them into the mix. Worldbeat, which combines rhythms and melodies from different cultures, is part of this trend. There are bands which even mix pieces of different styles within one song. The debate over whether Madonna is a feminist hinges in part on whether her submissive poses in certain videos are just traditional, degrading images of women or whether they are deliberate, ironic expressions of her own subjectivity, as she maintains. (On ABC-TV's "Nightline" Madonna asserted that she is in control of those images.) From a fan's standpoint Madonna as a role model creatively plays with this ambiguous boundary between subjective control on the one hand and corporate media manipulation and traditional images on the other, which is a large part of her appeal.

Music as a drug.   The media as contradictory forms of subjective expression allow for contested means of gaining pleasure and meeting needs through music. Some corporate interests use music like a drug to control people's moods, and listeners choose certain music to regulate their own feelings. Muzak, also known as dentist's office music, is also used by airlines and in malls as well as in waiting rooms. Its homogenized, soothing arrangements of familiar pop and rock songs medicate for anxiety and induce relaxation. But like a drug, its effect depends on the setting and the emotional state of the user. Some convenience store owners have used music as if it were a noxious chemical spray. By playing Mantovani through loudspeakers, they have managed to deter teenagers from hanging out in their mall. The federal government has used homogenized pop music as a weapon in psychological warfare, most notably when the army forced General Manuel Noriega to surrender in Panama in 1989 and when the Bureau of Alcohol, Tobacco, and Firearms surrounded the cult followers of David Koresh in Waco, Texas, in 1993.

But listeners use music to reflect or enhance their moods. In the 1980s hardworking professionals and managers began to relax to New Age music on the Windham Hill label and to minimalist composers like Steve Reich and Philip Glass. The music removes phrases from the context of a coherent melody and repeats endless circulating lines. One critic suggests that it reflects the nature of much bureaucratized administrative and professional work, which involves overseeing random self-referential codes devoid of narrative content and affect.[6] Fast-talking deejays on morning shows serve up chatter and pop music as stimulants in order to help people get up and function at work or in the house. As with advertising slogans and jingles, the repetitive airing of a hit song is a deliberate means of generating a taste or craving. The song's hooks, heard over and over, work their way into your nervous system until you find yourself hearing the tune and/or the words in your mind. Buying the song and playing it when you want is a way to control the experience, although it is also the outcome the music industry worked to attain as well. On the other end of the mood spectrum, light and soft rock stations are pitched toward office workers who require just enough stimulation to undercut the tedium of their routine without becoming an interference. In a TV ad for one New York soft rock station, office workers at their desk say they don't agree on much but all can agree to keep the radio at the spot on the dial which plays safe, sedating, inoffensive music as a bland, happy medium. For some who have lost all affect, there is music to maintain the experience. Some independent bands reflect the mood of youth who have come of age in the postmodern culture of uncertainty about the future, commitment, and political action. Rock bands like Galaxy 500 and Mazzy Star strip the music of its traditional drive and energy and play monotonous melodies while the lyrics speak of mundane things with little emotion.[7] The most explicit metaphor for music as a positive drug may be rapper Ice T's song "I'm Your Pusher," in which he tells the listener who wants to get high to throw that crack or smoke away and let the record play, since the "dope" he is dealing, music, is not smoked but felt.

Music and drugs.   Listening to popular music has been linked with mood-enhancing drugs themselves, such as LSD (sixties acid rock) and marijuana (reggae). In the 1990s marijuana seems to have made a comeback with its own t-shirts and cap styles and with hip hop rappers like Basehead, Cypress Hill, Redman, and Dr. Dre singing its praises. The drug Ecstasy also became popular around the same time among some gays who frequented disco clubs in New York, and it became associated with "house music." Some suburban youth who go to large dance spaces called "raves" also get stoned on marijuana or Ecstasy. But some music is almost inseparable from signs of the commercial, legal drugs alcohol and nicotine. For example, rock star Steve Winwood wrote the theme song for Anheuser-Busch's "Night belongs to Michelob" campaign. Michelob sponsored the Rolling Stones' Steel Wheels tour in 1989, and the band performed a TV spot for the beer. A typical 1989 issue of the New York *Village Voice* displayed music listings underwritten by legal drug companies: Michelob sponsors rock concerts at the New Ritz; Parliament cigarettes promotes Soundseries; Benson and Hedges offers a Blues series; Marlboro presents country music concerts; Stolichnaya vodka pays for jazz listings; and Absolut vodka presents jazz concerts.

Some in the music industry have tried to counter its drug image, at least its link with illegal drugs. In the late 1980s the rock video station MTV aired antidrug ads produced by a nonprofit group, Rock Against Drugs, which featured rock and pop stars speaking against drug use. But there was considerable skepticism about the credibility of some of the rock musicians who testified that they party without drugs.[8] Performance artist Eric Bogosian parodies the hypocrisy of the music industry promoting a drug-free image. In one of his sketches, disc jockey Ricky Rocket of WXXX emcees "the Krönenbräu Music Concerts series" of sadomasochistic heavy metal bands. He works his audience into a drug and alcohol frenzy, then reminds them to "drive safely" when they leave.[9] More sincere efforts are by rapper Chuck D., and the group, Public Enemy, who have sung about the way beer companies push forty-ounce malt liquors onto the black community.

Music making and drugs.   The emotional closeness of rock stars with their fans through concert and media exposure intensifies the stars' own subjective feelings of power and vulnerability. Drug use among musicians has an ambiguous legacy and may express the musicians' attempts to deal with this heightened sense of self. A number of prominent rock musicians have experienced bouts with alcohol and drugs and have lived to tell about it, like Belinda Carlisle, David Crosby,[10] John Phillips, and members of the heavy metal band Aerosmith. The ones who did not are well known: Jimi Hendrix, Brian Jones, Janis Joplin, Frankie Lymon, Jim Morrison, Gram Parsons, Elvis Presley, and Sid Vicious; in jazz, John Coltrane, Bill Evans, Billy Holiday, Charlie Parker, and Lester Young, among many others. But some musicians defend the use of drugs with music making as a means to enhance artistic expression. Some, like Greg Errico, the drummer for Sly and the Family Stone, feel that psychedelic drugs were a special part of the music of the 1960s.[11] Singer/songwriter Nick Gravenites was friends with Janis Joplin and with blues musicians Mike Bloomfield and Paul Butterfield, who also died of heroin overdoses. Yet he argues that drug use, except for cocaine, serves as a metaphor for the intellectual and spiritual restlessness of America: "It's part of our ability to create new things."[12]

Others explain drug use as a means for someone with an artistic temperament to deal with the pressures of stardom. Rock musician Alex Dore argues that drugs are one way to stay sane in the face of the enormous amount of euphoric emotional involvement a star has with the fans.[13] Nick Gravenites sums up the postmodern phenomenon in which the subjective desire of millions of fans becomes literally embodied in the person of the rock star, who feels both power and vulnerability: "It's tough to be in this materialistic world and at the same time to be so giving of your body and your soul, because people eat on it like it was cheese or something."[14] To extend this metaphor, the musician can nourish the fan's subjective life through his or her own subjective expression in a mutually enhancing way. The danger is that the hungrier the fans become because of the emptiness of their own lives, the more the star gets consumed and used like a drug. From the other side, an insecure star whose very identity and sense of self are dependent on the approval from his or her fans feels a loss of self the more he or she gives to the fans.

An American icon who may have overdosed on his own image, as well as on drugs, was Elvis Presley, who died in 1977. But in postmodern fashion his fans have incorporated him into their own subjective expression to such a degree that on some level he continues to live. One of the biggest examples of fan denial around a rock star and drugs which has become a cultural phenomenon is the myth, or belief, depending on your perspective, that Elvis is still alive.[15] Fans, mostly white working-class people, have kept him alive in their own way and have rescued him from the trappings of a banal, depraved, and disillusioning existence as a bloated, over-the-hill, show business star. Their collective effort at resurrection has generated a wealth of artifacts, images, performances, songs, books, talk shows, and stories which are a testament to the active creation of popular culture. Elvis sightings continue long after his death. Greil Marcus suggests that the appeal of Dead Elvis is due to fans' ambivalent feelings of both revulsion and obeisance; by keeping him alive they are remaking their own lives and assertively reclaiming something that was taken from them.[16] A part of the phenomenon is an angry response to his doctor who fed him the drugs. One memorial t-shirt displays his last high-dosage prescription for the singer. Perhaps more difficult than Elvis's death is for fans to confront the possibility that Elvis may even have taken his own life, as his brother maintains. In any event, the belief that he is still alive is a powerful cultural myth that flies in the face of his sordid demise from drugs: it was not an exit fit for The King and therefore cannot be true. Elvis Lives!

Addictive songs. Some of the content of popular music has addictive qualities. Until recently it was not hard to find explicit references to drugs like cocaine and alcohol among some rock lyrics, a favorite activity of right-wing groups bent on censorship and control. Of course many country and western classics present images of miserable people trying to drown their sorrows in alcohol ("Tonight the Bottle Let Me Down," "She's Acting Single, I'm Drinking Doubles," "Whiskey River Take My Mind"). Until recently images of the alcohol culture were predominant in country music and reflected the lives of its white working-class fans. The trend of the nineties in country, however, seems to be toward abstinence and sobriety; in Travis Tritt's video for the song "The Whiskey Ain't Workin'," his character refuses to drown his troubles in alcohol, and veteran honky-tonker Alan Jackson now sings that he is "hooked" on his baby's love in "I Don't Need the Booze (to Get a Buzz On)."[17] This trend is linked with less macho posturing and more sensitivity to feminist concerns among a number of influential male country and western stars like Garth Brooks and Clint Black.

A more subtle allusion to addictive qualities still found in many pop songs often sung by female vocalists is to codependent feelings toward a lover. In fact, when you consider all the songs in which the singer cannot go on or whose world is empty without the other, it is hard to find pop tunes which do not express codependency in some sense. (Robert Palmer said it outright: Better face the fact that you are "Addicted to Love.") Some hits refer to feeling out of control and being unable to perform simple things ("I Get Weak" by Belinda Carlisle), feeling the need to allow the lover to have his way despite how he hurt you ("Anything for You" by Gloria Estefan), and the feeling that without the other, you are nothing at all ("I Live for Your Love" by Natalie Cole). Although the lyrics of these songs convey the traditional role of women as weak, dependent, and masochistic, as music they are also powerful expressions of the desire for the erotic, romantic, and transcendental love which underlies many addictive cravings and which gives this kind of song its appeal. One of my favorite albums is by country singer and songwriter Nanci Griffith, "The Last of the True Believers" (1986), which includes a wistful song in which she wonders whether her missing her lover is due to the wine she is drinking, and an alcoholic fantasy (by a male songwriter) about an unavailable woman; on the record sleeve is a picture of Griffith holding a bottle of beer. But it may be country music which now signals the trend toward the image of more assertive, less codependent women in popular music. Singers like K. T. Oslin, Trisha Yearwood, and Reba McEntire sing about women who have careers, go back to college, and reject overly dependent men, and Mary Chapin Carpenter, in "Come On Come On," takes on issues like men's need to express their feelings and women's need for emotional space.[18]

Addictive Sports

Sports is another everyday phenomenon which can express addictive forms of control and denial within a postmodern configuration of pleasure and power. Sports today continues to be vested with the mythic, modernist image of a pure, wholesome means of self-expression separate from the daily problems of work, the family, or drug and alcohol abuse. "Do sports, not drugs," says one current bumper sticker. But the idea that sports offers superior natural highs and that it boils down to a choice of sports over drugs would strike many addicts as laughable. For an ex-addict, including cigarette smokers, exercise can provide feelings of euphoria and relaxation from stress but only after the person has made the decision to quit.[19] A former colleague who in her words was addicted to marijuana as a college student recounted how she would enjoy smoking a joint *after* jogging because her lungs felt more open and she was able to get a greater high.

The broader issue is that sports is not an innocent, viable substitute for drugs because in many ways sports itself has become addictive, and because many people do both sports and drugs, which gives the lie to the idea that sports is a sufficient substitute for drug highs. Sports, as part of leisure time, has been colonized as a commodity. In the industrial era capital divested work of its elements of play and subordinated it to the needs of profit. As compensation to working people play was transposed onto the terrain of leisure, but then leisure itself became subject to market forces.[20] Sports, for example, baseball, is not some innocent activity.[21] Because it has become commodified, it shares addictive qualities and has had strong tie-ins with drugs themselves. That is, commodified sports is pushed as a drug onto consumers or fans in the sense that it compulsively serves as a fix which medicates for feelings of boredom, frustration, or powerlessness. Sports in this sense substitutes for direct ways to deal with emotional deficits within everyday relations. Involvement with sports can take on addictive qualities such as perfectionism and the need for control to the point where it becomes destructive rather than playful and self-renewing. Postmodern culture through TV and movies sometimes promotes the myth of the purity of sports and sometimes explodes it, all the while transforming sports into a new addictive form. This occurs in complex ways.

Shooting up sports. As the media dissolve boundaries between fans and players, fans personally identify with players and sports itself, while players become more imbued with subjective attributes. Television radically transformed this relationship. In 1960 ABC began "up close and personal" coverage of college football, which led to high ratings, network bidding wars, and huge profits.[22] This new arrangement allows for more control over pleasure for both corporations and fans.

The idea that sports is a substitute for drugs is belied by the addictive way the media promote sports. On the consumer side fans have gained more control over their craving for sports information. Sports have become signifiers of self-realization without the need for people to play them. More people have become spectators and purveyors of information as more hours of TV programming are devoted to sports events and coverage of sports news. By the 1980s, with increased coverage, more intense scrutiny, and the use of new media forms, information about games and players was everywhere and at all times available to fans. Like happy addicts, fans could now be assured of getting their fix of sports information and could participate in sports by identifying with their favorite team or player and/or by betting. In New York a 24-hour all-sports station has fans calling in and commenting about the players, managers, and games; telephone sports hotlines are available, as are cable programs which provide continuous information on scores. In deference to the many gamblers who bet on games, pro football for a time used the video instant replay to verify or overrule field official's calls, since these affect the point spread.

As the corporate media have personalized professional sports, they have boosted the popularity and profitability of paraphernalia such as caps, cards, autographs, equipment, and designer clothing bearing the pro team's logos. But they also induce an addictive craving for these signs of personalized expression. In the ghettoes of Chicago, Los Angeles, Detroit, and New York, some young people who wear pro athletic jackets as personal fashion statements have been robbed and killed over their clothes.[23] During the late 1980s many black youths across the country, including some in gangs, began to wear black-colored pro sports clothing, in particular that bearing the pirate insignia of the Los Angeles Raiders football team, as a personal emblem. Some police officials attribute the trend to the Los Angeles drug gang, the Crips, who popularized the clothing around the same time they expanded their drug dealing around the country; others attribute it to rap music groups who began wearing the clothing on MTV videos, leading to what one rap producer terms a "nationalized culture" among black youth.[24] National Football League officials are concerned about the way the meaning of the emblem is being appropriated, and they prepared an ad campaign involving a rap music star who would "insist that youths can stand against violence and drugs and still wear team caps."[25] Sportswear, then, is an ambiguous cultural sign which can enhance self-expression or lead to addictive behavior. Youth can embrace it in creative ways as part of a nationalized culture. But when youth become overidentified with it as one fixed form of personal expression which is pushed on them as a measure of status, it can lead to violence and even death.

Personalizing the pros.   At the same time close-up media coverage has shown sports themselves, such as baseball, to be far from pure and athletes to be infused with the personal contradictions of the everyday, including addictive behavior. The media glorify star athletes, all the while undercutting their image. The foibles and problems of ball players, including drug and alcohol abuse and gambling addiction, have become magnified and personalized through the expansion of media coverage. In recent years baseball players like Keith Hernandez and Dale Berra have admitted to using cocaine; Yankee pitcher Steve Howe was banned a number of times after testing positive for the drug; All-Star player and manager Pete Rose was convicted of gambling on his own team; Mets Dwight Gooden and Darryl Strawberry went into rehab programs for cocaine and alcohol, respectively; former Yankee manager Billy Martin was killed in a drunk driver accident; Philadelphia Philles outfielder, Lennie Dykstra, smashed up his Mercedes-Benz and injured himself driving drunk; and basketball

star Michael Jordan ran up a huge gambling debt: all were headline news. The media also exposed the conflicts of the business of
baseball, including the players strike, which disrupted the 1981
season, the managers' lockout in 1990, and the discovery that
management was in collusion over refusing to sign free-agency
players in 1988.

Legal drug sponsorship.   The intensive media coverage of sports
which has gained major revenues for the networks has gone hand
in hand with profitable corporate tobacco and liquor sponsorship. For example, Virginia Slims cigarettes sponsors a tennis
tournament.[26] Cigar companies like Garcia y Vega are immune
from the TV ban on cigarettes and promote sports events (in any
event, the Marlboro Man is visible from center field during New
York Mets telecasts). In New York every time a Met or Yankee
hits a home run Anheuser-Busch has the announcers say, "This
Bud's for you," and sponsors the Budweiser Player of the Game.
Of course, the beer company owns the rival St. Louis Cardinals.
The "Bud Bowl," an animated intramural contest between Bud
and Bud Light run during the Super Bowl, draws as much attention as the game itself, and sometimes is more exciting. Their
rival, Miller, uses ex-baseball and ex-football stars to plug light
beer on TV. Beer commercials on TV often use images of sports

" THE MANAGER WAS THROWN OUT FOR GAMBLING, THE SHORTSTOP WAS SUSPENDED FOR STEROIDS,
THE PITCHER'S IN DRUG REHAB, THE CATCHER'S AT BETTY FORD AND THE REST OF THE TEAM'S
DOING A MILLER LITE COMMERCIAL! "

Reprinted with the permission of Doug Marlette, *New York Newsday.*

activities like volleyball, fishing, touch football, and softball. After baseball player Len Dykstra and his teammate Darren Daulton were injured in a drunk driving accident in 1991, a spokesperson for the National Council on Alcoholism and Drug Dependence charged that major league sports deny that alcohol is a problem among their athletes because of the close relationship with the beer industry.[27] National Football League commissioner Paul Tagliabue acknowledged that because professional leagues distinguish between legal and illegal drugs, it is more difficult to criticize alcohol abuse in the same way as illegal drug abuse.[28] The media themselves downplayed the role of alcohol after Dykstra's car accident and after the death of two Cleveland Indian pitchers in 1993 from a boating accident which was also caused by drunk driving. Sports, the touted antidote to drug taking, is tied to legal drugs every day.

The link between drinking and identifying as a sports fan is strong, in particular among men. Drinking is often an excuse for people to behave in ways they ordinarily do not, and has a history of being part of leisure time for working-class men. Drinking is also one way to recapture bodily feelings, to enhance the personal, vicarious pleasure of watching an athletic performance. Many men invest considerable emotional energy rooting for a team as an addictive substitute for their inability to deal with the changing relations in their own lives. For example some of them have little chance to develop the grace and command of their own bodies and to be winners in everyday terms. They may feel threatened by women's demands for equality or they may experience the loss of camaraderie and pride of skilled work brought about by changes in the workplace. As a means of escape, then, some identify with the aggressive nature of football, hockey, and boxing; fighting is almost a regular part of a hockey game (went to a fight and a hockey game broke out, goes one quip), and fights break out in other sports as well. As a consequence of all this—that some men use sports as a drug to escape, that they drink as spectators, and that drinking can lead to fighting—sports arenas have become socially acceptable places to drink and fight.

Concessionaires in sports stadiums and arenas do a brisk business selling beer to football, hockey, and baseball fans, whose excessive drinking sometimes leads to fights and personal injury as a matter of course. Yet in one case intensive media coverage of pro sports forced sports to distance itself from identifying with beer consumption. The incident was televised nationally, a 1988 football game between the New York Jets and the Buffalo Bills in which some fans brawled, people set fires in the stands, and five persons were hospitalized. As a result of the TV coverage the state authority which operates the stadium restricted the hours allowed for parking lot tailgate parties, where many get drunk before the game, and the hours during the game when beer may be sold.[29]

The temperance trend has continued, but the hypocrisy remains. In 1990 pro football began running ads urging fans to "stop rocking the boat," to drink responsibly and behave themselves at the game. Ballparks like Shea Stadium have designated nonalcoholic sections as a way to promote abstinence. Yet the same New York sportscasters who suggest grabbing a beer after every home run also tell the viewers in the next breath to "just say no to [illegal] drugs," an announcment paid for by a designer clothing company. Budweiser's campaign slogan, "Know when to say when," incanted by the sportscasters, is the height of absurdity for many problem drinkers.

The link between sports and corporate beer and tobacco sponsorship remains strong, and the corporations are able to resist challenges to this arrangement. In the face of congressional attempts to restrict beer and cigarette commercials, leaders of alcohol, tobacco, and advertising industries have protested in the name of First Amendment rights.[30] These industries have managed to limit restrictive proposals made by the National Collegiate Athletic Association (NCAA). For example, at the end of 1989 the NCAA signed a contract with CBS for exclusive rights to broadcast the college basketball tournaments for seven years, beginning in 1991, in which CBS agreed to reduce beer advertising from ninety seconds an hour to sixty seconds. The beer companies agreed to intersperse ads with equal numbers of spots promoting responsible drinking. The association at first wanted to ban beer commercials altogether or only have spots paid for by the brewers that urge drinking in moderation. But it yielded to the brewers, who are concerned that further restrictions could spread to other sports broadcasts. The TV industry, according to the commissioner of the Pacific 10 college conference, takes a hard line as well: "The television industry has said to us repeatedly that there is no substitute for beer advertising."[31]

Beer companies invest millions of dollars on promotions in auto racing, the second largest spectator sport next to football.[32]

They have come under attack in this market as well; the National Association to Prevent Impaired Driving criticized the brewers for linking beer with fast driving. But one fan defended the beer companies and his right to associate beer drinking with a sport he enjoys, while raising the issue of a double standard and class bias of those who promote temperance: "We sit out here drinking our beer and watching the race out in the open and they sit around their private yacht clubs and country clubs behind closed doors sipping their wine and champagne."[33]

Drugs and pro sports. As the media personalize sports and increase the pressure on athletes to serve as public figures and role models, they expose the problems of some athletes around drugs and alcohol. The profession has managed to downplay the fact that many ball players abuse nicotine. Almost half of major and minor league baseball players used spit tobacco in 1991, a form of intake in which the user absorbs more nicotine than the average cigarette smoker.[34] But the media have shown that some professional athletes have been implicated in other forms of substance abuse. Besides Phillies outfielder Lenny Dykstra, Denver Broncos' tight end Clarence Kay, Boston Celtics' Charles Smith, Minnesota Vikings quarterback Tommy Kramer, and Dallas Mavericks forward Roy Tarpley were involved in various alcohol-related incidents in 1991. The pressures of new media stardom and the difficulty of severing ties with people from the old neighborhoods who were involved with drugs may have contributed to some black athletes succumbing to cocaine and alcohol abuse, such as Dwight Gooden and Darryl Strawberry of the New York Mets, Micheal [*sic*] Ray Richardson of the New Jersey Nets, and Tony Elliott of the New Orleans Saints.[35] A number of pros become dependent on painkillers and amphetamines to get them through football and hockey games and other physically demanding events where big money is on the line. Although the National Football League (NFL) says that only 6 percent of the players tested positive for steroids in 1987 and 1988, a self-made expert and promoter of steroids says pro football players are the worst abusers of steroids.[36] In 1991 former pro player Lyle Alzado disclosed that he was a longtime user of anabolic steroids and implicated the drug as the cause of inoperable brain cancer, from which he died a year later. A former drug advisor to the NFL believes that about 20 to 25 percent of NFL players take steroids and that the league's policy of random testing is not working to eliminate the problem.[37] Human growth hormones (HGH) are popular with athletes who want a body-building drug because there is no effective test for it. In 1993 two professional football players were indicted by the Federal Drug Enforcement Administration for trafficking in hormones and steroids.[38]

Drug use in professional sports serves as a literal metaphor for the profession's own addictive desire for more competitive, more spectacular, and at bottom more profitable contests. The owners demand more from bigger, harder-hitting athletes, who in turn demand astronomical salaries. The increased pressure to win and earn more profits leads to greater media exposure and in turn more pressure. Like an addiction this process seems to be spiraling out of control. It follows the addictive pattern of increasing the dosage to get the same high, with dire consequences worsening over time. The attempt to tack on a punitive, no-use message to pro sports is futile and hypocritical. Pro sports' competitive, commodified nature remains addictive: the demand for more profits, the increased control over performance which leads to substance abuse and addiction among athletes, and the use of pro sports as a fix for fans' unfulfilled relations in everyday life.

One recent alternative to this addictive pattern has been the efforts of John Lucas, coach of the San Antonio Spurs basketball team. Lucas is a recovering drug addict who used drugs to escape the pressure of measuring his self-worth in terms of wins and losses. Since then he has established recovery and fitness centers for other recovering professional athletes. His commitment to a nonaddictive way of life extends to his coaching style in which he does not attempt to control his players but instead encourages them to have a significant say about strategies on the court and even personnel issues.[39]

Drugs and college sports.   The increasing professionalization of athletics and the lure of huge salaries place tremendous pressure on college athletes. This contributes to drug and alcohol abuse as a means to both medicate for the stress and to enhance performance. With the bonanza of TV coverage of college sports, schools are spending large amounts of money on athletes and athletic programs, some of it illegally.[40] Many athletes must spend more of their time on sports year-round. Joining a college sports program now has become the primary means for athletes to get onto pro teams, including minor sports such as golf, tennis, and hockey.[41] As a result some college athletes use drugs to deal with pressure or to give them the extra competitive edge. African-American athletes experience considerable pressure because many are channeled away from other professions and into sports programs in which only a few athletes can succeed. In the wake of the death of Len Bias, a promising black college basketball star who died from smoking crack in 1986, Jesse Jackson argued that in college sports "there are too many games, too much money involved and too much pressure to win at all costs. It's not just one school, it's everywhere."[42] Steroid use among teenage boys begins in the high school years, and many college football players take steroids in order to stay competitive.[43] The National Collegiate Athletic Association (NCAA) acknowledges the pressure which helps explain this use of performance-enhancing drugs. But rather than address this issue, the group chose to expand its drug-testing program of football players to year-round, and increased the penalties for abusers.[44]

As befits their ambiguous status as privileged campus heroes who are allowed only a scholarship and forbidden to work, student athletes are both lionized and unsupervised by the campus community, which often overlooks unruly or abusive behavior.[45] The male jock culture found in some college fraternities often is linked with excessive beer drinking. In recent incidents student athletes at St. Johns University in New York were accused of bringing a woman back to their house, getting her drunk, and sexually attacking her, and the University of Oklahoma quarterback was found to have sold drugs to an undercover agent.[46] Graduation rates among athletes are low, and some students are passed through and graduate without an adequate education. Meanwhile, athletic departments, coaches, local business communities, television networks, and beer companies all benefit financially from college sports.

The George and Billy Show.   Media scrutiny, which makes being a sports fan a personal means of self-realization, enabled fans in New York to share in the intimacies of one significant relationship which mixed baseball and alcoholic behavior: the one between Yankee owner George Steinbrenner and manager Billy Martin. For fourteen years Yankee fans were involved in the ins and outs of this symbiotic, love-hate affair, which was akin to an alcoholic marriage. Martin was an alcoholic who died in late 1989 in a car crash on his way home from a bar, driven by a friend who was found to be intoxicated. He was hired and fired as manager five times over a period of fourteen years by Steinbrenner. Sometimes Martin would start off the season and then self-destruct, or he was called in mid-season to clean up after another manager had failed, do well for a time, then fail again himself. He would belligerently stand up to Steinbrenner, get fired, then come back for more, playing the self-demeaning role of truculent hothead, troublemaker, and fool. He kicked dirt on umpires in an infantile rage. He bullied some of his players and brawled in bars, once with one of his own pitchers. He called Steinbrenner a liar. He first denied the fights and the statement, then admitted he lied.[47]

Martin evoked polarized feelings of love and hate from many fans. His defenders considered him a talented, exciting manager. They saw his feistiness as heroic, as a means of standing up to the big guys and of displaying a competitive attitude. They tended to dismiss his shortcomings and saw him as his own man. Steinbrenner and others had arranged for the funeral to be held at the pre-eminent St. Patrick's Cathedral in Manhattan, despite the fact that Martin had been divorced three times.[48] The media coverage of his funeral showed considerable discomfort and denial about his drinking by many. In the service the rector asked, "Why did it have to happen this way?"[49] But one answer is that Martin had a drinking problem. His numerous critics felt that he denigrated himself and the game through his behavior and was a negative role model for children.

But Billy Martin was only half the act. George Steinbrenner played his own part within this alcoholic system, sometimes as the authoritarian, controlling patriarch on whom Martin was dependent for a job, other times as the needy, forgiving partner who always takes the abuser back. Although he paid out large salaries to his staff, his control over them was absolute. He never trusted them enough to do their job, and at some inevitable point would impose his own opinions about what they should be doing, overriding their expertise and undermining their ability to perform. He spoke of his players' efforts in terms of productivity as if they were line workers. By criticizing his players and meddling in the clubhouse, Steinbrenner contributed to creating a climate of insecurity, tension, and low morale in which his team could not coalesce. In 1990 many Yankee fans got their wish for a short time: the baseball commissioner banned Steinbrenner from involving himself in Yankee business because he had hired a gambler to uncover dirt on a former Yankee player with whom Steinbrenner had been carrying on a litigious dispute. (Steinbrenner resumed de jure control of the team, which he had never lost in fact, in 1993.)

But other fans, as well as players, often expressed uneasy ambivalence about Steinbrenner while he wielded power. They would justify his behavior by acknowledging that he is the boss, he pays the salaries, he has a right to say and do what he wants. Steinbrenner appeared to be as dependent on Martin as Martin was on Steinbrenner. He alternated between controlling and bullying on one hand and patronizing and coddling on the other. To watch the two playfight at a press conference on the evening news evoked uncomfortable feelings akin to those which arise when one is forced to witness an intimate, troubled relationship in public.

Martin's dishonesty and infantile raging, Steinbrenner's power tripping and overstepping of boundaries, the destructive dependency cycle of anger and forgiveness, and the illusory thinking on the part of both that this time it will work out—these are symptomatic of an addictive system. If they were private figures, their behavior would be of little concern here. But because this was a public relationship personalized through the media, it implicated the feelings of the fans. Fans became drawn into the system: they, too, were dependent on Martin and Steinbrenner for providing them with entertainment and for fueling their fantasies and dreams of success through baseball.

Fans participated in the denial: maybe this time Billy will stay the season, keep his cool, and win a pennant; maybe this time George will button his lip and butt out of the manager's business. It is difficult to admit that baseball is not a pure innocent sport but a business like any other, that there are bosses and drones. To acknowledge that baseball can be disappointing and contain disturbed elements might expose something about the emptiness and failures of people's own lives. But on the other side, fans' negative feelings were made public through the media. They had some say in how the two carried on and by extension how the team did. The news media often solicited fans' opinions and reported on the various popular protests against Steinbrenner hatched in the stands at Yankee Stadium or through legal petitions. The Martin/Steinbrenner alcoholic system was reflective of an aging, modernist hierarchy. It may not be accidental that the two were gone from baseball within the same year, as the media publicized a troubled personal relationship while they personalized the public relationship of the fans.

Drugs and playing sports.   The media affect how people perform personal sports as well, which includes the playing out of addictive issues of control and denial. In some cases organized sports for youth such as Little League and high school football mirror professional athletics by imbuing kids with grave, adultlike roles of media-style stardom and status; the kids get to perform under pressure, while the parents live out their role as strategists and mentors. At its best children and adults can recreate themselves by appropriating positive media images of stars and coaches. But it is troublesome when those mass-produced images uncritically determine children's needs and feelings in each instance, as often happens in organized leagues. Sports itself becomes like a fix when adults treat a child who fails at competitive sports like a professional ball player in a corporate hierarchy who must deny feelings of shame and anxiety. When the child loses and fails to win the love of a parent or to bring glory to the family or coach, then the need to win at sports becomes a druglike substitute for the child's need for acceptance.

The 1989 antiwar movie, *Born on the Fourth of July*, presents a critical view of growing up in a modernist family and society where boys earn self-esteem, approval, and manhood through success at competitive sports. In a riveting, poignant scene which occurs in 1964, Ron Kovic (Tom Cruise), breaks down in tears after he loses a high school wrestling match in front of his family and girlfriend. That scene, with its critique of the use of competitive sports as a measure to prove self-worth as a person, could not have been made in 1964. Coaches, peers, and parents who pressure kids in militaristic ways to win at all costs—like former Green Bay Packers football coach Vince Lombardi, who said, "Winning isn't everything, it's the only thing," or like Woody Hayes, the Ohio State football coach who punched an opposing player after losing a televised big game—and who use humiliation and put-downs and demand strict obedience, represent a deteriorating hierarchy of control and denial. Hopeful signs of this change occurred during the 1992–93 collegiate athletic season when Colorado State fired its football coach and Army and California fired their basketball coaches, all because school administrators determined that the coaches had emotionally abused their players.[50] The profound irony about sports as a fix for drugs is that these humiliating coaching practices are precisely the kind that can place children and youths at risk of using drugs as self-medication because they induce experiences of anxiety and insecurity which drugs and alcohol help to relieve.[51]

One postmodern movie which resolves the addictive elements of baseball is the popular 1989 film *Field of Dreams.* The movie capitalized on people's need to view baseball as an innocent, nostalgic activity, especially in light of the way the media have exposed the glaring problems of the business in recent years. But what gave the story its timely appeal and the appeal with which many men identified is the Kevin Costner character's struggle to evoke his own idealized childhood and gain a rapproachement with his dead father. The father, like an alcoholic, was perfectionistic and controlling and tried to force his son to live out his own failed dreams of being a ball player. The son, with the aid of a perfect, understanding wife, succeeds at his adult-male-child-of-an-alcoholic fantasy and in the words of the movie eases his father's pain. In a realm of hyperreality in which dreams become true he resurrects his father, with whom he effects a kind of reconciliation, and also manages to retain the myth of baseball's innocence.

Finally, two adult athletic activities which became popular in the 1980s and into the 1990s, jogging and working out at health clubs, are postmodern forms of potentially addictive activity. They are postmodern in that identity becomes merged with style or image, in this case looking fit, and they can shade into compulsive, addictive behavior in that both encourage the participant to control the amount and kind of involvement. Jogging has been linked with the image of the overachieving workaholic professionals who became prominent since the Reagan era. It has inspired analogies borrowed from drug taking, like runner's high and addiction to running, whereby runners get a dose of addictive endorphins once they go past what runners call "the wall." It allows some to feel they can regain a sense of control over their hectic, fragmented lives and literally run from their problems, although the more they run the more they may need to keep running. Designer running shoes and flourescent synthetic apparel help complete the image.

The televised New York City Marathon captures the nation's imagination once a year. Runners display a driven sense of urgency, forbearance, and a quest for self-control and self-validation as they relentlessly pound through the streets of a city where the compulsive rat race for personal power and survival goes on every day. Baudrillard contrasts the New York Marathon, in which there are seventeen thousand runners, with the Battle of Marathon, in which there were not even seventeen thousand soldiers in the field. In a comment somewhat contemptuous of a popular cultural event, he observes that in the New York race

> each one runs alone, without even a thought for victory, but simply in order to feel alive. "We won," gasped the man from Marathon as he expired. "I did it!" sighs the exhausted marathon runner of New York as he collapses on the grass in Central Park. I did it! The slogan of a new form of advertising activity, of autistic performance, a pure and empty form, a challenge to one's own self that has replaced the Promethean ecstasy of competition, effort, and success.[52]

Triathlons, which add the skill of swimming and the strategy of cycling to the endurance of running, appeal to image-conscious upwardly mobile men, some of whom are "hooked."[53] The editor of a national triathlon newsletter says, "There's no doubt that it's a narcissistic sport," since triathletes develop their upper body and wear sexy, high-tech designer gear.[54]

Health clubs capitalize on many people's unhealthy daily routines: eating on the run, spending most time sitting at desks, in traffic, and watching TV, and feeling stressed out from jobs, bills, kids, and lack of free time. Although exercise does contribute to health, clubs exploit people's anxieties about their body image and marketability. There is pressure in the corporate and professional world to exercise and stay fit, not only as a means to reduce health care costs but as an indicator of status useful for climbing the career ladder. In some instances management has screened out overweight people.[55] In TV ads for health clubs Cher and rock singer Sheena Easton display pampered, trim bodies as the desirable standard. Many women continue to struggle with the "tyranny of slenderness"[56] which contributes to obsessive concerns over their body image. In this era of women's challenges to patriarchal privilege, the overblown bodies of Sylvester Stallone and Arnold Schwarzenegger may stand in as retrograde symbols of male power; some men, obsessed with their own image, use steroids and compulsively pump iron as a way to cover over their insecurity or sense of powerlessness with layers of muscle. More recently, due in part to publicity over the dangers of steroids, bulging biceps are out and subtle definition is in; sculptured arms have become a style tantamount to a fashion accessory.[57] Much health club equipment is designed for fitness image as opposed to creative play. The equipment fragments experience and removes it out of the context of whole bodily activity, allowing for greater personal control. The nautilus-type system is designed to isolate specific muscles, as if they were mechanical pieces, and the cardiovascular machines induce a singular, artificially repetitive, aerobic response. The machines in this way serve as extensions of the body, the image of which the club member can consciously work to change.

DUAL ADDICTIONS:
THE WAR ON DRUGS AND THE MEDIA

The corporate media are another significant example of a postmodern configuration which redistributes addictive qualities of control and denial. Government and corporate interests use the media as part of the war on drugs. Although the war in part represents many people's concerns about substance abuse and the illegal drug trade, the dominant interests have orchestrated the war in line with their own agenda and strategies. Former director of the Office of National Drug Policy Control, William J. Bennett, took a conservative approach to the drug issue. His stance itself had addictive qualities (Bennett himself was a nicotine addict, as gleefully parodied in *Doonesbury*). He regarded the problem in black-and-white terms and saw the only solution to be control of others. Bennett considered all illegal drugs and users, including casual ones, as evil. He urged that no tolerance be shown for the use of any illegal drugs and argued that extreme measures were necessary to control what he deemed to be a crisis. Bennett emphasized law enforcement over treatment and prevention and spent 70 percent on the first and 30 percent on the second. Law enforcement efforts included building more prisons throughout the country and using harsh police measures in Washington, D.C., a largely black and poor city he had promised would be a showcase for dealing with the drug trade.[58]

One treatment professional was critical of Bennett's addictive, all-or-nothing approach toward drug-using parents whom Bennett demonized as morally unfit to raise their own children:

Drug treatment, prenatal care, better schooling, shelter, jobs—
things that could actually enable drug-using parents to recover
and take care of their own children—these are not on his political agenda. They would be complicated, and the Bennetts of the
world love the simple truths: good versus evil; them versus us.[59]

Bennett's liberal critics argued that he misused drug data to justify
his extreme measures, refused to consider alternatives such as
decriminalization, and failed to stem the rising problems caused
by the murderous drug trade in Washington, D.C., and other poor
urban areas.[60] Radical critics claimed that since the war favored
law enforcement over prevention and treatment, it served as an
excuse to control and intimidate poor people of color and showed
little desire to help people deal with drugs through prevention and
treatment efforts.[61]

Media as Shapers of Policy

Like other wars, much of the war on drugs relies on the media.
The government uses the media to show the public that the problem is severe and that something is being done. One notorious
public relations event planned to dramatize the drug problem
occurred in New York City when then-Manhattan District Attor-
ney Rudolph Giuliani and U.S. Senator Alphonse D'Amato wore
disguises and arranged for themselves to be televised buying crack
in a Manhattan neighborhood; many, however, saw it as a sordid
publicity stunt. In the hands of conservative policy makers the
media reinforced the addictive aspects of the war, the quick-fix
approach, the attempt to control other people through force, and
the appeal to sensationalism, by reporting dramatic drug bust
operations. In fact, publicizing the dramatic actions of a drug bust
through the media in order to show quick results itself may have
contributed to fashioning a federal drug policy which favors using
short-term victories rather than attacking the long-term causes of
drug use and the drug trade. Some retiring agents from the Drug
Enforcement Agency (DEA) criticized the federal drug policy as
ill-conceived and futile.[62] One of them, Robert M. Stutman, the
agent in charge of the DEA office in New York City, argued that
federal policy leaders preferred a strategy of law enforcement over
prevention and treatment because law enforcement is more dramatic in the short run and has more political appeal than the less
publicized components of antidrug efforts; he charged that the

most highly publicized aspects of the federal policy are the least effective in fighting the drug problem.[63]

Media as a Drug

On this point of media publicity *New York Times* reporter Michel Marriot admits that there is a built-in resistance within the corporate media to cover drug stories within the context of broader social problems and a preference for short-term, dramatic events.[64] In this sense, the public "shoots up" the media coverage of the war as a quick fix. To present sensational images of swift, dramatic, short-term solutions without any analysis of why so many people sell and use drugs eases public anxieties about losing control over an intractable problem. With the news acting as a sedative, people then feel reassured for the moment that the objects of evil will be contained. With much of the war targeted against poor people of color in urban areas, the problem can be ghettoized along with those who suffer most from its effects. Of course, the fixes that corporate television offers, simplistic solutions and soothing effects, can be addictive themselves. Some viewers are addicted to TV and turn to it when they feel sad, lonely, upset, worried, or bored.[65]

Media as Antidrug Propaganda

Another role for the media is as a propaganda weapon to try to convince people not to use drugs. But there is considerable debate about whether the media reduce demand for drug use. One issue is whether the use of celebrities in antidrug messages convinces the general public to say no. The Entertainment Industries Council believes that young people will listen to a star and employs celebrities who give positive messages.[66] But many argue that quick public service spots, like the MTV Rock Against Drug series, which used rock stars like Ozzy Osbourne, give the false message that a few months of clean living can undo years of excessive drug use and the underlying needs that led to it in the first place.[67] Others who also disagree are former drug czar Bennett and the Partnership for a Drug Free America. The partnership argues that celebrity recovery addicts send a double message that not only can you recover from drugs but you can also be rich and famous, since, after all, they made it while they were on drugs for all those years prior to going straight.

The partnership employs a different strategy favored by Bennett and those who would demonize all illegal drugs. Its ads employ scare tactics such as the one which shows a fried egg ("this is your brain on drugs"), which has been satirized on t-shirts, and photos of people holding a gun up their noses with the caption, "cocaine." But a study could not show that these ads caused a shift in negative attitude toward drugs in media markets where they were run.[68] Another study by the Harvard School of Public Health criticized the partnership's scare tactics as ineffective and argued that viewers tend to tune out threatening messages or deny that they are relevant to them.[69] They also criticized the methodology of the partnership's research, which claimed success based on interviews done in shopping malls. The questionable research is supported by taxpayers through the National Institute on Drug Abuse.[70] Of most significance is that leading manufacturers of pharmaceuticals, tobacco, and alcohol products are major sponsors of the partnership.[71] Legal drugs then are scarcely targeted in the partnership ad campaign, for obvious reasons. Yet children are more likely to first encounter legal drugs, which account for hundreds of thousands of deaths each year.

These media strategies, the use of celebrities and scare tactics, try to reduce demand of illegal drugs through powerful images which key in to people's desires. But the ads themselves are like quick fixes which only drive home the message of refusal and do not address the issue of the appeal of drugs themselves. These strategies attempt to fix demand without confronting the reasons for demand, such as pain reduction and instant gratification as a result of living in a competitive society which does not meet many people's needs for security, self-acceptance, and fulfilling relations. The ads are like drugs themselves in that they attempt to control a problem through an extrinsic factor, in this case telling the viewer something is bad or scaring the viewer through fear. They reflect a hierarchy which presumes that people must be controlled or scared into doing something and deny the desire for mutual, self-enhancing relations. Unfortunately, foundations have tended to sink their money into these short-term public awareness ads. The ads draw resources away from school and community-based programs which are better able to deal with the long-term reasons why people take drugs.[72]

Absolut Bull

The Harvard study suggests that in order to reduce illegal drug demand the advertising industry should employ its own commercial marketing strategies, for example, target different audiences instead of relying on conventional public service advertising, which is run at the discretion of publishers and broadcasters. In other words, since the media effectively sell legal drugs and other products, they should use the same techniques to unsell illegal drugs. The point which first needs to be made is that the legal marketeers sell their own sometimes nefarious products, like legal drugs, through the use of mass media techniques which appeal to people's personal needs. In this sense they are similar to cocaine dealers, who also appeal to customers through personal contact while they communicate with them through the electronic media such as telephones and beepers. Most cocaine street dealers develop customers through personal reputation and word-of-mouth networks. The personal relation with the customer is important to both the dealer and the buyer.[73]

Legal drug dealers such as beer companies, for example, tailor their ads to the personal interests of specific groups. One offensive campaign not all that removed from the norm was an advertising supplement put out by the Miller Brewing Company aimed at college men who vacation during spring break at places like Daytona Beach and who represent a multimillion-dollar business.[74] The ads were so sexist (a segment on Lite Beer Pro Beach Volleyball asked readers, "Name something you can dink, bump and poke. Hint—it's not a Babe") that they generated student protests at the University of Iowa and the threat of a boycott at the University of Wisconsin, and led to an apology from Miller, which canceled the ad. But other less blatant, equally exploitive ads which appeal to the personal desires of particular target groups are found every day on TV and in magazines. Another example is the cigarette industry's effort to fight back against antismoking legislation and norms. In 1988 it launched a campaign to create a nationwide network of restaurants, hotels, and businesses that welcome smokers as patrons.[75] The heart of the campaign was that it depicted smoking as a matter of personal choice and portrayed the tobacco industry as the defender of smokers' civil rights.

Advertising colonizes the self as it becomes more a personal part of people's everyday activities. For example, some supermarkets offer consumers who enroll in a frequent-shopper program discounts and other incentives in return for partaking in a customer database which keeps track of what each person buys through scanner technology.[76] This allows the retailers to target individual shoppers and motivate them to change their personal shopping habits. A more pertinent example is that pharmaceutical companies now advertise prescription drugs directly to consumers through newspapers, magazines, and television instead of only to doctors.[77] Health advocates charge that the ads deny important information about the claims of the drugs and are more likely to deceive patients than to inform them; one study cites evidence that the drug ads in medical journals even mislead doctors.[78]

In other areas the line between commercial and noncommercial content is now smudged, as with some magazines which dissolve the boundary between liquor advertisements and editorials. Advertisers now want magazines to customize an ad so that it imitates the look and editorial tone of the magazine itself, and in a weak economy the magazines comply.[79] Some examples are J&B Scotch's "advertorials" and customized Absolut Vodka ads, such as a draw-your-own cartoon contest in the *New Yorker* and one which mimics the type face and format of the "Harper's Index" feature of *Harper's* magazine. In another example *Esquire* magazine editors collaborated with executives of the liquor importer for Absolut to select the winner for the Absolut Vodka Story Contest held in *Esquire*. In these cases liquor ads are like an enticing drink whose effect creeps up on the drinker and which helps dissolve the line between fantasy and reality. They insinuate themselves into the reader's chosen discourse of editorial content. It is not surprising that liquor and cigarette ads affect the content of a magazine itself. There is evidence that magazines that carry cigarette ads have consistently restricted story coverage of the dangers of smoking in order not to offend their cigarette sponsors, with the highest correlation being found among women's magazines.[80]

The larger point is that with respect to the media's war on drugs, advertisers who try to use their techniques of subjective appeal to unsell drugs cannot have it both ways. It is their foremost task to sell things which often are not in people's best interests, like junk food, alcohol, and cigarettes. It is hypocritical for them to be the ones to tell people to avoid bad things using the same tactics, let alone for them to be the ones to talk about the reasons why people take drugs. What makes their position even more convoluted is their outright denial that any connection exists between alcohol and cigarette advertising and consumption in the first place. Using double-speak, the vice president of Anheuser-Busch says that the "benefits" of advertising are to "provide information, foster competition and allow the introduction of new brands."[81] RJ Reynolds, the nation's second-largest tobacco company, defended its character Joe Camel against calls to withdraw the advertising campaign by the U.S. surgeon general, Antonia Novello, on the grounds that it influences children to buy Camels: "No linkage has been made between advertising and the consumption of cigarette products," the company said.[82] But it is nonsense to believe that the alcohol and tobacco industries would be spending hundreds of millions of dollars on "providing information," that is, on advertising, if they didn't think this benefitted their sales by influencing consumption. Even the president of "Just Say No" International argues that it contradicts common sense to suggest that exposure to thousands of beer ads does not have an impact on young people, and cites the logos of alcoholic- beverage companies on small-size t-shirts, posters, toys, and other youth-oriented paraphernalia as well as the companies' sponsorship of rock concerts and the use of celebrities and sports figures in their ad campaigns as efforts to influence children.[83]

One way the legal drug industry tries to remain on the antidrug bandwagon and get around the contradiction that it pushes unhealthy products is to endorse popular antidrug campaigns which do not threaten its own interests and also give it good public relations. For example, the Beer Institute, the trade association for American brewers and suppliers, has joined the anti-drunk-driving campaign.[84] By supporting designated driver programs and providing money for drunk driving prevention programs the brewers can attack one specific deviant behavior while still conveying the message that people can and should drink. In this way they need not deal with the broader problem of alcohol abuse and how they contribute to it. By narrowly focusing on the drunk driver as an individual deviant and contributing to groups like Mothers Against Drunk Driving (MADD) the industry can somewhat deflect the thrust of the new temperance trend toward declining alcohol consumption, demands for higher alcohol taxes, and more controls over alcohol advertising.[85] As another public relations move Anheuser-Busch distributed "Family Talk about

Drinking" booklets to consumers. However, "Just Say No" International refused to endorse them because they avoided important topics, in particular the nature and extent of the alcohol abuse problem and the effects of advertising on children, all of which the beer company denies.[86] The Tobacco Institute, also on the defensive, launched a campaign to discourage smoking by youngsters under eighteen, those most likely to take up cigarettes. But a top health official at the Department of Health and Human Services said the campaign was "just window dressing," and one researcher argues that the campaign in effect encourages children to smoke by highlighting smoking as an adult activity.[87]

In each area, music, sports, and the media, postmodern culture has redefined the relation between subjective desire and the nature of objects in the world through the fluidity of everyday signs. These changes promote the decay of the modernist hierarchy which dichotomizes individual subjective needs and the objective demands of society. This culture has begun to create new relationships which allow for both self-realization and democratic social involvement. Yet everyday pleasures may remain addictive to the extent that they induce the rigid need to control behavior and to deny information within a competitive hierarchy of power.

NOTES

1. Ad, *New York Times*, Feb. 4, 1991, p. B7.

2. John Rockwell, "Why Rock Remains the Enemy," *New York Times*, Jan. 21, 1990, p. H24.

3. Mark Crispin Miller, "Gonna Hawk around the Clock Tonight: How Television Stole the Soul of Rock and Roll," *Mother Jones*, Nov. 1988, pp. 36-42.

4. However, George Lipsitz makes the case that rock and roll originated as a working-class form and still allows for progressive oppositional voices to dominant ideologies in *Time Passages: Collective Memory and American Popular Culture,* Minneapolis: University of Minnesota Press, 1990, chapter 3.

5. Jon Pareles, "The Best Show? In the Court, Not the Concert Hall," *New York Times*, Dec. 30, 1990, p. H32.

6. Fred Pfeil, "'Makin' Flippy-Floppy': Postmodernism and the Baby-Boom PMC," in *Another Tale to Tell: Politics and Narrative in Postmodern Culture*, New York: Verso, 1990, pp. 97-125.

7. Karen Schoemer, "Music's New Catatonia: Don't Bother Getting Up," *New York Times*, Oct. 14, 1990, pp. H33, 43.

8. Keith Moerer, "The Music Industry's Drug Cures," *Bay Area Music Magazine*, No. 298, Dec. 16, 1988, pp. 24–28.

9. Eric Bogosian, *Drinking in America*, New York: Vintage, 1987.

10. David Crosby and Carl Gottlieb, *Long Time Gone*, New York: Dell, 1990.

11. Steve Solder, "The Body Count: Surveying the Casualties and Survivors Twenty Years Later," *Bay Area Music Magazine*, No. 298, Dec. 16, 1988, pp. 33–36.

12. *Ibid.*, p. 34.

13. *Ibid.* See also Richard Schickel, *Intimate Strangers, The Culture of Celebrity*, New York: Fromm, 1986.

14. *Ibid.*, p. 36.

15. See Greil Marcus, *Dead Elvis: A Chronicle of a Cultural Obsession*, New York: Doubleday, 1992.

16. Eric Lott, "Loving You," *Nation*, June 1, 1992, pp. 760–61.

17. "Country Rocks the Boomers," *Time*, March 30, 1992, pp. 62–66; Billy Altman, "Country Just Aint What It Used to Be," *New York Times*, Jan. 31, 1993, p. 24H.

18. *Ibid.*

19. "A Race to Kick the Habit," *New York Newsday*, Nov. 3, 1990, section 2, p. 7.

20. Cary Goodman, *Choosing Sides: Playground and Street Life on the Lower East Side,* New York: Schocken, 1979.

21. Warren J. Goldstein, *Playing for Keeps: A History of Early Baseball*, Ithaca: Cornell University Press, 1989.

22. Randy Roberts and James Olson, *Winning Is the Only Thing: Sports in America since 1945*, Baltimore: Johns Hopkins University Press, 1989.

23. "A Growing Urban Fear: Thieves Who Kill for 'Cool' Clothing," *New York Times*, Feb. 6, 1990, p. A20.

24. "Raiders Chic: A Style, and Sinister Overtones," *New York Times*, Feb. 4, 1991.

25. *Ibid.*

26. Feminist tennis player Billy Jean King defends Phillip Morris, the parent corporation of Virginia Slims cigarettes, for sponsoring women's tennis. As one of the original players on their pro tour, she loyally repeats the tobacco industry's claim that there is no evidence that sponsorship encourages nonsmokers to smoke and states that "we live in a diverse society with many conflicting points of view," an ingenuous position which ignores the impact of cigarette advertising on teenage girls and women and the inordinate power of tobacco corporations. Letter, "Give the Sponsor a Bit of Credit," *New York Times*, Dec. 20, 1992, p. S9. King's stance contrasts with that of Kathy Harty, chief of smoking prevention for the Minnesota Department of Public Health, who developed

media ads which encourage women who smoke to ask themselves, "Do I really want to make someone else rich and myself sick?" In one radio ad a woman thanks cigarette makers for portraying women as shallow and superficial, for making their hair smell, for staining their teeth, and for the 52,000 cases of lung cancer in women each year. "Cigarette Ads Skewered as Manipulating Women," *New York Times*, Sept. 6, 1992, p. 40.

27. "League Faulted on Alcohol Policies," *New York Times*, May 8, 1991, pp. B9, 12.

28. *Ibid.*

29. "Fans Drink Up Early Because of Beer Policy," *New York Times*, Oct. 10, 1989, p. D29.

30. "Basketball Pact Worries Brewers," *New York Times*, Dec. 8, 1989, p. D1.

31. *Ibid.*

32. "Beer Opponents Start Their Engines," *New York Times*, May 29, 1990, p. A14.

33. *Ibid.*

34. "Spit Tobacco and Youth—A Crisis in the Making," *Prevention Pipeline*, 6(2), March/April, 1993, pp. 18–19, National Clearinghouse for Alcohol and Drug Information, P.O. Box 2345, Rockville, MD 20847–2345. In the spring of 1993 major league baseball did forbid all minor league players, coaches, and umpires to smoke or chew tobacco anywhere in their ballparks or on team buses, but not major league players, who have rights under a collective bargaining agreement. "Tobacco Ban in Minors," *New York Times*, June 3, 1993, p. B10.

35. "Gooden, Hernandez, Back Strawberry," *New York Times*, Feb. 5, 1990, pp. C1, 6; Tony Elliott, "How Cocaine Took Control of My Life," *New York Times*, July 6, 1986, p. S2.

36. Peter Alfano with Michael Janofsky, "A 'Guru' Who Spreads the Gospel of Steroids," *New York Times*, Nov. 19, 1988, pp. 1, 49.

37. NBC-TV, "Now It Can Be Told," New York, Jan 22, 1992; "N.F.L.'s Steroid Policy Too Lax, Doctor Warns," *New York Times*, July 3, 1991, p. B7.

38. "D.E.A. Says More Players Are at Risk," *New York Times*, Jan. 15, 1993, pp. B9, 12.

39. Harvey Araton, "The Twelve Step Coach," *New York Times Magazine*, April 11, 1993, pp. 18ff.

40. Roberts and Olson, *Winning Is the Only Thing, op. cit.*; David Whitford, *A Payroll to Meet: A Story of Greed, Corruption, and Football at SMU*, New York: Macmillan, 1989; Rick Telander, *The Hundred Yard Lie: The Corruption of College Football and What We Can Do to Stop It*, New York: Simon and Schuster, 1989.

41. "In 'Minor' College Sports, Big Pressure," *New York Times*, Jan. 9, 1990, p. A1.

42. "U.S. Drive on Drugs Urged," *New York Times*, June 26, 1986, p. B12; see Lewis Cole, *Never Too Young to Die: The Death of Len Bias*, New York: Pantheon, 1989.

43. Felicia E. Halpert, "Business as Usual," *Nation*, Jan. 22, 1990, pp. 96–98; "Teen Steroid Use Rises," *Sunburst Drugs and Alcohol Newsletter*, Pleasantville, NY, Fall 1990, p. 2.

44. "N.C.A.A. Stiffens Drug Penalties and Expands Testing in Football," *New York Times*, Jan. 11, 1990, p. A1.

45. Tony Elliott, "How Cocaine . . ." *op. cit.*

46. Halpert, *op. cit.*

47. Ira Berkow, "Remembering Billy Martin, Battler," *New York Times*, Dec. 30, 1989, p. L45.

48. "Mourners Pack Cathedral for Martin's Funeral," *New York Times*, Dec. 30, 1989, pp. L45, 46.

49. *Ibid.*

50. William C. Rhoden, "Coaches Need to Learn Respect," *New York Times*, Feb. 15, 1993, p. B7; "Tirades Spell End of a Coach," *New York Times*, Feb. 15, 1993, pp. B5, 7.

51. National Association of Elementary School Principals, "Report to Parents, Sports: Recreation or Obsession?" flier, 1990; see also Tony Elliott, *op. cit.*

52. Jean Baudrillard, *America*, New York: Verso, 1991, p. 20.

53. Michael Norman, "Overachievers Stay on Track and in the Swim," *New York Times Magazine*, April 1, 1990, pp. 26ff.

54. *Ibid.*, p. 32.

55. "In the Air, a New Battle over Weight," *New York Times*, April 2, 1990, p. A12.

56. Kim Chernin, *The Obsession: Reflections on the Tyranny of Slenderness*, New York: Harper, 1982; Wendy Chapkis, *Beauty Secrets: The Politics of Appearance*, Boston: South End Press, 1986.

57. "Jockbeat," *Village Voice*, May 12, 1992, p. 150; "The Arm Fetish," *New York Times*, May 3, 1992, pp. V1, 13.

58. "Bennett to Resign as Chief of U.S. Anti-Drug Effort," *New York Times*, Nov. 8, 1990, p. A22.

59. Ernest Drucker, "In Dickens' America," *Family Therapy Networker*, Nov.–Dec. 1990, p. 45.

60. Franklin E. Zimring and Gordon Hawkins, "Bennett's Sham Epidemic," *New York Times*, Jan. 25, 1990; Anthony Lewis, "The Czar's New Clothes," *New York Times*, Dec. 14, 1989, p. A39; Representative Charles B. Rangel (D-NY) in "Bennett to Resign . . .," *op. cit.*

61. Clarence Lusane, *Pipe Dream Blues: Racism and the War on Drugs*, Boston: South End Press, 1991; Juliet Ucelli and Dennis O'Neil, "The Cost of Drugs: Toward a Progressive Agenda," *Forward Motion*, May 1990, pp. 2–9.

62. "Retiring Agents Sharply Attack Drug Policies," *New York Times*, Mar. 1, 1990, pp. B1, 4; Robert Stutman and Richard Esposito, *Dead on Delivery: Inside the Drug Wars, Straight from the Street*, New York: Warner, 1992.

63. Retiring Agents . . . ," *ibid*. See Craig Reinarman and Harry G. Levine, "Crack in Context: Politics and Media in the Making of a Drug Scare," *Contemporary Drug Problems, 16* (4), 1989, pp. 535–77.

64. Lynn Chancer and David Forbes, "From Here to Panama: Face it, We're Addicted to Lies," *Village Voice*, Jan. 24, 1990, pp. 31–32.

65. "How Viewers Grow Addicted to Television," *New York Times*, Oct. 16, 1990, pp. C1, 8.

66. "Can the Rich and Famous Talk America Out of Drugs?" *New York Times*, Nov. 12, 1989, p. E5.

67. Keith Moerer, "When and Why You Should Say No to Drugs," *Bay Area Music Magazine*, No. 298, Dec. 16, 1988, p. 95.

68. "Coalition Opening Ad Drive to Stem Drug Abuse by Young Blacks," *New York Times*, Nov. 11, 1989, p. B16. A partnership spokesperson acknowledges there is no sure way to establish any direct link with prevention ads and decreases in drug use or changing attitudes. "Frequent Prevention Messages Are More Effective," *Alcoholism and Drug Abuse Weekly*, 4(49), Dec. 23, 1992, p. 4.

69. "Talking Too Tough on Life's Risks?" *New York Times*, Feb. 16, 1990, p. D1.

70. "Weird Science," Letter, Dave Fratello, Drug Policy Foundation, Washington, *Nation*, May 11, 1992, p. 614.

71. Cynthia Cotts, "Hard Sell in the Drug War," *Nation*, Mar. 9, 1992, pp. 300–2.

72. *Ibid*.

73. Terry Williams, *The Cocaine Kids: The Inside Story of a Teenage Drug Ring*, Reading, MA: Addison-Wesley, 1989, pp. 48–51.

74. "Miller Beer Drops Ad after Protest," *New York Times*, Mar. 13, 1989.

75. "Tobacco Industry Counterattacks," *New York Times*, Nov. 23, 1988, Bus. pp. 1, 43.

76. "Shifts in Marketing Strategy Jolting Advertising Industry," *New York Times*, Oct. 3, 1989, pp. 1, D23.

77. "Drug Makers Set Off a Bitter Debate with Ads Aimed Directly at Patients," *New York Times*, Mar. 3, 1991, p. 34.

78. "Study Says Drug Ads in Medical Journals Frequently Mislead," *New York Times*, June 1, 1992, pp. A1, B7.

79. "Messages from Sponsors Become Harder to Detect," *New York Times*, Nov. 19, 1989, p. E5; "Advertising's Marathon Auditions," *New York Times*, June 6, 1993, section 3, pp. 1, 8.

80. "Coverage of Smoking Linked to Tobacco Ads," *New York Times*, Jan. 30, 1992, p. D22.

81. Letter, Stephen K. Lambright, Vice President, Anheuser-Busch Companies, *New York Times*, Feb. 16, 1991, p. 26.

82. "Top Health Official Demands Abolition of 'Joe Camel' Ads," *New York Times*, Mar. 20, 1992, pp. A1, D21; "Smoking among Children Is Found Linked to Cartoon Advertisements," *New York Times*, Dec. 11, 1991, p. D22.

83. "Notes from 'Just Say No' International," *"Just Say No" International Newsletter*, 4 (1), Fall 1991, p. 4.

84. Ad, "Drunk Driving Is One Problem the Brewers are Facing Head On," *New York Times Magazine*, Dec. 7, 1989, p. 32.

85. Craig Reinarman, "The Social Construction of an Alcohol Problem: The Case of Mothers against Drunk Drivers and Social Control in the 1980s," *Theory and Society*, 17 (1), 1988, pp. 91–120; "Industry Headache; Americans Drink Less, and Makers of Alcohol Feel a Little Woozy: Concerns of Drunk Driving, Health, and Sales to Youths Force Producers to Adapt," *Wall Street Journal*, Mar. 14, 1984, pp. 1, 18.

86. "Notes from 'Just Say No,'" *op. cit.*

87. "Tobacco Campaign Set to Warn Off Teen-Agers," *New York Times*, Dec. 11, 1990, p. D1. See also "2 Studies Attack Tobacco Industry," *New York Times*, Sept. 2, 1992, p. D18.

PART 3

Prevention

CHAPTER 5

The Self

Living far from one's nature is not unusual in our culture, which is why the drug conquest of America is virtually complete.

Alice Walker

SCHOOLED DAYS

When I was sixteen I wrote an opinionated article under the pseudonym Will B. Free in my high school paper criticizing the guidance department (this was the mid-1960s.) As a teenager I did not always know what to call my feelings of anger and alienation, but I knew something was amiss about my elitist high school, a revered place which served as nothing less than the alpha and omega of the repressive upper-middle-class suburb where I lived. I wanted a more responsive and honest milieu instead of the competitive, indifferent, and emotionally evasive atmosphere in which I was mucking about. In the piece I pointed out that the school lacked supportive services such as discussion groups where students could talk with adults about some of the pressures they were undergoing. I felt that the school overvalued academic concerns and that guidance placed too much emphasis on getting students into a good college to the exclusion of helping them with other issues they faced. When a teacher wrote a letter to the paper challenging me to come out in the open and support my argument with facts, I did so in a more informed article which described some counseling services in other districts which seemed to better address the needs I had in mind.

Today I work in a school-based drug and alcohol prevention program in which I provide some of those kinds of opportunities for students in classrooms as well as in individual and group settings. Prevention professionals work to establish spaces within the school in which students feel safe enough to discuss some of their personal issues in the presence of adults without being judged on the basis of formal, correct answers or the need to please authority. I have heard colleagues and teachers share my sentiment, that they too wish they had had an accepting, caring place to sort out things that were bothering them when they were teens. Recently I learned that my old high school now has a flourishing student assistance program which even runs support groups for children of alcoholics.

Although I find prevention work gratifying, it is also frustrating in part because of its low priority within the education system, since schools continue to subordinate these so-called affective concerns in favor of the cognitive realm of hard academic subjects, as they did when I was in high school. The point, however, is not to make the case for the validity of a supposedly separate affective sphere in contrast to a cognitive one, since this approach only perpetuates a specious, dualistic model of human development which is symptomatic of modernist education and culture in general.

The cognitive/affective model is ideological; in modernist education the cognitive realm is often a code for formal learning which entails the study and memorization of traditional canons of the works of Great White Men. The cognitive/affective dichotomy sets up a false hierarchy which holds formal learning to be absolutist, universal, and more valid than tacit or intuitive knowledge, the everyday kind of understanding which people gain through interacting with family members, peers, informal community networks, street life, and popular culture. School knowledge evolves around fixed, abstract forms detached from sensuous, bodily experience, whereas street knowledge is more visceral and linked with desire.[1] The dichotomy elevates academic, logical, scientific, and rational learning, expressed through formal writing, over and above the cultural knowledge of subaltern groups. According to this way of thinking, many working-class people, women, and some third world cultures learn through physical labor and rely on oral, visual, artistic, and emotionally expressive forms. The prevalent myth is that thinking is superior to feeling, and that people who are wealthy, white, and male think while women, people who work with their bodies, and third world cultures feel. This ideology has implications for defining the nature of citizenship, since it follows that those who are most rational are best qualified to decide what is good for society.

Schools tend to perpetuate this modernist dualism, reflected in the hierarchical structure which contraposes the classroom to the guidance department and teaching to counseling. Most classroom teachers believe that personal issues and experiences which students bring from outside the class ought to remain there. Teachers often feel they must cover certain formal material and cannot afford to digress by discussing a less useful kind of knowledge which is not relevant to the factual subject matter at hand. With the push toward teaching the basics in math, reading, and the sciences there is evidence that teachers may be more resistant to use class time for social problems such as drug abuse.[2] Yet nowadays schools have had to assume more responsibility for educating children in social and personal areas which in the past had been the charge of the family and the church, such as personal safety, physical and sexual abuse, and sex education. Good teachers do make use of students' experiences as part of a lesson plan, for example, on literature; they encourage them to express personal opinions which they can hold up to critical inspection; and they take into account the personal problems of many students in forming a classroom milieu responsive to student lives. But many teachers with whom I work confess to feeling overwhelmed by the personal needs of students. They protest that they are not social workers and are more comfortable with the circumscribed formal approach to classroom learning in which they were trained. For the most part teachers do not legitimate student personal knowledge, let alone subject student needs to critical scrutiny as part of the curriculum. Instead, they relegate students' personal concerns to the domain of school social workers, guidance personnel, and drug and alcohol abuse prevention counselors.

By the same logic human service professionals such as drug abuse prevention counselors in schools often focus on student feelings, which they abstract from an analysis of broader social relations. Counselors tend not to evaluate feelings in terms of formal, academic frames of knowledge, for example, by analyzing anger or depression with respect to the power relations implied by such terms as *class, gender, racism,* the *nuclear family,* or other historical, political, and sociological categories. Affective education is often relativistic and shuns critical analysis of values. Counselors discuss feelings as things which simply seem to well up from inside a person; they just are. In the best of programs students do inspect their feelings in the context of everyday relationships and learn to evaluate what to do with them. But counselors as a rule do not encourage and help students construe feelings as data which they can subject to the kind of reasoning skills they are required to learn in the classroom. Drug abuse prevention workers tend to help students adjust to the bureaucratic demands of schooling without raising the issue of how some of the petty, arbitrary, and degrading aspects of academic life themselves may contribute to the need for drug and alcohol experimentation among some students. Some counselors can mitigate the harsher aspects of schooling. They sensitize teachers on topics which affect children through in-service training, promote a systems or relational view of the school community, and act as student advocates who argue that certain school practices can prevent a student from doing his or her academic best. But on the whole their purview remains that of the emotions and interpersonal relationships, a distinctly less valued realm than that of classroom learning.

The cognitive/affective model is inadequate, is antiquated, and fails to meet the needs of children growing up today. Postmodern culture has radically transformed the nature of knowledge and redefined the expression of emotions. The failure of the model is typified by the student who gets an A in a health course on alcoholism and then gets drunk and smashes up a car on the weekend, or the boy who memorizes the names of the reproductive organs in a sex ed course and then refuses to wear a condom with his girlfriend. The world of formal facts remains arid and detached from the everyday reality of students' lives outside of school while daily life remains a flow of unreflective experience. The challenge is to recombine so-called cognitive and affective aspects of learning in a new way which does justice to the multiple forms of relating which characterize postmodern culture. It requires educators to reevaluate what counts as legitimate knowledge and to situate everyday understanding within a reconstituted curriculum in which students can appropriate the traditional canons for their own purposes.[3] The other side of this is that students need to interrogate the knowledge of their own personal history and culture by applying formal skills of critical thought. A postmodern approach to drug and alcohol abuse prevention begins with the everyday experience of youth. However, this means that the boundaries between knowledge and personal life are renegotiated and realigned, not obliterated. Well-intentioned educators and counselors can sometimes overstep boundaries and meddle in students' lives in a controlling way in order to meet their own unaddressed needs.

The key idea behind most traditional prevention is to assist youth in the development of an autonomous self, and drug and alcohol abuse prevention professionals tend to rely on modernist views of self-development which divide thinking from feeling. But now it is necessary to reconstrue self-development and prevention in light of changes in the culture. The following discussion focuses on adolescent development because adolescence is crucial to the formation of a self and because much of the drug and alcohol abuse prevention field targets teens in its work in schools, since they are at the peak age for initiating drug use.[4]

MODERNIST AND POSTMODERN ADOLESCENCE: THE TRANSFORMED SELF

Modernist theories of human development see adolescence as a universal stage of development between childhood and adulthood. But adolescence itself is a historically determined phenomenon and a feature of modernist life. Until the last century it did not exist as a separate stage of development; growing children learned to take their place alongside adults in the world of work and childrearing. Adolescence emerged in the twentieth century as the family shifted from serving as the basic unit of commodity production to becoming the center of personal life. In addition, advances in technology eliminated the need for child labor, compulsory schooling was lengthened in part to keep teens out of the work force, and childhood was extended as a time to prepare for the more complex demands of adult maturity. Corporations began to target youth as a new market for leisure and consumerism. As a consequence, within modernist culture teenagers have experienced considerable contradictions. Many, especially those in their mid and late teens, are physically capable of adult work and of having babies but for the most part remain out of the job market and under the legal control of their family and the government. Living in a suspended, uncertain nether world and in a state of enforced dependency, neither innocent children nor fully vested adults, teens form their own norms within subcultures, for the most part modifying and experimenting with the roles and values of their class.[5] Most teens seldom have the chance to assume significant responsibility and decision making or to practice critical judgment on important matters. Then, at twenty-one, they are suddenly expected to be mature enough to deal with adult issues without having had the opportunity to exercise such real-world skills.

In normative models of development such as Erik Erikson's the task of adolescence is to integrate different aspects of one's self and form a coherent, stable adult self or identity.[6] With respect to this task, mental health professionals regard adolescence as a time for youths to distance themselves to some degree from the values of their parents and experiment with other ways of behaving and thinking. In object-relations terms, teens dissolve the parental ego-ideal.[7] As their ego-ideal becomes fragmented, teens look for other objects to idealize, emulate, and desire, including their own selves. For example, the video of Whitney Houston's hit song, "The Greatest Love of All," depicts the successful merging of a young girl into her grown-up personage, who sings that the greatest love of all is love of your own self.

During the process of experimenting with different self-objects as part of identity formation, teens experience fragmented, unformed selves which some professionals describe as "piecemeal" and "patchwork."[8] The psychoanalyst Peter Blos believes that the teenager, in seeking self-objects with whom he or she can interact in order to consolidate a cohesive self, has "an avaricious desire which leads to constantly changing superficial attachments and identifications. Object relations at this stage lead automatically to transient identifications."[9] From this perspective teens temporarily choose people or images in forming a self not so much because they are valued in their own right but because they meet the teen's own immediate narcissistic needs. The nature of these rapidly changing identifications is ephemeral and superficial, with fluid, merging boundaries between the object and the teen's self. When a teen tries on the persona of a rock idol or hero, or attaches himself or herself to a close friend, the teen sometimes doesn't know where he or she ends and the other person begins. The next week the focus may be on an altogether different object and the old one is forgotten.

Much of the normative theories of adolescent development which depict the storm and stress of teenage identity fragmentation square with the experience of many people growing up in the West during this century. But in classic modernist fashion most theorists present teenage angst as if it were an eternal truth rather than a time of instability and disenfranchisement in people's lives which has occurred under certain historical conditions. Now, however, postmodern culture underscores the historical nature of the phenomenon of adolescence by standing it on its head: not only is there no longer any promise of solid identity formation for many youth at the end of the teen years, but much of childhood and adulthood is also taking on the piecemeal, patchwork qualities of modernist adolescence. These include the demise of stable social formations, the constant search for rapidly changing, transient objects, and an emphasis on surface appearances as a reflection of identity. If adolescence arrives early and never leaves, there is no longer a formation of the self as we have known it. The self, through the development of new modes of information such as the electronic media, has become a nexus of shifting relations.

Postmodern culture holds suspect the very process of the formation of a self, the modernist task which signals the end of adolescence and the beginning of maturity. A sceptical postmodern perspective not only rejects the stable formation of a self but celebrates the very denial of any unchanging self which holds across time and space. From this standpoint there is no stable, enduring self but multiple representations of alternating appearances; these simulacra may even be nonhuman, commodified objects which stand in for a self. The self has become filled with images and voices from various relationships in which it partakes from everyday life. Christopher Lasch, a cultural conservative, bemoans the dissolution of the self, which he believes has now become conflated with disposable commodified images:

Reprinted, with permission, from *The City*. © 1991 by Jon Backderf.

> [The consumer] knows the world . . . largely through insubstan-
> tial images and symbols that seem to refer not so much to a pal-
> pable, solid, and durable reality as to his psychic life, itself expe-
> rienced not as an abiding sense of self but as reflections
> glimpsed in the mirror of his surroundings.[10]

But in postmodern culture agency, responsibility, and desire are not necessarily dissolved one-dimensionally into commodified signs whose meanings are superficial and determined solely by mass tastes and corporations. Peter McLaren argues: "It is one thing to say that individuals do not exist independently as body/ subjects, from surrounding social structures. Yet it is quite another to claim that they are simply the product of a monolithic engage-ment or identification with social texts."[11] Rather, as I have argued earlier, postmodern culture has realigned the relationship between selfhood, or subjectivity, and the commodified world such that objects as signs reflect and create subjectivity just as signs are imbued with meaning by creative subjects. The point here is that the modernist stage of adolescence, which until recently has come to involve the process of forming a self, is transformed because of this reconstituted relationship between self and object, and post-modern culture in which children are becoming adults today in some ways smacks of modernist adolescence itself. Although this is a problem in terms of the modernist demand to consolidate a sta-ble self, it allows for different kinds of self-development which can no longer be construed in traditional terms of linear, individual progress but instead occur within a new ground of relations.

The Self Transformed

A critical aim of modern drug and alcohol abuse prevention strategies is to strengthen the self. Modernist theories describe what it takes for a mature, functioning individual to develop a self in this society. Modernism, Gergen explains, supplanted romanti-cism and "reasserted the importance of individual reason and observation for human action; one should listen not to authorities or groups but to the evidence of one's own reason and senses. The ideal human being under modernism was self-reliant, self-moti-vated, and self-directing."[12] But much of this perspective must now be interrogated from the standpoint of postmodern culture. Postmodern culture transforms the nature of childhood and adult development. Self-development is a more open process and must be fought over in order to assess what kind of relations children need.

In modernist terms, educators and mental health profesionals believe that in order for a youth to develop a solid sense of self a number of things are necessary. First, a youth needs significant and *solid adults* around, typically parents or guardians of both sexes, who have accomplished the task of identity formation themselves and who then embody or model a possible future selfhood. A youth needs to be inducted into *solid cultural institutions* and social forms in which these vibrant adults participate and which speak to the young through living symbols and rituals instead of empty ones which preserve dead formalities from the past. These may include neighborhood volunteer associations and other groups based on religion and family ties, as well as basic institutions such as the family and the workplace.

Second, an important requirement in forming a self is that the youth gain greater awareness and control over his or her *feelings* and moods. Modernism is clear that feelings are internal, subjective states which need to come under the control of more objective, rational processes. Teenagers are potentially subversive to the social order in that they embody self-involved, here-and-now pleasure through the enjoyment of sexuality (raging hormones), rock and roll, and obsessive consumption. Because they are without power and disengaged from work, bills, mortgages, and other adult responsibilities, they are more given to express threatening subjectivity such as boredom, apathy, or anger at the injustices of society, as well as to indulge inner moods, volatile utopian dreams, and fanciful alternatives which challenge stable, traditional forms of social ties. Socializing a teenager into an adult self by such pleasure-denying agencies as the school usually means that the youth abandons certain impulses and fantasies which may be disturbing to the social order and focuses on outer rather than inner reality, such as responsibilities toward one's employer, family, and country.

A third necessary ingredient for youth as they mature is *self-esteem*. Modernist theories believe that youth should have a high regard for themselves, to accept themselves and feel confident about their abilities and skills. Many professionals and parents believe that self-esteem is a necessary requisite for later adjustment and success. According to Abraham Maslow, esteem needs such as self-esteem are necessary before one can attain self-actualization. On his pyramid of need hierarchy they occur at the next highest level after social needs. Professionals sometimes blame low self-esteem for those poor and working-class youth who fail to achieve or advance in school or in work. Youth need to feel pride in their ethnic heritage in light of the belittlement of many cultures within American society. In order to gain self-esteem, youth need adults who accept and affirm them for who they are across all classes and ethnic backgrounds.

Fourth and last, educators and politicians alike condemn *peer pressure* as inimical to forming a viable adult self. According to modernist norms of developing maturity, youth need to abandon their reliance on their peers and gain more autonomy. Such norms favor middle-class youth resisting peer pressure by practicing individualistic skills and by pursuing a professional career track; they encourage poor and working-class youth to abandon antisocial peer behavior by settling down, getting a steady job, and/or raising children. The belief is that all youth need to develop independent decision-making skills and assume greater individual responsibility for their lives.

These elements of developing a solid self are problematic in light of postmodern culture. The following discussion on each of these four needs explores the difference between modern and postmodern thinking on the issue of self-development, which has been a cornerstone of modernist prevention aproaches. Educators can creatively take what is legitimate from modernist thinking and hold it up to everyday experience in order to develop a progressive postmodern approach to drug and alcohol abuse prevention.

1. Solid adults, stable community?   Today it appears that the entire culture is going through something akin to modernist adolescence as it sheds its own ego-ideals. Teens are losing adult role models and a sense of the future as social ties become unmoored. More adults themselves are self-absorbed with changes in their own lives and are undergoing crises on a number of levels as they experience uncertainty over what were once stable values and expectations around work, housing, career, love, marriage, parenting, upward mobility, and the security of the future. Changes in the workplace and the shattering of stable working-class communities, with their attendant problems of unemployment, homelessness, crime, and drug dealing, have impoverished cultural organizations such as unions and neighborhood voluntary associations, which no longer provide any viable continuity with the past or promote a vision of a future for many youth. The large number of downwardly mobile working- and middle-class families suffer feelings of anger and sadness which affect all members of the family.[13]

As a result of these and other changes I have described earlier, many teens and children grow up within chaotic, unsupportive, and often violent environments which are themselves fragmented and unstable. Adolescence begins earlier in childhood and extends longer into adulthood. Younger children go through emotional ordeals which were once the domain of adolescence. Feelings more typical of teenagers, such as anxiety, depression, and boredom, now occur in younger children, as do crime, sexuality, pregnancy, suicide, and drug and alcohol use.[14] Substance abuse prevention professionals in New York State argue that all children, not just select groups, are "at risk" of abusing drugs.[15] Although this description can be dismissed as self-serving (now everyone needs our help), it does do justice to the precarious nature of postmodern childhood. I have seen a number of children who themselves must emotionally care for adults who are overwhelmed with their own lives, including children of alcoholics and substance abusers. This image appears often in popular culture. For example, in the 1986 John Hughes movie *Pretty in Pink* the adolescent girl (Molly Ringwald) assumes a parentifed role with her unemployed and depressed father, a single parent. Many children who come through our program are overlooked by adults and spend hours home alone without adult supervision, playing Nintendo and watching TV. Yet they are exposed to adult problems of divorce, sex, drugs, alcohol, and violence at increasingly younger ages.[16] Another Hughes movie, *Home Alone*, became an unexpected box office smash in 1990 because it hit close to home for many audiences. The movie is a comedy about a young boy (Macauley Culkin) accidentally left behind by his parents on a trip to Europe; however, his efforts to fend for himself in an adult world of crime, violence, and adult and family pettiness is often not funny. In other families parents who are troubled by their own problems may turn to drugs and alcohol and emotionally, physically, and sexually abuse their children. This in turn can generate youthful runaways and throwaways, unwanted children who become too much of a financial or emotional burden to their parents and who are forced to grow up in a hurry, leaving them without mature skills to face the adult world.

Some anxious working- and middle-class parents who face a shrinking job sector pressure their children to achieve in school or in other areas at young ages. The push can begin as early as infancy with parents who provide babies educational toys designed to enhance their performance on an IQ test which can now be administered to infants. The aim is to put the child on a success track beginning with placement in the more desirable childcare centers, which in turn can lead to a slot in the elite, so-called gifted classes or better schools later on.[17] Those young children soon become career conscious and may experience considerable anxiety, as did a number of junior high students with whom I worked in a competitive fast-track program. Some of these students are at increased risk for drug abuse and suicide. Many students in affluent suburban high schools deal with intense demands such as getting into the right colleges, wearing the right clothes, having the right car, and in general trying to live up to the expectations of their parents. The parents, though, may buy their kids off with expensive items, as they tend to work long hours, travel extensively on business, and are not always available to their children.[18]

Still, for many young people in downwardly mobile families their parents' economic problems leave them in a position of "elongated adolescence" in which they live at home longer, attend hometown junior colleges, and work at marginal jobs.[19] As the modernist vision of the future recedes for many working- and middle-class children, a number of them reject the demands imposed on them or are themselves discarded by the system which winnows out those few who will succeed. Many of these are pessimistic about their place in a future, which is discolored by unemployment, homelessness, the fear of AIDS, the threat of nuclear holocaust, a crumbling infrastructure, and environmental destruction. Some model themselves after their worried, self-involved parents in their own way and spend most of their time listening to rock music, doing or dealing drugs, or just hanging out.

The culture recreates adolescent processes of rapid change, surface appearance, and interchangeable components geared to immediate desires in contrast to a modernist sense of history, continuity, or stability. These changes in turn affect the workplace. According to the complaints of one business management consultant, young workers have low productivity because they continue to exhibit adolescent traits of self-absorption, lack of commitment, and short attention span. His advice to managers—treat workers under thirty like teenagers—is telling about recent cultural changes (as much as it is about authoritarian business practices): keep meetings short and focused, assign just one task at a time, give constant feedback to bolster their "shaky identities," and "do not accept any exceptions to the rules."[20] The consultant foolishly believes that young workers prolong their adolescence for two reasons, first, because more youth today attend college before entering the work force, which allows them to remain committed only to themselves, and second, because more parents subsidize them by letting them live at home. But of course the first reason ignores the fact that college can foster independent thinking in future workers, such as questioning the purpose of the mindless work and authoritarian hierarchies the consultant favors. His second reason ignores the economic necessity for many students of living at home, a common occurrence among many families and brought about in part by the selfish, short-term (that is, adolescent), profit-seeking strategies of American business in the first place. In the 1980s deindustrialization and capital flight occurred on a large scale and destroyed the generational continuity and stable sense of the future for many working-class youth, who once could expect to follow their parents into the local plant or factory. On the other hand, these same forces which drive the transnational character of capital have exposed the redundancy of much of industrial wage labor and its accompanying culture. They have contributed to revealing the interdependency of people around the world and have generated technologies which make for the possibilities of self-realization on a new plane.

The rite of getting that first full-time job marked the entrance into adulthood for many teens in modernist culture. But for those youth unlikely to gain adequate employment, their life passages are now chronicled by cycles of consumption, the hallmark of leisure time. Some experiences of growing up in postmodern culture mirror the adolescent nature of commodity consumption and extend on into the adult years. The form and content of consumption are adolescent in this modernist sense: the glittering, superficial, rapid-fire presentation of ever-changing objects which appeal to the narcissistic demand for immediate gratification. The logic of consumption creates a constant procession of fads, styles, and trends, with the latest one erasing the memory of last year's. The tempo of this process accelerates so much that the halflife of a generation has shortened; as product and service life cycles shrink, each generation experiences a world different from the last one. For example, Benetton clothing stores instantly change future clothing color, shapes, and patterns on the basis of computer-generated data of yesterday's sales in all branches around the world.[21]

But children today have more control over consumption cycles and can choose clothes and other commodities as forms of personal expression. Benetton also represents itself as a multicultural or transcultural signifier which appeals to people from different ethnic groups. Children can select from a wide range of movies and music as well as interact with complex video games which allow them to explore an extraordinary variety of places. A colleague remarked how children now can get instant pleasure by seeing a movie such as *The Wizard of Oz* any time they like by playing a video which has been taped, rented, or bought, in contrast to when we baby boomers had to wait for its yearly appearance on television. My young nephew owns a childrens' cassette player on which he easily learned to play his favorite tapes at age three, something I can scarcely imagine doing when I was a child. His younger sister, not to be outdone, had been given her own at age two and insisted on continually replaying a tape of a story their grandmother had recorded for them, carrying it around the house all the while. She created an odd effect, managing to disperse and alter the presence of her grandmother through sampling the taped voice in order to suit her own taste.

The upside of postmodern culture today with respect to the destabilizing of identity formation is the awareness that children are people too. More parents and other adults recognize that children are already selves with their own rights, opinions, perspectives, tastes, and desires, not passive or unformed objects to be controlled or shaped according to adult needs. Children develop complex relationships with the family and the rest of the culture through direct interplay with media technology and other children who themselves interact with popular culture. They have more opportunities to explore different selves in different relations with a variety of discourses. Yet they still require adults to help them evaluate and make choices. Adults, too, are more able to reconnect with their playful, creative, impassioned, childlike sides (the metaphor of the inner child) and explore a range of selves without becoming locked in to one predetermined identity.

2. Feelings?   In postmodern culture feelings are disappearing, that is, feelings in the dualist sense of words which reflect an internal, private state. Modernist mental health professionals believe that adolescents need to determine and label their inner feelings and then take appropriate action to deal with them in a responsible manner. The rationale for drug and alcohol abuse prevention is that youth who are more conscious of their feelings of pain, boredom, anxiety, or sadness are less likely to act out by using drugs as a means to medicate for these emotions, and more likely to find appropriate ways to solve their problems. But in postmodern culture statements of feelings become displaced by other means. Emotional qualities are expressed through cultural signs which no longer need to refer to a private, internal state. This affects the way educators and youth employ drug and alcohol abuse prevention strategies because it requires different forms of expression to match the experience of adolescents.

Postmodern signs express dynamic qualities which can now represent and stand in for what were once references to the person's emotional inner life or self. Inner and outer states are realigned, and feelings are translated into dynamic signs which are publicly accessible. Visual images such as those found in videos, billboards, TV and magazine ads, and clothing are a significant form of emotional discourse, as are representations of high tech, computer, and media communication. One example is a series of TV ads for New York Telephone. Each ad shows a businessperson who describes in highly technical argot his or her company's inadequate and outmoded phone system and how New York Telephone brought in a superior computerized one. As the person speaks, the viewer sees a dryly humorous subtitled translation in everyday language of what he means. At the end of one ad the convinced businessman recounts that he asked the telephone company representative, "Where do I sign?" The subtitled punchline is, "We have a positive feeling about it." The double irony of the ad is that not only do people still need outmoded modernist subtitles to understand what is going on but that it is no longer necessary to refer to an inner state such as a positive feeling in order to carry out everyday interchanges.

For many youth of today, including children from middle-class homes as well as those from impoverished ones, there is no discourse of inner life. These children do not have access to the patient ear of an adult who can read back to them the emotionally

expressive qualities of their body language or tone of voice or of
the social context in terms of words which describe feeling states.
They spend more time in a milieu which is shaped and transmitted through visual images and actions, often violent ones. The
chaotic, destructive, and painful nature of everyday life for many
urban children elevates their anxiety and prevents them from dis-
passionately concentrating on and analyzing their own plight.
One drug abuse prevention counselor working in the East Flatbush section of Brooklyn with a child who was in trouble in
school was frustrated in her attempt to discover and describe the
child's alleged landscape of feelings, supposedly wedged between
hearing a put-down from another child and the reflexive response
of punching out that child.

> "What were you feeling when she called you that?"
> "She dissed [insulted] me, so I had to hit her."
> "But what were the feelings you had when you heard it?"
> "When you get called something like that you got to get back at
> them."

The child is unfamiliar with the language the counselor tries
to introduce. For the girl, to punch someone back after he or she
insults you involves no intermediate feeling, and is no different
than the automatic, affectless response of "You're welcome,"
after someone says, "Thank you." The counselor attempts to create a subjective space between the appraisal and the response in
which the child comes to discover that she has a feeling she can
name. The modernist assumption here is that there is an already
given feeling lodged somewhere in the child's consciousness which
the proper language would then be able to reflect. In the positive
sense the aim is to slow down the process so that by learning to
apply terms such as *hurt* and *angry* to herself the child can learn
that there are then different things she can choose to do, by
weighing the consequences. She then is no longer yoked to just
one course of action; aggression is not determined by nature but is
now subject to choice. But the child is unconvinced. To be able to
say "I am feeling hurt and angry" to yourself is a luxurious privilege even for many adults in this society, let alone youth, who are
then even less likely to be able to say it to the other person as a
viable alternative response. This form of discourse is not universal
or guaranteed as being the one most true to social reality and
tends to reflect the language of the experience of middle-class pro-

fessionals. Instead, expressive action is a common signifying form within the everyday culture of many youth and is best understood in the relational context of children's lives. Its various forms, such as role-playing, are starting points to increase their awareness that there are competing discourses and that what they do is not fixed but contestable. This is because meaning is not simply reflected by language but is produced within it, and language in turn is bound up with the power relations of everyday life.

Children need representational forms other than language, what Paolo Freire calls "codes," which show their situation back to them in a familiar way. Often these codes come from popular culture, the language of many youth from all classes and ethnic backgrounds. A few years ago I worked with a street-smart Italian-American male of thirteen who was extremely angry at his parents and with whom I was not getting very far by talking. We finally hit upon a form of communicating in which he would choreograph for the two of us elaborate scenes of murder, regret, and restitution involving the use of his entire body in both fast action and slow motion. Through this nonverbal dramatic interchange in which we improvised vignettes borrowed from *Star Wars,* gangster movies, and other familiar pieces of popular culture, and which included the use of rap beat box sounds at which he was surprisingly skilled, I was able to earn a degree of trust and establish a common bond between us. By involving my own body in his scripts, I came to understand more of his world and also earned more credibility and respect. Within this new realigned context I could then offer him alternative ways, both verbal and nonverbal, to help him deal with his relationships.

For many of today's youth the electronic media provide an emotional language to describe their experiences through songs, TV shows, videos, and movies. A white twelve-year-old boy from a working-class neighborhood whom I was counseling in school was living with his divorced mother and was struggling to come to terms with his aggressive, macho father who lived in another state. The boy was seldom able to talk directly in terms of feelings, for example, about his ambivalence toward his father, which included fear and distrust as well as desire to accept him on some level. Instead he would recount with much animation his dreams, which often incorporated frightening figures from movies such as *Halloween* and *Predator.* At other times he would provide me with elaborate details of these kinds of film. By staying within the media images and letting him imagine himself as director or hero, I encouraged him to replay alternative plots and overcome the bad guys. I would then help him relate the stories to his own life when it seemed suitable; we would discuss the contradictory aspects of the films as well as of his relationship with his father.

Many sexually burgeoning girls of eleven or twelve who participate in our program's after-school discussion groups are also fascinated with horror movies, which often exploit girls' anxiety about sex by showing amorous teens meeting grisly deaths. For the girls the movies reflect the frightening yet arousing aspects of an adult world of sexuality. Some of them rent these films and watch them together, which allows them to control the experience in a supportive setting. Instead of regarding their interest in these films as diversionary, educators can use it as an invitation to relate feminist issues around images of women, power, and sexuality to the girls' lives. These instances suggest that there is no one guaranteed language of subjective feelings, just as there is no one theoretical discourse with fixed meanings; the experiences are open to contested interpretations. Adults need to help children explore and evaluate emotional forms within new cultural patterns of expression.

3. Self-esteem?   Self-esteem is no longer some subjective quality fretted over only by mental health professionals.[22] It has entered the public arena as a topic for debate and has become a political football between liberal and conservative forces in education as well as an issue on the Left and in the women's movement. In 1987 California State Assembly member John Vasconcellos, a liberal Democrat, sponsored a Task Force to Promote Self-Esteem and Personal and Social Responsibility, whose final report in 1990 made detailed recommendations for enhancing self-esteem in the family, school, workplace, courts, hospitals, and welfare bureaucracies. But conservatives argued that promoting self-esteem in schools is a waste of taxpayers' money and is a means of smuggling in subjective, liberal values to the detriment of teaching basic academic skills. Phyllis Schlafly's group, the Eagle Forum, believes that the family, not the school, is the place to engender self-esteem and that school-based programs offend traditional values. When the report came out, the cartoon strip *Doonesbury* lampooned the task force as an endeavor which took itself too seriously. A radical perspective argues that calling for people to draw on their own resources and develop self-esteem fits with budget cutbacks and government austerity as a way to throw the burden back on poor and disenfranchised people in need of services.23 In modernist terms liberal, conservative, and radical perspectives each have some merit. It seems to make intuitive sense that youth need to have sufficient self-regard in order to succeed, but self-esteem becomes a slippery, value-drenched concept when educators attempt to turn it into a quantifiable, predetermined, and commodified skill. It can also be used to justify reactionary policies.

Still, the concept appears useful for many adults today. The power dynamics within people's family of origin often were and are reflective of the dynamics of oppressive hierarchical relationships of modernist society, especially in terms of class, gender, and race. The theory is, the lower one's status within the social hierarchy, the less self-esteem one has. This experience, as well as the conditional way people are raised as children (for example, I will love you if you please me), contributes to many growing up with an internalized sense of inadequacy about themselves. Self-esteem has become part of everyday culture and is no longer a quality reserved for the privileged. At one workshop during a conference in honor of Paolo Freire's birthday in New York in 1991 a group of Latina activists described how they were unable to proceed with political work with other women from their community until they went back and helped them with their self-esteem through experiential exercises and discussion. The women apparently had lacked sufficient confidence in themselves to feel they could carry out the political skills they were learning.

This example turns Maslow's hierarchy of needs on its head and exposes its vulgar materialist assumptions. In Maslow's pyramid one must first have survival needs, then needs for safety, followed by need for belonging to a group, before one has self-esteem needs. Yet for these women self-esteem had to come first before they could proceed to develop their social and survival needs. In postmodern culture the personal sense of inadequacy is not necessarily overcome after one resolves one's material needs. We all know people from relatively privileged backgrounds who experience lower self-esteem than some poor people despite their material advantages and which prevents them from realizing themselves in more satisfying ways. Maslow's model clings to a modernist dualism which privileges survival needs as necessary before creative, expressive needs are possible. The model has parallels with some of the Left's strategy to construe economic survival needs (the base) as something which must come before personal and cultural needs (superstructure). This has often led to an impoverished model of existence which offers lifeless, drab goods and services devoid of imagination, creativity, and play.

But in postmodern culture bread and roses are inseparable, and the commodified, imaged package is of a whole with the material entity itself. If a self is now formed and defined through multiple, simultaneous relational contexts, then self-esteem no longer can be relegated to a secondary need allowed only after people gain a measure of crude material satisfaction, but is instead a necessary, immediate element. However, the other side of the dualist coin is the argument, recently revived by Gloria Steinem, that self-esteem is the driving force of all social change, including the feminist movement.[24] Steinem, a leader of the women's movement, now emphasizes personal change, to be gained through yogic breathing, artistic expression, and guided meditation. In a critical review of Steinem's book, Deirdre English, a leftist feminist, takes up this dualist bait and finds it disturbing that "the strategic vision of social revolution here has all but been replaced with a model of personal recovery. . . . To improve the lot of America's women, the pressing need is not an ever greater focus on the self."[25] English contraposes the focus on the self with political activism such as figuring ways to force employers to pay attention to women's needs and addressing sex discrimination and harassment. But in neither Steinem's nor English's arrangement is there a sense of the reconfiguring between self-esteem and political activism which is changing both the nature of the self and of traditional politics. The battle over self-esteem gets joined whenever the parties see the term in the modernist, dualist narrative of an autonomous, inner self opposed to outside societal structures, instead of viewing the issue from the postmodern perpective of selfhood as saturated by social relations and of social relations as embodying subjectivity.

This relational feature of the self in postmodern culture illuminates the specious nature of one other classic dualist, modernist dilemma for many human service professionals, the conflict over having to provide so-called concrete services to clients as opposed to what most professionals prefer, helping people change their consciousness and increasing their self-esteem through psychotherapy, education, or training. For example, a group of service providers working in prevention programs with Children of Substance Abusers (COSAs) reported that they were frustrated with the lack of interest among parents and children in the professionals' efforts to improve their self-esteem. They first had to do case management services to help children and parents with what they considered as basic survival needs such as shelter, medical care, safety, and clothing. Some took comfort in remembering Maslow's hierarchy of needs, "because they know they are not failing when they find little participant interest in prevention programs aimed to improve self-esteem and knowledge."[26] Here the providers conceptualize what they term basic survival needs as separate from and prior to training parents and children in "more appropriate or prosocial ways to behave." But this dualist, hierarchical framework exposes the way some professionals impugn the lives of many poor people by construing their needs as ones of bare survival. It diminishes the complexity of everyday culture by reducing dwelling, eating, wearing clothes, and healthy living to primary needs devoid of qualities of aesthetics and sociability: the danger is that a home becomes a roof or shelter; eating becomes passing out surplus cheese; clothes are worn throwaways; health care means access to an overcrowded clinic. The framework denies the fact that to provide practical services is itself a significant prosocial act performed as a relationship and involving self-esteem, as any benevolent despot or corrupt godfather knows. It also implicates the professional agenda of providing so-called appropriate and prosocial behaviors themselves which are supposedly superior to the less hierarchically advanced needs of the clients. The problem is often that professionals define such behaviors and "positive social interactions" in normative terms removed from the everyday relations of the people they aim to help, who for these reasons often resist them. The question, then, is not the false choice between higher-order prosocial needs and primary survival needs but how to determine the kind of relationship between the parties involved, how power and information are to be negotiated and shared, and how self-esteem gets transformed in the process.

Self-esteem is also tied up with the politics of identity. In its extreme form identity politics presumes that people have some authentic, delineated social self such as African-American, gay, or Christian. The social movements of the 1960s demanded recognition of individual identity, and this demand infused racial politics, the women's and gay movements, and the human potential move-ment.[27] Some proponents of multiculturalism today hold to a modernist, essentialist notion of self. The belief that predefined, authentic, unchanging, and delineated identities or selves exist fuels the demand to hold those selves in high regard as a counter-force to the dominant cuture which belittles them.

Self-esteem, though, cannot be based on some preconstituted, stable self which is neither constructed nor negotiated within var-ious social contexts. There is no pure, correct identity for each particular ethnic group or sexual orientation, and the question of who gets included is a contested one. Ilene Philipson asks, "Are people who are half black and who can 'pass' as white to be included in the identity defined as African-American? Are bisexu-als to be included with gay and lesbian groupings? Are Jews who display Christmas trees and ignore Jewish holidays to be included as Jews?"[28] In a brief essay I wrote which explores the identity of a "Brooklyn-American" I similarly ask, "Is there really one cor-rect way a Chinese- or Arab- or other hyphenated American is supposed to think or behave? What is the cultural essence of kids whose parents are Irish-Italian or Granadan-South Carolinian who go to school together and experience the multi-culture of Brooklyn?"

On this account, self-esteem is neither simply some essential-ist, positive entity which educators and mental health profession-als instill and measure nor something which identity politics can unequivocally identify. It may be, to take an extreme example, that George Bush and Saddam Hussein score high on self-esteem measures or otherwise demonstrate high self-regard on some sup-posedly objective scale. This would prove nothing to those who oppose their respective policies and would render the term irrele-vant. Rather, self-esteem is implicated in a network of relation-ships involving the larger culture, family, school, and personal relations and is inseparable from goals and values which must be evaluated and contested in personal and political terms. Self-esteem, including ethnic pride, may be a significant part of help-ing children become active learners, and there is an interplay between successful learning and self-esteem, with each one feed-ing on the other.[29] But self-esteem must be grounded in the every-day relations of students or it becomes hypocritical or meaning-less. It is not a separate skill which can be taught while the rest of the school milieu undermines it.

In postmodern culture a self can become oversaturated with one representation, as with people who overinvest their esteem in work or one relationship, like a drug which props up their sense of self; when the one image dissolves, self-esteem goes with it. The modernist solutions, either a focus on internal feelings or a direct effort to measure and teach objective skills, ignore the relational aspect of self-esteem, how the self is now dispersed and absorbs a variety of self-images. Ellen Herman argues, "If self-esteem is to mobilize people for progressive change, rather than just simply equip them to endure new variations of old injustices, the dualism between internal and external transformation will have to be rejected as false and useless."[30]

Children need to explore and develop self-esteem as a relational quality which is neither *subjective* nor *objective* in the modernist sense of the words. It is not certain whether the modernist term *self-esteem* even can be meaningful in a postmodern context, since the nature of the postmodern self has more to do with fluid social constructs than with a fixed, stable, essential entity, and esteem is less a property or attribute of such a self and more a quality of social regard. Whereas a skeptical postmodernism would do away with the self altogether, an affirmative one would declare the dignity and value of all persons not only through their particular assets but also through their essential sociability. That is, a self, by virtue of coming into being through an ensemble of relations, is more than a bundle of accumulated attributes and on this account alone is esteemed. A self is no longer a private autonomous entity which competitively accumulates skills to enhance its esteem in the modernist sense. Instead it increases in esteem through the quality of its relationships. An affirmative view would allow for a democratic way to evaluate this quality of relatedness. A self could have access to all the unique ways it is affirmed through its participation in relations of which it has not even been aware; that is, it can enhance esteem through knowledge about itself from others who are more knowledgeable of its qualities than itself. In a culture where all children are held in high regard and who have access to knowledge about how to enhance their particular relations, difference is respected and the modernist version of self-esteem as competitive acquisition and ownership of a positive attribute would disappear.

4. Peer Pressure?   Why do so many teens get into trouble or experiment with drugs and alcohol? Because of peer pressure, say many educators and mental health professionals. But this answer is pat and superficial and itself needs explaining. It tends to lead to individualistic strategies which deny the social needs of teens and adults in general by assuming a basic antagonism between the monadic individualized self and the group. Peer pressure is as much a phenomenon of adulthood as it is for teens. In a competitive, mobile society where one must sell one's personality and where it is possible to cash in on popularity, conformity is a premium.[31] Being accepted, going along with others, is social insurance, a hedge against uncertain factors which one could not afford to face on one's own. Lasch argues that people feel pressured to acquire the skill of impression management, learning to see themselves with the eyes of strangers and projecting a winning self-image, given the prevailing pressure to "shape the self as another commodity offered up for consumption on the open market."[32] Adults, then, who criticize teen peer pressure but who fail to acknowledge the adult behavior which teens emulate try to have it both ways. If adult conformity is the key to success on the corporate ladder, in politics, and in the neighborhood, then many teens will follow suit. If smoking, drinking, sexual scoring, and buying luxury cars are hallmarks of maturity for adults teens will perform them with a vengeance.

Teen peer behavior is a contradictory phenomenon which reflects youths' varying degrees of agreement with and resistance to the broader norms of the society. Societal agencies themselves are ambivalent about teen peer behavior. Manufacturers of beer, wine coolers, cigarettes, soft drinks, clothing, sneakers, and the recording, television, and motion picture industries target teens because they have leisure time and disposable income. Peer pressure is not a threat to these corporations; in fact they rely on and foster peer influence among teens in order to increase sales. But because teens represent the pleasures of consumption certain kinds of teen peer pressure can threaten modernist norms of productivity and social order such as the work ethic and family and societal responsibility:

> The truth of youth culture is that the young *displace* to their free time the problems of work and family and future. It is because they *lack* power that the young account for their lives in terms of play, focus their politics on leisure. Youth culture matters for the old too: it is young people's use of leisure that raises the

problems of capitalist freedom and constraint most sharply and most resonantly. Youth is still the model for consumption.[33]

Adults whose task is to socialize teens within schools and mental health agencies may be threatened by the intense loyalty and sharing which characterizes some peer relationships. Teens are expected to outgrow these positive forms of bonding and transfer their loyalties to supposedly more mature forms such as the privatized nuclear family and the corporatized workplace. But in adulthood there are fewer chances to interact as a member of a group in the freely given, caring, and collective way that some teens do with their peers.

Some of the peer behavior which poses a problem for normative educators is class based.[34] For middle-class students to succumb to peer conformity contradicts skills of autonomy, decision making, creative problem solving, and leadership, which are in accord with professional and managerial careers that require their own conformity. For working-class youth, peer pressure in the form of antisocial rebellion undermines respect for authority, the acceptance of one's status, and the need for self-denial and presentability—values which are in line with their future role as blue-collar workers. Educators have appealed to the concept of maturity as a way to combat peer pressure, a strategy which cuts across class lines.[35] They have emphasized loyalty to the school by encouraging school spirit and involvement while restricting expressions of youth subcultures within school involving music and dress. They have tried to assure teens of their steady progress toward adulthood by building in rites of passage which lead up to graduation. But teenage peer groups are no worse at promoting conformity than schools and other nondemocratic adult institutions such as corporations and the military. These socializing agents do not hesitate to use peer pressure if it is in their own interests.

Youthful peer pressure to take drugs helps fatten the profits of the illegal drug market, undermines traditional authority, and undercuts productivity. It becomes a threat to conservative interests such as those represented by Ronald and Nancy Reagan and former secretary of education and drug czar William Bennett. The "Just Say No" movement which Nancy Reagan started aims to help youth to resist peer pressure around drug experimentation. It relies on generating its own form of peer pressure among certain sectors of youth to influence them to abstain from drug taking. The professionals and urban children I have worked with find the idea of just saying no laughable; but according to "Just Say No" International there is a nationwide network of over 12,600 clubs which has more than 360,000 members.[36] Their obsessive focus on the drug as an intrinsic object of evil induces the technocratic need to train children to resist the temptation. This ideological move obscures the social context which creates contested meanings of drugs, drug taking, and drug pushing and prevents youth from freely examining the issue as a problematic rather than as a handed-down absolute truth. The cynicism of this moralistic crusade becomes further evident when one looks at the Reagan and Bush administrations' lack of commitment to drug and alcohol abuse prevention and to tackling a litany of social ills which contribute to youthful drug abuse in the first place.

There appear to be at least two opposing trends in youthful peer relations today. Peer configurations based on older established ties of class and ethnicity still exist alongside postmodern formations which are pastiches of class, race, and gender styles and which oppose the old modernist distinctions. Assertions of multiculturalism, the women's movement, a depressed economy, and a hostile society which promotes racism and xenophobia have contributed to both polarizing affinities and forming new ones which allow for a fluid merging of styles. Some working-class youth in segregated subcultures hang out among their own kind and protect each other against those whom they see as different. The worst kind feed on violence. Gangs of white racist youth have attacked blacks in Brooklyn, Boston, and other urban areas. In some inner-city neighborhoods black gangs, including girls, pressure youth to rob and kill for coveted jewelry, expensive clothes and other commodities.[37] In these troubled groups a youth derives a sense of self from surface values which are expressed through the group and which have a long history in American society: racism (having white skin) and conspicuous consumption.

In the second trend some peer groups freely borrow and adopt interracial and cross-gender styles of clothing and music and are contemptuous of the traditional loyalties on which their parents based their peer relations. For some youth in this grouping the sense of self seems to be derived almost entirely from fads and images from the mass media and corporate culture. At a high school conference organized by our program the students in one workshop described these patterns among their peers, the ease with which some felt they can mix different styles of clothing and the obsession of others with owning and wearing clothes from select stores such as The Gap or with having the most expensive sneakers.

Educators need to acknowledge and legitimate some of the fears, anxieties, and values of youth in segregated subcultures while challenging the ways they try to get their needs met. They can help youth saturated with images from popular culture understand something of their own subjective history and the traditions of their parents as well as to critically examine media signs. For such youth, McLaren says, "Lacking a language of resistance, resistant students simply become signs of themselves, and can only encode the anxiety of the present and the apprehension of the future." They need to "construct a language that refuses its own limits, that is capable of locating gaps and fissures within the prevailing cultural hegemony."[38]

Peer pressure is not intrinsically negative. Gergen argues: "If individuals are by definition elements within relationships, they can neither stand apart from the social world nor be pushed and pulled by it, any more than the movements of a wave can be separated from or determined by the ocean. The sense of being threatened by the oppressive group becomes not a case of 'me against the group,' but of the conflict between one form of relatedness and another."[39] In this sense peer pressure becomes a problem when it threatens the rights of choice and tramples on democratic processes. It can take its place alongside the topics of gender inequality, demagoguery, the media, schooling, and other forms of social influence in a postmodern curriculum which speaks to the everyday lives of youth and their role as full citizens.

In sum, prevention approaches which presume a modernist self are fraught with problems because the self has become a socially constructed narrative. The postmodern self is shaped less by stable structures of work and family and more by new, shifting relations generated within popular culture. Emotions are not simply private, subjective, inner feelings but assume new expressive forms. Self-esteem is neither strictly subjective nor objective but is dependent on relations which transcend the inner/outer dualism. And peer relations are not something to be outgrown but are an integral part of any self. The self contains a multitude of voices, and signs within popular culture are imbued with personal meaning. The self has become a politicized construct in its own right.[40]

NOTES

1. See Peter McLaren, *Schooling as Ritual Performance*, New York and London: Routledge and Kegan Paul, 1986; Robert B. Everhart, *Reading, Writing and Resistance: Adolescence and Labor in a Junior High School*, Boston: Routledge and Kegan Paul, 1983.

2. William J. Bukowski, "School-Based Substance Abuse Prevention: A Review of Program Research," in Stephanie Griswold-Ezekoye, Karol Kumpfer, and William J. Bukowski, eds., *Childhood and Chemical Abuse: Prevention and Intervention*, New York: Haworth Press, 1986, p. 100.

3. Stanley Aronowitz and Henry A. Giroux, *Postmodern Education: Politics, Culture, and Social Criticism*, Minneapolis: University of Minnesota Press, 1991, pp. 3–23.

4. C. L. Jones and C. S. Bell-Bolek, "Kids and Drugs: Why, When and What Can We Do About It?" *Children Today*, 15 (3), 1986, pp. 5–10.

5. Dick Hebdige, *Subculture: The Meaning of Style*, New York: Metheun, 1979. Mike Brake, *Comparative Youth Culture*, Boston: Routledge and Kegan Paul, 1985.

6. Erik Erikson, *Childhood and Society*, New York: Norton, 1986.

7. For object-relations theory, see Margaret S. Mahler, *The Psychological Birth of the Human Infant*, New York: Basic Books, 1975.

8. Joanne Magdoff and Steve Barnett, "Helpless in the 80's? Treatment Strategies for New Wave Youth: Integrating Self Psychology and a Systems Approach," paper presented at Orthopsychiatric Association, New York, April 1985. David Elkind, *All Grown Up and No Place to Go: Teenagers in Crisis*, Reading, MA: Addison-Wesley, 1984.

9. Peter Blos, *On Adolescence: A Psychoanalytic Interpretation*, Glencoe: Free Press, 1963, p. 9.

10. Christopher Lasch, *The Minimal Self: Psychic Survival in Troubled Times*, New York: Norton, 1984, p. 34.

11. Peter McLaren, "Schooling the Postmodern Body: Critical Pedagogy and the Politics of Enfleshment," in Henry Giroux, ed., *Postmodernism, Feminism, and Cultural Politics: Redrawing Educational Boundaries*, Albany: SUNY Press, 1991, p. 161.

12. Kenneth J. Gergen, *The Saturated Self: Dilemmas of Identity in Contemporary Life*, New York: Basic Books, 1991, p. 240.

13. Katherine S. Newman, *Falling from Grace: The Experience of*

Downward Mobility in the American Middle Class, New York: Vintage, 1989.

14. Elkind, *op. cit.*, pp. 6–8.

15. Conference sponsored by New York State Association of Drug and Alcohol Abuse Prevention Professionals, Fordham University Graduate School, New York, April 10, 1986.

16. Elkind, *op. cit.*

17. "Race to Enter Top Public Schools Intensifies," *New York Times*, May 29, 1989, pp. 25, 27.

18. "A High School Looks Hard at Values," *New York Times*, June 2, 1986, pp. B1, 6.

19. Katherine S. Newman, cited in "Trapped in the Impoverished Middle Class, *New York Times*, Nov. 17, 1991, pp. F1, 10; Barbara Ehrenreich, "Angry Young Men," *Utne Reader*, 45, 1991, pp. 78–80.

20. "Teaching Young Workers to Grow Up," *New York Times*, Nov. 17, 1991, p. F13.

21. Steve Barnett and Joanne Magdoff, "Beyond Narcissism in American Culture of the 1980's," *Cultural Anthropology*, 1 (4), 1986, pp. 413–24.

22. "Hey, I'm Terrific!" *Newsweek*, Feb. 17, 1992, pp. 46–51.

23. Ellen Herman, "Toward a Politics of Self-Esteem?" *Z Magazine*, Jul.–Aug. 1991, pp. 42–46.

24. Gloria Steinem, *Revolution from Within: A Book of Self-Esteem*, Boston: Little, Brown, 1991.

25. Dierdre English, "She's Her Weakness Now," *New York Times Book Review*, Feb. 2, 1992, p. 13.

26. Karol Kumpfer, Ellen Morehouse, Bob Ross, Candace Fleming, James Emshoff, and Lisa DeMarco, "Prevention of Substance Abuse in COSA Programs," Office for Substance Abuse Prevention (OSAP), n.d.

27. Ilene Philipson, "What's the Big I.D.? The Politics of the Authentic Self," *Tikkun*, 6, (6), 1991, p. 51.

28. *Ibid.*

29. Rosemary L. Bray, "Self-Esteem: Hoax or Reality?" *New York Times Education*, Nov. 4, 1990, p. 23.

30. Herman, *op. cit.*, p. 46

31. Jules Henry, *Culture against Man*, New York: Vintage, 1963, pp. 147ff.

32. Lasch, *op. cit.*, pp. 29–30.

33. Simon Frith, *Sound Effects: Youth, Leisure, and the Politics of Rock 'n' Roll*, New York: Pantheon, 1981, p. 201.

34. William Graebner, "Coming of Age in Buffalo: The Ideology of Maturity in Postwar America," *Radical History Review*, 34, 1986, pp. 53–74.

35. *Ibid.*

36. *"Just Say No" International Newsletter,* 4 (1), Fall 1991, p. 1.

37. "For Gold Earrings and Protection, More Girls Take Road to Violence," *New York Times,* Nov. 25, 1991, pp. A1, B7.

38. McLaren, "Schooling the Postmodern Body . . . " *op. cit.,* p. 167.

39. Gergen, *op. cit.,* p. 242.

40. Henry A. Giroux, "Introduction, Modernism, Postmodernism, and Feminism: Rethinking the Boundaries of Educational Discourse," in Henry A. Giroux, ed., *Postmodernism, Feminism, and Cultural Politics: Redrawing Educational Boundaries,* Albany: SUNY Press, 1991, pp. 1–59.

CHAPTER 6

School-Basing

In our society today we are crossing over the border from a modern to a postmodern culture. The concept of *border pedagogy* as developed by Aronowitz and Giroux is useful here for two reasons.[1] First, it calls on educators to combine modernist traditions of emancipation and democracy with the postmodern resistance to dominant narratives and structures. It takes the best of modernist principles and reworks them within an emerging culture with different referent points. Second, the practice of border pedagogy means that people as learners constantly cross over the borders of different historically constructed and socially organized rules and norms of meaning, "maps of knowledge, social relations, and values that are increasingly being negotiated and rewritten as the codes and regulations that organize them become destabilized and reshaped."[2] For example, although there are borders of class, race, gender, ethnicity, and sexual orientation which speak of power relations, there is not necessarily one fixed way in which a person is a member of these categories, nor is there a predetermined relationship between the person and the way he or she must think or act in various personal, cultural, and political terms. To rewrite the borders of knowledge allows for contradictory, multiple, and complex interpretations and cultural forms. It rejects the binary thinking which characterizes much of modernist thought, that there is one best way, or one universal truth or interpretation of reality, as defined by those elites who have privileged access to knowledge and power.[3] It is also in contrast to the either/or quality of addictive thinking, in which a person must be in control of all the right factors and deny or suppress all other aspects which contradict the official story, theory, or party line. We must work the border between certain modern and postmodern forms of drug and alcohol abuse prevention approaches in order to promote radical democratic and emancipatory processes. Although there are historical differences between the two, traditional prevention programs contain significant and useful aspects which can be interrogated and appropriated along with emerging postmodern approaches.

Traditional prevention professionals often take a modernist, dualist approach to the self in their efforts to prevent drug and alcohol abuse among youth. Besides assuming the characteristics of the individual self discussed earlier, they also tend to see individual behavior in terms of either health or illness. They are especially concerned with identifying youth who they deem to be *at risk* of substance abuse. The term comes from a medical model which views an underlying personal problem as an objective disease which, like a medical problem, supposedly has predictable etiological, developmental, and epidemiological characteristics. Professionals believe that if they can identify the causes they can then develop a strategy to prevent the disease and promote health. The medical model theorizes that addictive drug use is pathological and, once its antecedents are identified, can then be prevented in other cases. If smoking cigarettes, abusing alcohol, and becoming dependent on illegal drugs is unhealthy, then it makes sense to prevent those causes which lead to these behaviors and to promote healthy alternatives.

But the problem with the medical model is that the use and abuse of drugs is not simply a biological occurrence but a social and cultural one which involves contested meanings and struggles over power relations. The medical model—in fact, any preventive model—must involve ideological and political assumptions about what are good social relations associated with nonabuse. In most drug and alcohol abuse prevention (and treatment) programs the desired behaviors to be promoted are spelled out but often appear in unexamined moral terms which are presumed to be given truths.

Traditional models of health prevention tend to favor the formation of an autonomous, authentic self, a self that would not need to be dependent on drugs. The modernist take is that drugs and alcohol are extrinsic entities which substitute for missing skills, attributes, or needs of the self. Prevention programs regard the individual as monadic and needing to develop personal skills to ward off inappropriate group norms and values. The more self-sufficient the person, the stronger the sense of self and the less susceptible he or she is to peer pressure. But the youth should also be less egocentric and more socialized to other, more appropriate norms of society, usually those defined by the professionals. The cultural milieu, the everyday matrix of social relations of those labeled "at risk," is often left out of the picture. If professionals do consider culture, they tend to see it in narrow terms of stereotypical ethnic background, a predetermined, extrinsic, or environmental factor which is brought to bear on the autonomous individual and which requires sensitivity and understanding on the part of the health educators.

Programs assume that individual youth are at risk of becoming addicted to drugs when their selves are not well formed and they are unable to properly handle their own troubled feelings such as boredom, anger, anxiety, and sadness. For example, mental health professionals describe how some troubled teens fear a loss of self through fragmentation and disintegration and exhibit extreme defensive postures such as an attitude of omnipotence, isolation, and detachment, and a preoccupation with inner reality which the professionals might label as schizoid, a psychopathological personality disorder.[4] In similar fashion, for some youth drugs serve to function as surrogate defense mechanisms to stave off the dissolution of a threatened, fragile self. Marijuana, cocaine, and alcohol can be effective because they provide the user with the experience of the same schizoid defenses. Cocaine as a stimulant creates the feeling of being all-powerful; marijuana enhances aloofness and preoccupation with one's own thoughts; alcohol allows for the temporary sense of confidence and of feeling together by escaping one's anxiety. To prevent this kind of phenomenon, traditional programs would offer teens personal skills to shore up their sense of selves, enhance their self-esteem, and allow them to successfully deal with their inner phenomena without drugs. In a more therapeutic domain they might provide individual counseling and/or family therapy to effect a relational shift in the family system in which a youth's troubled self functions.

Prevention researchers tend to follow a medical narrative of cause and effect and rely on normative values to label high-risk children. They speak of etiological causes of early onset in terms of atomized factors which they attempt to define, isolate, and control. For example, according to the research, the clearest indicator of high risk of substance addiction is early drug experimentation; youth who use drugs at a young age are more likely to become addicted later on.[5] This is a circular finding which begs the question by stating that those who take drugs are more likely to start to take drugs. But the broader point is that the medical model, in first defining and then trying to describe the causes of this social phenomenon, glosses over the social context by using a neutral, totalizing language which mimics the natural sciences. The meanings of the words cannot be fixed in unequivocal terms but are socially constructed. Is use the same as dependency? Does all drug use lead to dependency later on? Is drug dependency always a health problem?

Researchers tend to apply the term *high risk* to children who do not conform to ideal white, middle-class norms. For example, they suggest that children characterized by family history of alcoholism, poor family management practices, family conflict, early behavior problems, rebelliousness, antisocial behavior, and school failure, all arguable terms themselves, are most likely to experiment with drugs and alcohol at an early age.[6] In this sense a high-risk child is often considered the Other, a poor, working-class, or third world child, a child from a single parent or deviant family, one with a substance-abusing parent, and/or one who does not adjust to the norms of schooling and the dominant values of society. Because they have determined that these children have deficits, professionals attempt to supply them with the proper health-promoting elements, such as individual knowledge and social competence skills, as a preventive or risk-protective strategy. Programs with young children and adolescents accordingly focus on a comprehensive approach to social development which enhances deficits in parenting skills through support, training, and therapy and create school programs which promote individual achievement, good behavior, and normative bonding to the school, all in accordance with the dominant narrative of social health. Prescribed acceptable alternatives to drug abuse supposedly include steady work, leisure activities which offer natural highs, and mature family, community, and social relations. Some researchers label protective factors which are precisely reflective of the modernist self. These include positive attachment to responsible, caring adults, shared beliefs and rituals, investment in the future, strong beliefs about right and wrong, and strong internal controls.[7] Yet these prescriptions are at sea in a postmodern culture in which clear-cut moral norms, a linear sense of the future, and a stable, internal self, among other factors, are problematic. When programs view all children to be at risk for drug abuse and require normative preventive measures which infuse the general school curriculum, then debatable political and ideological forces are at work on a broad scale.

Prevention professionals protect children when they intervene in troubled relationships, engage them at a significant level, teach useful skills, encourage new awareness of relations, and help free them from addictive patterns. But in many cases professionals seldom question the extent to which preventive programs reinforce mainstream narratives which are not useful to disaffected youth or families, nor do they question the extent to which programs verge on being a form of social control which maintains dominant power relationships. It is rare for programs to collaborate with the target population on how they define their needs beyond a superficial level, nor do they tend to critically engage them in terms of their own sense of themselves as *active creators of culture* and how they can contest and reconstrue their place in school and society. This is because programs tend to assume that people exist as autonomous selves who possess objectively determined, stable, high-risk attributes which need to be modified toward what the professionals determine to be more appropriate, healthy ones, also called "resiliency factors." They also tend to assume that institutions such as the family, the school, and the workplace are predetermined structures which are not subject to contested rearranging. In an earlier article I wrote a fable describing the successful results of a state-funded, broad-based, traditional prevention campaign which managed to get everyone in the state to stop taking drugs of all kinds. The campaign typically denies the relational context of drug and alcohol use and focuses on individual behavior. Here is an excerpt which describes the aftermath of the campaign, in which all personal drug use stopped while the social relationships and cultural institutions remained the same:

> Although school was still competitive and high-pressured for upper-middle-class kids and dull and restrictive for working-class and poor kids, students no longer smoked marijuana. There remained a dearth of childcare and after-school programs and the usual pressures on single working mothers, but no women drank or popped tranquilizers. Many wage earners still had little say over workplace conditions and no less stress from speedups, layoffs, and boredom; nevertheless, they didn't turn to amphetamines, cocaine, alcohol, or marijuana to get them through the day. Millions of city dwellers continued living with decaying or rapidly overdeveloped neighborhoods, crime, poor

transportation, and bad housing; the suburbs stayed a hiding place for many bored children, isolated homemakers, and workaholic commuters. But in neither town nor country were drugs to be found. The media still tried to coax consumers into debt by encouraging new addictions to cars, junk food, lottery gambling, and violent movies, as well as alcohol and cigarettes, all the while stoking anxiety over one's sexual saleability. But substance use was steadfastly avoided. And the federal government continued its cutbacks in human services, education, civil rights, and health and safety while it boosted military expenditures, fostered jingoism at home, and pursued adventuristic policies abroad. But the people of the state refused to medicate themselves in the face of it all.

Instead, citizens took on greater individual responsibility for their lives. Inner-city kids worked at personal accomplishments such as cheerleading and sports and felt good about themselves. They knew they had what it takes to overcome the poverty that surrounded them. They each applied "saying no" techniques to the pushers on the corner as they returned to school. Bored kids from working-class neighborhoods no longer hung out in the streets and parks swilling beer, dragging on joints and butts, and complaining about their strict or indifferent parents. They were found instead working on their communication, assertiveness, decision-making, and other "life skills" with their peers, families, and teachers. At other times they actually did their homework. Yuppies-in-training stopped snorting coke with their Wall Street dads and quit filching mom's booze from the cabinet. Instead, whole families jogged together, leaping over bodies of the homeless while discussing the latest class of their investment course.[8]

The preceding description parodies the kind of society which drug-free advocates favor, one in which individuals abstain while their troublesome relationships remain intact. It is analogous to what recovering alcoholics call a "dry drunk." The alcoholic is now sober but has not dealt with changing the quality of his or her relationships. A dry drunk abstains, but now it is really how he or she learns to deal with others that makes the crucial difference; whatever social inadequacies the alcoholic first had which were masked by drinking are now compounded by the discomfort of sobriety. The federal government's no-use message which it and prevention researchers advocate for curricula and for school and community policies does not acknowledge that drugs and alcohol serve to meet people's need for security and other social needs given the lack of fulfilling relations.[9] It flies in the face of an addictive culture in which drug use of one form or another is an everyday reality. What follows are some examples of prevention programs and curricula which aim to produce dry individuals. The programs ideologically demonstrate unreflective, technocratic approaches to their target population. They aim to bring the targeted group to some predetermined goal in line with traditional, normative narratives of individualistic self-development. But these narratives do not see the self as embedded in and contributing to troublesome competitive, hierarchical relations which themselves must change and which people are able to transform.

Substance abuse prevention professionals traditionally divide prevention into three levels based on the model from public health.[10] In primary prevention educators aim to influence everyone to abstain from any form of substance use by providing information and teaching social skills needed to resist use. In secondary prevention professionals identify and target those they consider to be at risk for taking drugs. Tertiary prevention work is equivalent to treatment for those who already have a problem with drugs and aims to prevent a chronic condition. These divisions are not clear-cut; for example, one researcher speaks of primary prevention strategies aimed at high-risk students.[11] The first two examples in the following discussion target high-risk youth, and the rest aim to reach all students. Most prevention programs include individual counseling, an eclectic practice which often shares the assumptions of the field as a whole.

COAS/COSAS

A significant number of prevention strategies target the presumed high-risk groups of children of alcoholics (COAs) and children of substance abusers (COSAs). COAs are considered a high-risk population for developing physical and mental health problems in the short run and for developing alcoholism in later years. To a considerable extent these are groups who do not necessarily identify themselves as needing help, in part because they experience the shame of the stigma of their parents' behavior. COSAs have the added stigma that their parents' drug use is often illegal. According to researchers and clinicians, these children grow up in families where one of the cardinal rules is "Don't Talk, Don't Trust, Don't Feel." They are unlikely to trust a researcher in presenting a picture of their problems and may have a difficult time identifying emotional problems in the first place.[12] When professionals decide unilaterally that these families and children need to be taught certain skills for their own good, they are likely to be resisted, as I discussed earlier. Yet when such students identify themselves after classroom drug education and agree to participate in intervention groups, many children from alcoholic and substance-abusing families benefit from programs and groups in schools and agencies which provide them information, support, counseling, and structured activities. They get feedback about themselves and their experiences which helps combat the sense of isolation, and they learn skills to help them cope with their families.[13] The very acknowledgement of their predicament for many is a relief and is part of the ongoing realignment of personal and public realms, whereby shameful private selves can be expressed within a safe social discourse.

One danger of identifying children in this manner, however, is that the label COA or COSA itself can become a restrictive and stigmatizing badge rather than a means of freeing a person from unhappy relations. The tendency to totalize one particular identifying relationship which then defines the person primarily in those terms is evident in this kind of approach. Some people feel they can never escape their identity and must always remain at risk of either alcoholism or some other troublesome emotional pattern. Besides, not all COAs necessarily suffer from the symptoms which professionals ascribe to them. There is debate as to whether children of alcoholics in fact have unique emotional patterns and problems from other children; some researchers argue that the characteristics of COAs, that they feel different from others, are reluctant to stand up for themselves, and don't enjoy life as much as they would like, are worded in such a vague and universal way that many people identify with them.[14]

A more provocative argument is to suggest that many people identify with qualities of COAs, not because the characteristics are vague or because they may be from other kinds of so-called dysfunctional families, but because children of alcoholics may be prototypical of many people who grow up in a culture which itself is like an alcoholic family.[15] If this is so, that many people to some extent are brought up in arbitrary power relationships in which people control others and deny self-expression, then it speaks to the need to discuss and act on these political and personal issues among all children and adults, not only among a stigmatized subgroup. Yet do to so would require a political analysis of family relations and not only one which reduces experience to psychological causes.

MUTUAL AID

One contradictory school-based prevention program aimed at high-risk students is based on a well-respected mutual aid model in which peers help each other out under the auspices of the school. In one application of this model, Catholic school students are required to participate in supervised peer groups because of their known drug use.[16] But the program rationale appears to favor individualism and conformity: despite the stated need to help the school reach out to the teen, a reading of the program description shows that it is the individual student who must in the end adjust and cooperate, not the system of relations which must change. A traditional narrative is operative here: substance-abusing students are believed to have been "unsuccessful in gaining acceptance in the conventional and socially acceptable way. . . . It is not an absence of motivation that isolates these youngsters so much as their inability to recognize their stake in their nurturing systems and reach out to them for help effectively, whether that system be the school, the family or the peer group."[17] The imagery here is that of idle but intact, workable families and schools merely awaiting engagement by the unskilled student. The project aims to help teens "develop coping skills necessary to lead more productive lifestyles within the mainstream of society."[18] The author reemphasizes the need for adolescents to "rediscover their stake in the system" no less than three other times throughout the account.

The thrust of the service is "helping the drug using student or the student considered at high risk of drug use to use the school more effectively and cope with the developmental issues inherent in the educational experience in adaptive ways, rather than by withdrawal through substance abuse."[19] But this disguises the failures and inadequacies of the schooling process itself by psychologizing them, that is, by treating them as predetermined, developmental features of a natural system. The student must learn to adapt, and it is his or her cooperation which becomes the measure of success.

The project involves a counselor who helps the students to find and achieve new ways to deal with problems of daily living accomplished with the help of peers. It is not surprising that a good part of the cited discussion of one group is about the unhappiness members feel about their stigmatized status as reluctant participants. The counselor denies the issue of psychological manipulation by insisting that he or she cannot change another person. Instead the student must examine and change his or her drug use with the help of peers. The entire project is referred to as work accomplished through a contract, which further ensures a noncoercive, impersonal mystique. It seems unlikely that the students have a say in questioning the power arrangements behind these terms within the counselor-led peer group sessions. The burden of change is put back on the students, and the complex of relationships involving the school escapes critical scrutiny.

INOCULATING EVERYONE

One of the ongoing debates within the field is whether to focus on so-called high-risk students or try to cover all students. Many school-based prevention programs and curricula do aim to reach all children in schools, not just special populations. Three of the more popular approaches in recent years are providing information about drugs, offering alternatives, and improving youth's broad coping and social skills through affective education. From the standpoint of empirical evaluation there is no clear evidence that these approaches prevent or decrease substance use. The most promising normative prevention approach in terms of showing modest quantitative success at reducing cigarette smoking in the short term is a social learning model: educators teach children social skills to resist peer pressure around drug use and provide information about the immediate negative consequences of use.[20] From a qualitative standpoint many of the better prevention programs open a space within school which allows and encourages children to talk about things like family and personal relationships, some within new social formations such as structured voluntary discussion groups. But the larger point is that prevention programs are ideological: they tend to promote normative values which privilege the autonomous self and regard many students' oppositional behavior to traditional meanings of success as indicative of personal deficits. They tend not to help students interpret substance abuse and addictive behavior in the context of the concrete cultural relations of which they are a part in order to change them.

LST

The Life Skills Training (LST) of the Cornell University Medical College is a highly touted program which aims to prevent cigarette, alcohol, and marijuana dependency by helping students develop "basic life skills" and improve "personal competence."[21] The theoretical underpinnings of the approach come from social learning theory and problem behavior theory. According to these approaches, drug use is a "socially learned, purposive, and functional behavior which is the result of the complex interplay of environmental and individual factors."[22] The training adopts two models within these theories to explain why children would use drugs. One is the coping model; for example, the researcher suggests that drug use may be a way to cope with expected failure or anxiety. The second is a social influence model, in which according to the researcher drug users are individuals with low self-esteem and low self-confidence who are more susceptible to the influence from high-status role models or advertisers.[23] The idea would be then to teach alternative coping skills and ways to resist social influence as preventive measures to decrease the chance of drug-taking behavior.

But the researcher's conclusions for why youth use drugs are not warranted by these theoretical models. He loads the examples of the models with negative traits (anxiety, low self-esteem) because he begins with the premise that drug use is health compromising. The assumption is that people who would knowingly engage in behavior which compromises their own health are likely to be socially or emotionally deficient in some way. He does not take one aspect of social learning theory at its word, that behavior is purposive, and that drug users do not necessarily construe their action as health compromising. (Even when they do they do not necessarily stop if they perceive the benefits to outweigh the costs.)

Instead he employs the other aspect of the theory, that behavior is functional, in order to justify his own judgment. By not allowing that drug use provides some positive benefits for the users, that is, that users construe positive meaning to the drugs, he stacks the deck with his own framing of the issue from the outset, that drug use must function as a way to deal with deficiencies in coping and resistance to susceptibility. In other words, youth who use drugs may not necessarily have a problem with all coping skills or be susceptible to all forms of social influence in areas that are important to them. It is the researcher's idea that certain behaviors are unacceptable in normative terms which leads him to conclude that the youth therefore must be deficient in coping and resistance to susceptibility skills in general. But what kinds of coping and social influences the youth find salient has to do with their cultural frame of reference of everyday relations, which are not necessarily those of the researcher. Drug-using students may well have good coping skills in certain social contexts, for example, in the streets, and know very well how to resist certain direct social influences, including, say, the harangues of teachers and principals.

Nevertheless, the LST's counterstrategy is to try to increase students' general coping skills and decrease their susceptibility to social influences. The LST trains teachers to give their students information on cigarettes and to teach them individualistic skills such as personal decision making, assertiveness, resisting peer pressure, anxiety reduction, and improvement of self-image. The researchers believe that such success-oriented skills are incompatible with maladjusted behaviors such as drug use, and cite evidence that students who use drugs also tend to get lower grades, are less likely to participate in organized extracurricular activities, and are more likely to engage in what they term "antisocial behavior." Drug users, they claim, also tend to be low in assertiveness and impatient to assume adult roles. The researchers attribute these negative traits to what they call "a lack of social competence" and believe that teaching individualized social skills can prevent students from developing them.

But this set of deviant attributes is a gloss which describes many poor, working-class, and otherwise dissafected youth of all classes. The LST in effect promotes normative skills which are in line with middle-class values, done so from the top down and without respect to the cultural milieu of student lives. For example, being assertive and resistant to peer pressure can be maladaptive within

certain working-class experiences if by doing so the student is dis-
loyal to his or her group. By the same token, cooperation with peers
in resisting schooling may be preferable to learning autonomous,
competitive skills which break down dynamic cultural meanings
and practices into static attributes of the person.[24] The program
minimizes the positive cultural meanings and perceived benefits for
students of drug use from the outset. For many students cigarette
smoking may be a direct way to reassert the sensuous nature of the
body in an adult way which is denied by repressive relations within
the school and the family; or it may be a way to identify with the
subculture of the family, especially if other family members smoke.
If the program acknowledged these kinds of relations, it would then
enable itself to work with students to consider the merits and disad-
vantages of competing alternatives. Instead it takes what it believes
to be a scientific, objective approach but which in effect is one particular narrative which may or may not prove useful to students in
certain contexts of their lives.

DUSO

The program Developing Understanding of Self and Others-Revised
(DUSO) is an elaborate affective educational package designed by
Don Dinkmeyer and Don Dinkmeyer, Jr., for use with children in
the first and second grades (DUSO-1) and third and fourth grades
(DUSO-2). According to the authors, the aim of the program is to
help the students understand themselves, to encourage them to
develop positive self-images, to increase awareness of their relationship with other people, and to recognize their own needs and goals.
The authors explain the rationale for the program in terms of
abstracted feelings:

> The feelings that accompany learning have a significant effect
> on how well children learn. If they have positive feelings, chil-
> dren tend to participate with a high degree of motivation and
> involvement and are more likely to derive permanent gains from
> their efforts. If children's feelings are negative, they are poorly
> motivated, participate on a minimal basis, and are less likely to
> derive permanent gains.[25]

The program encourages discussion of stories, various activities,
and singing in order to bring about its effects. It comes in hard

plastic kits which are slickly packaged, elaborate, and expensive. DUSO also puts out a separate K–4 curricular package aimed at creating "drug-free" kids with similar materials; this package specifically teaches resistance to peer pressure, assertiveness, communication, and decision making skills, and ways to say no to drugs. But the generic package itself is compatible with the approaches of much of the drug and alcohol abuse prevention field. In fact, our program invested in purchasing the kits for use by school prevention counselors in their work with young children.

As purchasers of the product, our agency was entitled to an orientation session on how to implement DUSO. The company spokesperson described the philosophy of the program as "Adlerian" in the sense that it is nonjudgmental, is self-affirming, and favors democratic processes and social skills. Alfred Adler believed that our failures are a consequence of doubts in ourself and others; the diminution of self-doubt and sense of inferiority and the development of self-confidence should then allow one to develop a sufficient social interest to cope with one's place in society.[26] This is a crystalized account of a particular version of modernist thought: it promises that a solid sense of self is the foundation for success and adjustment to an appropriate social position instead of seeing the self as taking shape within a nexus of social relations.

The curriculum has sections on self-understanding using neutral but loaded language such as "developing realistic attitudes about one's capabilities," "developing self-acceptance," and "learning to manage anxiety." Some of the lessons include messages on positive thinking which are akin to the individualistic, victim-blaming philosophy of American business. (One song says, "When things don't go the way you want them to, don't look for someone to blame. You're responsible, the one responsible. The only one who can do something about it is you." Another says, "When you feel you have a problem and you don't know what to do, A problem never needs to get the best of you.")

But in the absence of grounding concepts like *realistic attitude* and *self-acceptance* in a critical understanding of everyday power relations, teachers and counselors are likely to supply these terms with a normative framework. One example is a curriculum-related activity subsumed under the goal "Developing Feelings of Belonging with the Peer Group," entitled, "How Does That System Work?"[27] The stated purpose of the activity is to increase student's awareness of ways people work together in jobs. The activity calls for the students to list jobs in which a number of people work together, and then think of all the different tasks that must be done "in order for that system to function smoothly." It suggests some systems to discuss, such as steel mill, assembly line, hospital, city government, police department, newspaper, and school. But like the debate in sociology which favors a Parsonian model of normative systems over a conflict model, the language of this exercise favors the notion of smoothly functioning, conflict-free systems. Each one of these systems is problematic in terms of how people actually work or do not work together nowadays. The exercise makes no reference to anything like labor-management divisions, unions, bureaucracy, layoffs, job stress, or accountability, that is, debatable real-world controversies around who decides how things get done, by whom, and for whom, issues that children are able to understand in concrete terms.

The curriculum does address the issue of conflict and suggests ways other than violence to resolve disputes to be learned through discussion and role-playing. But it focuses on individualistic alternatives, some of them idiosyncratic. One story describes a king and queen who were always competing with each other to see who had the biggest army or who could grow the most wheat. The queen accused the king of stealing a jewel and sent him a nasty letter and a pie in his face. In the follow-up discussion there is no attempt to help children deconstruct the story of competitive royalty who summon people to swell their armies because of a personal dispute. DUSO favors an individualistic approach to social conflict, focusing on what each individual can do to increase or lessen conflict, instead of learning how to concretely analyze the relational aspects of disagreements. In a curriculum-related activity DUSO says the queen could have tried using yoga to help calm her angry feelings, and goes on to suggest teaching yoga exercises as a way to lessen intense feelings of inner conflict. But the original conflict was not necessarily within herself but a relational one between herself and the king. It depends on how the queen or in effect how the children construe the conflict. Offering yoga as a way to deal with her angry feelings in this case may not get at the conflictual issues within the competitive relationship and may reinforce the belief that if individuals follow this sort of self-referential action in similar cases they can resolve their problems.

LIONS-QUEST

Another elaborate curriculum entitled, "Skills for Adolescence," developed by Quest, an educational organization, and the Lions Club, the service organization, is being peddled as an effective school-based drug prevention program throughout the country.[28] The school system which our program serves paid for teachers to take the training course to learn how to use the curriculum in the classroom. The rationale is that if youth have certain "internal" conditions such as a sense of self-worth and self-control plus "external" conditions such as skills and information then they will develop "positive behaviors" such as self-discipline, responsibility, good judgment, and getting along with others and make "positive commitments" toward one's family, school, positive peers, and community. The idea behind developing positive social behaviors and commitments is that these factors are supposed to be crucial in preventing antisocial behavior such as drug taking and that they are more likely to be present in youth who will lead "productive, healthy, drug-free lives." The modernist elements are all here: a construct of an internal self, supposedly objective external factors, normative, antisocial behaviors, and unproblematized social structures. The curriculum aims to develop the modernist self: to teach students how to effectively manage their emotions, to foster "positive peer pressure," to engender positive perception of family interactions, and to teach personal skills such as decision making around drugs, learning how to say no to peers, and setting and achieving goals.

The last skill, realizing goals, is supposed to help increase students' sense of control over their lives and lead to self-confidence. According to the curriculum, it is related to other desirable individual traits such as "being productively involved in meaningful work" and "developing positive, optimistic thinking." In discussing these skills the curriculum acknowledges the importance of "economic reality" in terms of a child's sense of personal control over his or her life. But despite this, the authors say, with the conviction of hucksters peddling a book on positive thinking, the teacher and the "Skills for Adolescence" course can help change students' attitudes and have a positive impact on them. The framework is not relational but dualistic: the individual, pitted against harsh material forces, can overcome them by dint of the proper training. Sure enough, one of the lesson plans is a discussion of an article by the industrialist W. Clement Stone, a man whom the curriculum tells us was inspired by Horatio Alger books and whose life story demonstrates the "value and importance of a positive attitude." In sum, the curriculum is a recycled and repackaged version of the modernist American Dream, the belief that any individual can overcome his or her environment armed with the right technocratic skills, positive attitude, and demonstrated loyalty to the enduring institutions of family and school.

LEARNING TO LIVE DRUG FREE

The United States Department of Education put out this curriculum model for use in schools and encourages schools to revise, adapt, or integrate the model to meet their needs.[29] It aims to infuse the general school curriculum with the drug prevention message that illegal drug use is wrong and harmful. The program material is grouped according to grade levels as well as geared to six specific subject areas: language arts, social studies, mathematics, art and music, health and physical education, and science. Besides lessons plans it contains one to two pages in each section which suggest ways teachers can work with parents and with community groups such as merchants, law enforcement officials, religious leaders, the media, and other civic leaders. As with other curricula one of its purposes is to enhance life skills that keep youth from using drugs, such as learning how to resist peer pressure. Another stated emphasis is to promote responsibility, both individual and civic, in order to help students become "caring and productive citizens."

Much of the model tries to teach individualistic skills like problem solving and takes a modernist approach to growing up in this society. For example, it suggests a lesson for grades 7–8 on Goals for the Future in which each student draws a time line segmented into stages and places important events from his or her life along it. The curriculum offers up its depressing philosophy of history to the students by way of directions to the teacher: "Explain that each person's life is like history itself: filled with mundane daily happenings that are sparked by extraordinary events that change the course of life." The students are then to add in specific goals they would like to accomplish. The teacher is to point out "the value of looking at life as a continuum," and is encouraged to discuss questions about life goals.

But there is no sense here of people's lives as part of networks of relations, or of history as something which people make together in complex ways involving power and conflict, or that everyday life can be anything other than mundane, nor that it is something capable of qualitative, nonlinear transformations. In short, there is no sense that life is anything other than a random series of individualized, linear time lines which occasionally flare up with some significant event. The model of linear lives punctuated with normative occurrences like marriage, job, and retirement is a distinctly modernist model. Instead today's world in which youth are growing up is marked by cycles in which many people begin careers, families, relationships, and selves over again in new contexts. One of the characters in the 1991 comedy movie *City Slickers,* having lost his job and his marriage, is convinced by his friends that his situation is similar to playing ball as a kid when the player makes a mistake beyond the rules of the game: he gets to have a "do-over." There is none of this sense of possibility and choice in the government curriculum.

Another government object lesson in modernist self-development is an activity for grades 9–12 on Growing Up which teaches that "adolescence is a time for developing relationships and discovering the world, and that this period should be put into the perspective of a whole lifetime." As if teachers could convince adolescents of this belief, even if it were still true of being a teenager today, students are to read *Our Town* by Thornton Wilder, a hackneyed and antiquated work about small-town white America. The curriculum does tell the teacher to make sure to discuss how "life options" for young men and women have changed and to contrast today's attitudes to the roles of men and women of previous years; but it offers the teacher nothing in the way of helping students with an analysis of the changing nature of everyday culture or of their own lives, only a means to squeeze today's experience into outdated models of teenage development.

NEW YORK STATE DRUG EDUCATION CURRICULUM

This curriculum consists of a booklet for each grade K–6 and one each for junior and senior high. Like the federal model, it coordinates topics with academic subjects such as science, English, art, and social studies and encourages parent and community involvement. The philosophy is similar to others in adopting individualistic and normative premises: if young people acquire basic concepts on health-related issues, a positive view of themselves, supportive family and friends, fulfilling experiences in schools and families, and experiences in decision making, then they are less likely to use drugs.[30] It includes activities designed to improve self-concept and to develop communication and decision-making skills, especially with regard to drug use.

What distinguishes the curriculum somewhat is that it encourages a variety of active teaching methods which allow for students' creative and physical participation, such as brainstorming and role-playing. The lessons are also more pedagogically sophisticated and nonideological; that is, they do not inevitably lead up to the correct messages the students are supposed to learn (no-use, I am responsible) but are more open-ended. For example, the junior high booklet in the section on drugs and society suggests that students interview school officials about school drug policies and report back to the class, asking questions such as how and why the policies were formed and who was involved in developing them. They can then discuss their own ideas for a policy using a fishbowl method which divides up the class into small-group discussions. They then rewrite the policy and "present the product to authorities for consideration." These processes hint at a critical pedagogy which treats school policy as an open-ended topic, not as some mysterious, immutable law handed down from on high but as a social endeavor written by certain people for certain reasons which are contestable. The curriculum also suggests that students discuss the issue of health versus law, that "the body doesn't understand drug laws or policies, it only responds to the laws of science." This encourages questioning the rationale for certain drug laws. With further practice in deconstructing statements, students might also begin to question the part of the statement about whether the body always responds to the laws of science in exactly the same way, in order to explain individual and cultural variations in response to drug use.

The curriculum offers other critical pedagogical activities. In the junior high booklet a section on understanding motivation for drug use suggests that students interview people they know (but maintaining their anonymity in the report) who use alcohol, smoke cigarettes, or "misuse drugs" in order to find out the reasons why, and draw their own conclusions and opinions about the subjects' involvement with the substance. Another suggested activity is a role-play in which a student who smokes marijuana converses with a parent who smokes cigarettes, which allows for questioning why one drug is more acceptable than the other. A third is a discussion which seeks to elaborate differences between drug experimentation, recreation, and abuse. This exercise asks students questions which encourage nuance of meaning, such as, When does recreation become abuse? and, How do we decide when an activity can be done safely as experimentation or recreation? These exercises promote mutual critical inquiry and independent thinking. They allow students to reach varying conclusions from differing interpretations without implying one correct answer. Another more directive lesson is on "medication for feelings" in which students brainstorm the costs and benefits of substance use. The lesson aims to elicit from them the significant understanding that as long as a person perceives the benefits of substance use to outweigh the costs, the use will continue. This kind of approach contrasts with the message from other curricula that all drug use is bad and is a much more supple and heuristic means of combatting addictive behavior because it does not deny users' and students' experience but instead allows students to develop their own conclusions.

But the curriculum does not encourage this kind of interpretive pedagogy throughout, and for the most part promotes normative conclusions. For example, in the senior high booklet, one activity on drugs and society lapses into a standard antidrug message which reverses the pedagogical approach of the earlier cost/benefit exercise and preempts the process of independent thinking. It has the teacher prepare and prominently display a chart which purports to reflect the "social, economic, political, psychological and physical costs of drug abuse." It presents statements which reflect the dominant concerns of certain groups as if they were objective, indisputable truths. For example, economic costs include "job absenteeism" and "loss of productivity"; but costs to whom, workers or management? Social costs of drug abuse are said to be "family disharmony," "disruption of school routines," and "crime." But this implies that were it not for drug abuse family and school would be harmonious entities, unaffected by other disruptive social forces which may even be salutory in some respects. As for crime, again, the question is, who benefits, and a well-researched list would yield banks who profit from money laundering. But this kind of inquiry is not likely to come about from an activity which leaves no room for multiple readings.

A second normative example is a lesson which promotes what the curriculum calls the "alternatives concept," the use of more socially acceptable constructive alternatives to drug use which provide natural highs, such as yoga and running. But the curriculum does not discuss the potential for those or any other activity to also become addictive. It only tells the teacher "to bring out that it is natural and healthy for people to experience a range of emotions, rather than to strive for happy or 'high' feelings at all times. Emotions should be appropriate to events, without becoming controlling factors in people's lives." Perhaps they should, but in this culture feelings often do become controlling factors. Besides, who decides what is an appropriate emotion to an event, and how do we decide? But these and other issues which are part of the nature of everyday relations, the crux of the matter, remain unexamined in this curriculum.

CONFLICT RESOLUTION

A recent prevention program in the New York City schools is Resolving Conflict Creatively. It aims to teach students how to communicate, how to deal with anger, and how to act as peer mediators in order to help others resolve conflicts without violence. The program, along with another project in Santa Monica, is part of a broader trend toward "emotional literacy," which educators used to assume was the domain of the family.[31] Students learn to speak in an assertive manner without being aggressive, to listen to the other person without interruption or insults, and to paraphrase the other's perspective and feelings. They also practice cooperation, compromise, and taking turns as well as learn ways to prevent prejudice. Some learn the art of mediation and negotiation and help resolve fights between other students that occur in the school yard, cafeteria, or classroom.

Two trainers from Educators for Social Responsibility who work on the Resolving Conflict Creatively project in New York gave some of our drug prevention program staff a two-day workshop. We discussed some techniques and then role-played a number of situations, such as between a counselor and principal and between two angry students, and tried to apply what we had learned. Part of the problem for me and some of the staff was the technocratic aspect of the training. We sensed that the trainers were on an earnest mission to teach The Way, and this, along with their use of a few sensitivity exercises for which we were not prepared, induced in us a feeling of resistance to being controlled rather than of being empowered. One of the role-play scenarios felt like a forced resolution between the two parties which did not first acknowledge the differences between them. A colleague who practices family therapy raised the issue that many people are addicted to conflict and that it is not just a case of applying certain formulas and techniques to get them to stop, especially because people often fear the emptiness of having to deal with each other after the familiar conflictual behavior is gone. This sophisticated point, which the trainers were not prepared to address, raised the issue for me that trying to train people to help manage other people's conflicts also had somewhat of an addictive or codependent quality to it, the fervent need to control and solve other people's problems through a rational formula that if consistently applied could make the world a nice place. It smacked of a certain intolerance for ambiguity and irresolution. The trainers seemed to me somewhat reluctant to acknowledge that not all conflicts can be resolved, especially during a time which, as another colleague pointed out, nonviolence is not a popular concept and Malcolm X is more popular than Martin Luther King. To their credit the trainers were responsive to some of our issues and in their follow-up report posed them as unresolved problems. For example, what if the other party is more powerful? If the negotiation/mediation process doesn't get at the roots of conflict, is it worth doing at all, and what are the benefits and limitations? Some of their follow-up list of suggestions, though, were written in a cookbook style which suggested precise, technocratic ways to practice and promote the mission of conflict resolution. An important, open-ended issue to address is what the educator as bearer of this process gets out of it all.

A primary problem is that the mission to create peace and harmony, one of the curricular lessons in the program, can become an imposed, positivistic ideology. It can become a technique to manage the private realm of emotions and control student conduct without acknowledging the contradictions within the broader cultures of the school and everyday life. The program has claimed to have helped create a more peaceful and cooperative climate in a number of schools. But it would be a mistake to view it as a cure-all technique which educators technically apply without extending the process to broader power relations of everyday life, such as gender and race relations, let alone the way adults treat students in school. A comprehensive conflict resolution curriculum which questions violence would need to examine the violent nature of everyday life for many residents of the inner city, the ways violence is promoted by people in power, and what people can and cannot do about it. It would acknowledge that for some people for a range of reasons violence is often the only way they feel powerful, the only way they feel heard. A curriculum would examine the current ways sexuality has been linked with violence against women, ranging from the way women are shown as objects of abuse in rock videos to date rape to sexual harassment in schools. It would need to discuss when, if ever, violence is necessary and to help create a vision of what nonviolent neighborhoods, societies, and a world would look like.

RAP GROUPS

The heart of the prevention program where I work is the rap or discussion group (not rap music), a teacher-led, voluntary group in which students get to draw up an agenda of topics and discuss them in confidence. The groups are available to all students after school hours beginning in the fifth grade in schools where there is interest from the principal and a sufficient number of teachers who wish to become group facilitators. The groups each consist of around eight to twelve students and run for ten weeks, with each session lasting forty-five minutes to an hour. The preventive rationale for the groups is the modernist theory of drugs as medication for feelings. This approach acknowledges that drugs work to alleviate painful feelings such as anxiety and depression; but it claims that if students can identify their troubled feelings and have them validated through the group and with the help of an accepting adult, they will be able to develop alternative ways to deal with them instead of turning to drugs. The belief is that if students can gain some self-esteem through positive support and skill building in the group they will have a better sense of themselves and will be less susceptible to the influence of negative peers offering them drugs.

Almost all children who join groups are very serious about the group process and confidentiality. For many it is the first time they have participated as members of a structured group in which the norm is that they are to be respected and to respect others. It is rare for them to be in the presence of a tolerant adult who listens instead of admonishing, lecturing, or ignoring them, as do many of their parents and teachers. In the groups students discuss sex, drugs, relationships, friends, family, and school in the context of their own concerns and focus on how they can help themselves when a problem exists. They use the group to weigh decisions such as whether to have sex or try drugs. They make friends and practice social skills like careful listening, speaking up for oneself, and giving supportive feedback to others. Many find they are not the only ones with a substance-abusing and/or abusive parent or relative, and they learn survival strategies from others. Although there is no unequivocal evidence that group experience reduces drug experimentation on a significant scale, anecdotal accounts show that children value the groups in their own right and display some of what they learn in other settings. Children have also disclosed experiences of physical and sexual abuse to the facilitator within the group; often it is the first time they have shared their secret with an adult. The prevention program then works with the child in order to report the abuse to the state and to ensure proper follow-up. The value of this aspect alone cannot be overestimated.

The program trains interested teachers and other school personnel to become group facilitators. Trainees learn about the stages of group development, such as how to develop initial trust and how to terminate a group. They also study the prevention rationale of drugs and alcohol as medication for feelings and discuss adolescent development. They practice leadership skills such as how to encourage democratic participation, how to listen with empathy, how to intervene when certain group problems arise, and how to focus on group interaction, or process, instead of content. The program emphasizes process in order to get teachers to shift their concern with subject matter and right answers to how group members relate to each other.

Teachers learn that it is the relationships within the group and with respect to the group that are of the utmost importance, not whether some particular topic is covered or whether a member gives an answer which is acceptable or correct according to some objective or moral standard. They practice turning the nature of the group interactions into the content of group discussion itself when appropriate. Like the women's movement in the 1960s, which began to insist that the Left attend to the way people treat each other and not simply focus on the correct political line, the training stresses the quality of feelings, interchanges, and power dynamics within the group and encourages the facilitator and group members to do the same. Many teachers who take the training and run groups find they can apply some of the skills within the classroom setting. They discover they are more aware of students' issues and can enhance their classroom work by attending to ongoing relational dynamics and addressing them with their new skills.

On the face of it the practice of running student rap groups shares similarities with the practice of critical pedagogy.[32] The groups begin with student's self-determined issues; they emphasize problem posing instead of the right answer; they stress collaborative and supportive efforts; and they strive to operate through democratic processes, careful listening, and mutually respectful dialogue. The difference is that the groups end there. Rap groups are consigned to the affective domain, which does not penetrate the realm of critical inquiry, the everyday task of the school. In those relatively few schools that avail themselves of our training, the groups meet after classes and run ten weeks, a small part of the school year. The groups themselves have little overall impact on the school but to some extent function more as an emotional safety valve, since students have few chances for self-expression during school and afterwards are usually confined to empty apartments where they watch TV or do homework. In fact, most principals and teachers, even enlightened ones, would not want to see too many of the skills students practice in group, such as assertiveness and democratic processes, go on during school time. In any event, because it is a voluntary activity it cannot always reach those kids who may need it the most.

Nor are the groups themselves always successful. Sometimes teachers struggle with their nonjudgmental role and ignore group process in favor of driving their own point home. But this may say less about teachers' ability to maintain an idealized facilitator role than it does about the natural difficulty of separating personal issues and values from the formal process of education, a line in the sand which both educators and counselors strain to honor.

To accept student voices but fail to legitimate them as an integral part of the school culture widens the false split between affective experience and structured learning. In recent years I have tried to help bridge this gap by introducing to teachers and group facilitators the critical pedagogical practice of problematizing some of their children's statements. As a way to legitimate and then critically interrogate student voice in order to help transform students' lives, teachers can take some of the things group members say which strike them as trivial or as immaterial and convert them into a controversy which can lead to further study and action. Some of the teachers are exasperated with the way rap group members get obsessed about the way the opposite sex looks, or with gossip and chatter about clothes shopping, TV shows, or rock stars. I encourage facilitators to probe these subjects in ways which get at the unspoken power relations, with the purpose of vesting the students with power. For example, when the talk turns to who is good-looking, ask at some point how boys and girls regard looks and why; how important it was for their parents or even grandparents; why looks count, and who influences their judgments; how people's looks are used in family and other everyday relations, by whom and for what purpose; how they would deal with their own children in the future who might have different tastes and values from them; and whether the future will even be the same as today.

This can lead to discussing power relations concerning gender issues, sexuality, the media, family structure, racism, and history, as well as the nature of friendship and love. It can lead to discussing the backlash against women's recent gains in terms of the "beauty myth," a form of social coercion which defines women's value in terms of appearance.[33] By considering the relation between popular culture and embodied selfhood, students can explore the ways they both take in and resist popular representations through their body. This allows for new ways to increase their own power to resist restrictive relations, such as girls being addicted to thinness or to approval by boys, and boys succumbing to violence and possessiveness, and to create more mutually enhancing ones.

But it is important to remember that the Freirean project of critical consciousness or empowerment remains suspect unless group members trust each other and the educator.[34] Unlike many so-called empowering projects, a successful rap group first establishes the basis of a trusting relationship. (Often children don't care what you know until they know you care.) Only when this occurs can a group then allow for the genuine expression of differences and shared perspectives of knowledge and action. There is a need for both critical thought and trust in others as part of the process of joining knowledge, pleasure, and power.

NOTES

1. Stanley Aronowitz and Henry A.Giroux, *Postmodern Education: Politics, Culture, and Social Criticism*, Minneapolis: University of Minnesota Press, 1991.

2. *Ibid.*, p. 119.

3. Henry Giroux, *Border Crossings: Cultural Workers and the Politics of Education*, New York: Routledge, 1992, p. 51.

4. W. R. D. Fairbairn, *Psychoanalytic Studies of the Personality*, Boston: Routledge and Kegan Paul, 1952.

5. J. David Hawkins and Richard F. Catalano, "Risk-Focused Prevention: From Research to Practical Alternatives," High Risk Youth Update, OSAP, April 1989, pp. 2–4f.; J. David Hawkins, Richard F. Catalano, and Janet Y. Miller, "Risk and Protective Factors for Alcohol and Other Drug Problems in Adolescence and Early Childhood: Implications for Substance Abuse Prevention," *Psychological Bulletin, 112*, July 1992, pp. 64–105.

6. *Ibid.*

7. Hawkins and Catalano, *op. cit.*

8. David Forbes, "Saying No to Ron and Nancy: School-Based Drug Abuse Prevention in the '80s," *Journal of Education, 169* (3), 1987, pp. 81–82.

9. "Prevention Plus III: Assessing Alcohol and Other Drug Prevention Programs at the School and Community Level," Office for Substance Abuse Prevention, U.S. Department of Health and Human Services, n.d.

10. M. Gonet, "A Three-Pronged Approach to Substance Abuse Prevention in a School System," *Social Work in Education, 12* (3), April 1990, pp. 208–16.

11. S. Schwartz, "School-Based Strategies for the Primary Prevention of Drug Abuse," *Social Work in Education, 11* (1), Fall 1988, pp. 53–63.

12. Karol Kumpfer, Ellen Morehouse, Bob Ross, Candace Fleming,

James Emshoff, and Lisa DeMarco, "Prevention of Substance Abuse in COSA Programs," OSAP, n.d.

13. Ellen R. Morehouse, "Working in the Schools with Children of Alcoholic Parents," *Health and Social Work,* 4 (4), 1979, pp. 145–61.

14. "'Wisdom' on Alcoholic's Child Called Stuff of Fortune Cookies," *New York Times*, Feb. 19, 1992, p. C12.

15. See David Treadway, "Codependency: Disease, Metaphor, or Fad?" *Family Therapy Networker,* Jan.–Feb. 1990, pp. 39–42.

16. Sally A. Shields, "Busted and Branded: Group Work with Substance Abusing Adolescents in Schools," in Alex Gitterman and Lawrence Shulman, eds., *The Legacy of William Schwartz: Group Practice as Shared Interaction*, New York: Haworth, 1986, pp. 61–81. See Forbes, *op. cit.*

17. *Ibid.*, p. 62.

18. *Ibid.*, p. 63.

19. *Ibid.*, p. 64.

20. Elaine Norman and Sandra Turner, *Adolescent Substance Abuse Prevention Programs: 1980's Literature Review and Annotated Bibliography*, New York: Fordham University Graduate School of Social Service, 1991.

21. Gilbert J. Botvin and Thomas Willis, "Personal and Social Skills Training: Cognitive-Behavioral Approaches to Substance Abuse Prevention," in *Prevention Research: Deterring Drug Abuse Among Children and Adolescents*, NIDA Research Monograph 63, pp. 8–49.

22. Gilbert J. Botvin, "The Life Skills Training Program as a Health Promotion Strategy: Theoretical Issues and Empirical Findings," Cornell University Medical College, 1985, p. 13. This is a contradictory definition which says little by saying too much. Anything and everything can be said to be a complex interplay, but more important, if behavior is purposive, that is, meaningful, then it is not simply functional and a result of social learning. In later studies researchers refer to cognitive-behavioral theory, another dualistic approach which tries to graft purpose and function together using pseudo-scientific language.

23. *Ibid.*

24. Forbes, *op. cit.*

25. Don Dinkmeyer and Don Dinkmeyer, Jr., *DUSO–2: Developing Understanding of Self and Others, Teacher's Guide*, Circle Pines, MN: American Guidance Service, 1982, p. 12.

26. Rudolf Dreikurs, "Individual Psychology: The Adlerian Point of View," in Salvatore R. Maddi, ed., *Perspectives on Personality: A Comparative Approach*, Boston: Little, Brown, 1971, pp. 260–72.

27. Dinkmeyer, *op. cit.*, p. 205.

28. *Skills for Adolescence,* Granville, OH: Quest International, 1988.

29. *Learning to Live Drug Free: A Curriculum Model for Prevention,* Rockville, MD: National Clearinghouse for Alcohol and Drug Information, 1990.

30. *Drug Education Curriculum,* Albany, NY: State University of New York/The State Education Department, Bureau of Health and Drug Education and Services, 1986.

31. "Pioneering Schools Teach the Lessons of Emotional Life," *New York Times,* March 3, 1992, pp. C1, 7.

32. Ira Shor and Paolo Freire, *A Pedagogy for Liberation: Dialogues on Transforming Education,* South Hadley, MA: Bergin and Garvey, 1987.

33. Naomi Wolf, *The Beauty Myth: How Images of Beauty Are Used against Women,* New York, Anchor, 1992; Susan Faludi, *Backlash: The Undeclared War against American Women,* New York: Crown, 1991.

34. Elizabeth Ellsworth, "Why Doesn't This Feel Empowering? Working through the Repressive Myths of Critical Pedagogy," *Harvard Educational Review, 59* (3), 1989, pp. 297–324.

CHAPTER 7

(Po)Mo' Better Prevention

In postmodern culture adolescent self-fragmentation is diffused throughout the society and across different age groups. The one cohesive, rational self gives way to multiple selves and everyday culture reconstitutes inner self and outer world with fluid boundaries. Modernist selves which people formed according to traditional structured roles such as woman, worker, or child are dissolving and are laced with contradictions as people have more of a hand in creating themselves. The self no longer develops apart from the influence of the electronic media and popular culture but now incorporates images and meanings from music, TV, videos, ads, and fashion.

Drugs then play a different role, and any notion of prevention must take these changes in the culture into account. Drug taking may ritualize the rapid surface transformations which occur in the culture. Taking a drug to alter the self is isomorphic with the kind of instant image changes which people now create for themselves. In this sense drugs no longer just serve as external threats against a self or as props to shore one up; they are able to represent, displace, and constitute a sense of self themselves. People can produce themselves by appropriating drugs as self-signifiers, as part of cultural images which are manifest as different selves in different social contexts. Some teenagers describe using alcohol as a way to feel put together when they are out of sorts; on one ABC special a boy describes it as liquid courage. When someone takes cocaine for self-confidence, he or she becomes a self-confident person at that moment, just as wearing fashionable clothes makes a person fashionable. The debate over alcohol and cigarette ads, including Camel cigarette's Joe Camel, is important because they are now personalized signs which can represent the various meanings of the substances for the self and for ways of relating to people; for example, a Camel smoker is a cool character, and a beer drinker is popular and sexy. Youth now creatively appropriate everyday cultural symbols as part of their changing identities. In postmodern culture advertising images are important means of socializing children which provide images of self-identity for youth, and so they need to be understood and contested.[1]

People can present different social selves which they creatively appropriate from popular culture. The question then is not how one strips away false veneers and find an authentic self, or how one finds a true self apart from the pressure of peers, the media, or society, since the self only appears in myriad forms with respect to these relations. To see it otherwise is to presume an invariant, underlying structure of selfhood which is supposed to develop and emerge through normative, universal, scientifically determined, or politically correct ways and in inevitable opposition to undesirable social forces. Rather, the question is, given that selves are now both reflected in and reflect popular culture—that is, they have a relational quality—which selves are better constructs for presenting chosen expressive features; and given that selves are relational, what relationships enhance self-expression and mutuality.

Becoming addicted is an embodied, relational pattern in which a person is controlled by something, someone, or some way of relating which limits his or her range of self-expression. In postmodern culture addiction takes the form, to adapt Gergen's phrase, of the self becoming saturated with one or another of its representations. When the self is overidentified with one form of expression, it loses its relational nature. Despite their modernist narratives, many school-based prevention approaches often do help youth question addictive patterns. Group work and creative use of curricula offer children alternatives to addictive drug use, provide information on drugs and alcohol, and teach practical skills. In fact, the lived reality of prevention programs is postmodern in a number of ways, for example, when teachers adapt a piece from an individualistic prevention curriculum and apply it to the reality of their students' lives. (Some in the prevention field oppose the creative modification of curricula and instead favor "fidelity of implementation."[2] They argue for the need for teachers to carry out the program the way the researchers designed the curriculum. But in this sense teachers, instead of working as intellectuals, are reduced to technocrats of packaged products designed by technologists.)

The progressive kernel of prevention is its challenge to modernist drug pushing and drug abuse. But modernist prevention models tend to treat the individual self devoid of its relational nature. They consider the family, school, community, and peers as influences on the individual. But in postmodern culture the self only exists within these relations, which themselves are infused with power and have been transformed through creative interplay with the electronic media and technologies within popular culture.

Substance abuse prevention is an immanently ideological field which proposes healthy or moral ways of behaving; postmodern culture is an immanent challenge to modernist narratives. To propose a radical postmodern curriculum which prevents addictive relations then is to launch an explicit attack against those modernist, rationalist, and elitist narratives and relations which control people's behaviors and which deny people's full-bodied experiences. It opposes addictive relations of all kinds. It appreciates and uses irony, humor, and playfulness. A prevention curriculum stands for relationships which enhance choice over being controlled by someone or some substance or idea; in certain cases this may even include the choice to remain addicted as well. It stands for creative, full relationships which promote access to knowledge over the restriction or denial of information. The concept of addiction itself is not predetermined but is open to varying interpretations in particular contexts.

Addictive relations include a bureaucratic and cultural network which restricts people's creative and sensuous expression in various ways. To practice a postmodern prevention curriculum is part of what Giroux and McLaren call a "postcolonial cultural politics" which works to eliminate all forms of oppression and injustice.

> To conceptualize curriculum as a form of cultural politics is to acknowledge the overriding goal of education as the creation of conditions for social transformation through the constitution of students as political subjects who recognize their historical, racial, class, and gender situatedness and the forces that shape their lives and are politically and ethically motivated to struggle in the interest of greater human freedom and emancipation.[3]

This project calls for analyzing concrete power relations in terms of the corporate nature of work, the interests of those holding state power, and institutional and interpersonal forms of racism and sexism, among others. However, as Giroux and McLaren point out, this project cannot afford to lapse into a traditional leftist narrative which proposes a rational overview that predefines the meaning of historical forces and the goals of freedom and emancipation. It is one thing to analyze and challenge power relations through an understanding of everyday relations and to work together to create an alternative, liberating vision; it is another to claim advance knowledge as vanguard educators about what that future ought to be and how to get there.

Progressive postmodern prevention requires, among other things, that educators explore and create relationships which constitute expressive selves through interplay with images, discourses, and modes of knowledge from popular culture. The self is not a singular identity but itself consists of continually reconstructed, contradictory, open-ended, and fluid relations.[4] Prevention works to recapture those aspects of the self which have been appropriated and colonized by patterns of control and denial. It encourages students to critically explore their various selves in tems of gender, peer, family, cultural, and international relations and to reconstitute themselves as fully participating citizens within new relationships. It means that educators and students create new narratives. They retell people's lives in ways which speak of their power and ability to overcome domination by restrictive and addictive forces.

A prevention curriculum employs both dialogical and bodily ways to seize and share knowledge. Drug abuse can result from a desperate attempt to reaffirm sensuous knowledge which has been denied through restrictive patterns of relations. Some children experiment with drugs, beginning with cigarettes and alcohol, as a means to resist and escape from the sterile, disembodied worlds of school and conditional families, and others emulate their families' ways of dealing with stress and insecurity through substance use. Those that get hooked on the feeling from these and other drugs discover their connectedness with their bodies in a way which is still sanctioned by part of the larger culture through cigarettes and alcohol.

The process of prevention no longer means that educators lead students to predetermined outcomes or conclusions or induce certain behaviors or attitudes. The process itself aims to be free of addictive, controlling elements and is a collaborative effort between the educator and the participants. The knowledge of the teacher or prevention professional is always partial, and he or she becomes a part of the process of constructing new narratives. This process cannot be taken for granted but must be grounded in trust and a respect for differences.

A postmodern prevention curriculum deals with both relationships and critical learning in order to enhance students' and educators' sense of their lives. One way to bridge these traditionally divided realms is to *critically investigate unspoken addictive relations in everyday life and work to change them with others.* This approach legitimates the study of everyday relations; it interrogates everyday culture in order to both criticize and transcend it, to acknowledge its authentic expressive forms.[5] It is situated in students' lives and includes topics such as peer relations, gender, sexuality, schooling, family life, and popular culture (for example, music, dance, the media, clothes, food), and can include the topics of work and the state. It addresses them through the tools of critical teaching such as problem posing, dialogue, and mutual inquiry. Certain so-called cognitive and affective approaches such as memorization and focusing on feelings and group processes become reconstituted within a pedagogy which aims to promote self-enhancing relationships and which links knowledge with power.

There are as many creative prevention programs as there are dedicated educators and prevention specialists. The following describes a few projects which are in the postmodern spirit.

SHOWeD

One Freirean program developed by Nina Wallerstein and colleagues at the Alcohol Substance Abuse Prevention Program at the University of New Mexico employs critical questioning of everyday relations and incorporates the goal of social action into prevention of substance abuse.[6] The program uses a code or trigger to start the process, a representation of a problem or issue such as a picture, cartoon, story, song, video, dialogue, or skit. It then generates a structured discussion based on a five-step protocol with the acronym "SHOWeD": See, Happening, Our, Why, and Do. For example, one of their projects is to reduce drunken driving among youth using a video story about youth facing the problem of drunk driving as the code. The first step is to ask youth what they see, to describe what the story is about. They are then encouraged to talk about what is happening in terms of what the characters are feeling and how they deal with the problem. The third step is to ask how our feelings are similar: Do you know others with this problem? Fourth, youth critically discuss why this problem occurs: What are the different levels of explanation on personal, family, community, and societal levels? Finally, youth decide what they can do to prevent the problem or bring about changes in personal, community, and societal terms. The protocol brings the youth to the point of taking action after considering how the problem relates to them and after exploring its causes.

RELATIONAL LITERACY

One piece of an alternative prevention curriculum might be to teach a kind of relational or antiaddictive literacy. Through discussion, role playing, studies of popular media material, reading, and research students would become familiar with the various uses of words which characterize relations and self-expression. Students could script the words, a technique in which they interpretively act out the meanings of a word in various contexts. A list of significant words which are both personal and political might include *control, denial, addiction, manipulation, intimidation, dependency, anxiety/insecurity, depression/powerlessness,* and *shame.* The words can be interrogated from the standpoint of power relations like class, gender, race, and other categories and can be applied to the study of students' everyday relations. Arnold Wesker, the British dramatist, proposes a similar project, a list of essential words for survival literacy. He tells the story of his son, who was bullied by two older boys and who, bewildered by their taunts and eventual physical abuse, did not know how to respond to them. Wesker's example underscores the dialectical nature of words which refer to interpersonal relations, the way each respective self contains some aspect of the other within the relationship. He wonders,

> Would discussion of the word 'intimidate' in my son's school have made him understand that it was not the thug intimidating him, but he—with his long hair, colourful clothing, disregard for the school uniform, extensive vocabulary, his entire personality and output of confidence—it was *he* who was intimidating the thug. Such understanding of the word "intimidation" can't keep a swelling down; but it might have prompted him to move

on at the first sign of danger, or to have faced it squarely to show he was going to hit back.[7]

Relational literacy also means that people become proficient in the different relational discourses of everyday culture, and just as important become aware of their relational selves, the ability to cross different cultural borders by listening and making themselves understood. For example, in a prevention group some young Haitian-American students in Brooklyn acknowledged the stress of dwelling in at least three difficult cultures with three different discourses: at home they are expected to speak Creole and relate formally to their immigrant parents; in school they must deal with white teachers and speak standard English; and in their Brooklyn neighborhood they must speak black English and the language of the streets in order to survive. This remarkable awareness that they are perpetual immigrants, crossing over and dwelling within different cultures, not only discloses the relational, shifting nature of the self, that there is not necessarily one true or pure self apart from cultural relations, but speaks to the possibility of literacy regarding the relation of the relations, the critical awareness of how one develops through different cultural discourses and which then allows for the skill of expressive choice, the melding of knowledge, power, and pleasure.

From a modernist standpoint these three cultures are not all equally valid but fall within a normative hierarchy of legitimacy. On the bottom, street culture is condemned as an inferior and unacceptable way of life. At the next level immigrant family values and patterns are outmoded as a whole and need to be overcome as quickly as possible. Only the school culture of white middle-class teachers, whose task is to help the students assimilate to the dominant discourse of American culture, holds status.

But in postmodern culture this hierarchy has toppled. Classroom discourse is now only one of a number of contested languages which itself needs to be critically evaluated in terms of the shifting relations of students' and teachers' lives. By the same account street and hip hop culture has gained a significant degree of legitimacy by virtue of its powerful and expressive forms of knowledge which have impacted on everyday life, and multiculturalism has fought to recognize the valid kinds of knowledge within different ethnic cultures in contrast to imposed assimilation. An educator in the postmodern sense who nurtures the students' critical awareness of these cultures as ones which deserve serious consideration can help students further interrogate them through intellectual inquiry and research: What are the troublesome and enhancing aspects of each one? How have they been historically shaped and formed? The educator can also encourage this literacy through nonlinear forms of expression such as poetry, theater exercises, and collaborative video pieces, among others. Not only can the students become fluent in learning to cross over and flourish within cultural discourses, but their awareness of this process and of their skill in performing it then allows them to consciously and creatively negotiate, restructure, and cross-pollinate the cultures as they enrich and elaborate their own selves.

One thing that distinguishes relational literacy from the Resolving Conflict Creatively program is that it regards popular culture as part of personal life. Relational literacy does not treat the media as just some outside evil influence which opposes values of cooperation and nonviolence. Nor is relational literacy just a form of individual behavior management; instead, it questions the everyday power relations within the school. In other words, it does not accept the dualist model in which emotions constitute some separate, personal sphere apart from the rest of the world, including school and the media. The self is filled with contradictory images and pieces of popular culture and is in turn an integral part of power relations. Repetitive TV images, lines from rock and rap music, and statements and actions from parents, teachers, and kids on the street can saturate the self and galvanize students to make expressive choices or can induce addictive, compulsive behavior.

Educators and students need to acknowledge and interrogate popular cultural images, sensations, and patterns from the standpoint of active people able to make self-enhancing choices. This point links up with Kellner's call for a critical literacy of images within popular culture, by which students learn to unpack the relations between commercial images in cigarette ads and the lifestyles they endorse through their products.[8] In this way students engage in the politics of everyday life whereby they come to resist and redefine the kinds of relations promoted through popular culture. For example, the debate around what to do with Joe Camel, the mascot for Camel cigarettes known for his overtly phallic facial features, brings forth modernist arguements pro and con. Some argue that the ad itself is not important, that it is a smokescreen for the real enemy, the tobacco corporations, who are poisoning youths with a toxic product. The opposite strategy of this materialist approach is to ignore the political economic forces and teach youth individualistic skills such as how to resist advertising and how to rationally analyze the manipulative techniques which try to influence them.

But in a postmodern framework the self itself is not a pure entity which can stand outside of popular culture (in fact, Joe Camel has as high a recognition as Mickey Mouse among many children). Instead the self is formed in part from its relation with various media images such as Joe Camel and within corporate relations of power and organization. Students need to become literate in reading the different ways the image does and does not speak to their lives, and educators need to help them explore and deconstruct in concrete terms the different relations which the image represents, such as being cool, smooth, self-confident, well-dressed, and masculine, as well as the way they are already implicated in a power relationship with tobacco companies as targeted potential consumers. In this way students are freer to come to terms with the legitimate and enhancing aspects of the relations in which they develop, as well as to change the disturbing, addictive, and exploitative features. This absolves neither tobacco corporations nor individuals but places the need to challenge problematic relations and create expressive ones on a different cultural and political ground in which the nature of the self is reconstituted.

A political cultural perspective is crucial if educators are to avoid falling into teaching apolitical, individualistic techniques which are not linked up to the everyday relations of school and popular culture. This view also acknowledges the addictive nature of conflict in many cases. It does not try to deny this by forcing resolution, itself a suspiciously addictive process of trying to control for and solve other people's problems, but respects the process of people learning to give up futile attempts to control others, including the educators themselves.

GIVING UP CONTROL

The heart of an alternative prevention approach is both the critical study of everyday addictive relations and the challenge to create practical alternatives. I worked with a woman colleague,

Nancy Roberts, also white, on a project in the East Flatbush section of Brooklyn with young black males in the seventh and
eighth grades of a Catholic school, most of whose parents were
Haitian and from other Caribbean islands. We met with them in
their classroom once a week for one period without their teacher
for the better part of a school year. The goal was to establish a
safe, respectful relationship so that we could discuss personal
issues of importance to them as black males but also shift toward
formally examining these issues as more structured topics, for
example, through reading autobiographies, newspaper articles,
and other texts. We had modest success toward establishing this
sort of hybrid arrangement largely because of our limited, outside
position with respect to the cognitive/affective division in school
and the corresponding expectations of the students toward us. We
did manage to achieve a working level of mutual respect and
understanding, made difficult in part because we began after the
school year had started and were not integrated into the structure
of the school as full-time staff vested with power; we were from
outside the everyday culture of the school.

As part-time outsiders it was especially challenging to create
an island of democratic collaborative learning within a sea of
more traditional education, despite the support of a principal
open to innovative approaches. Students at first resisted or passively cooperated when they saw us as part of the established
school authority; they sometimes acted up when they saw we were
not going to discipline and treat them in the conventional ways.
After all, if we are teacher types vested with traditional, formal
disciplinary or academic power who ask them to discuss their personal issues, they are not likely to feel safe in front of us or their
peers, for whom they must risk performing and disclosing themselves in a competitive, academic setting; on the other hand, if we
are feelings oriented, accepting, counselor types who are encouraging them to formally read and write about the topics we discuss,
they are not likely to take the assignments as seriously as if it were
coming from a teacher who would grade them. These barriers
may be less an issue for a classroom teacher or on-site counselor
who tries to integrate these perspectives on a regular, consistent,
and frequent basis than for part-time outside consultants.

Nevertheless, we plowed ahead, not knowing how things
would turn out. We introduced topics for discussion and structured the meetings but tried to avoid steering the group in one

rigid direction. We first worked to establish a mutually agreeable climate in which people respected each other as well as felt safe enough to discuss some personal issues. We did this through group activities, for example, by making membership voluntary, agreeing on ground rules, and engaging in icebreaker exercises. We encouraged everyone to listen and share feelings and opinions; as leaders we were prepared to share our own feelings and opinions with the group when we thought it was relevant.

At this stage we spent some time talking about how the students treated each other, especially the practice of dissing, teasing, and putting each other down. The discussion clarified that some of it was harmless and was actually a way to express closeness but that some of it was hurtful. We discussed to what extent it is a black thing, a male thing, who else disses who in the larger society, and whether it is natural and necessary. We linked up the way they felt disrespected by the school with the way they treated each other, discussing similarities and differences. We talked about what drugs are capable of diminishing the feelings of being dissed and why someone might take a drug. We also discussed their precarious status as young black males within society as well as the school. In one session we explored the word *intimidation* and what it is like when some white people appear to be afraid of them on the street, as well as their own fears toward white people in certain circumstances.

At a later point we considered dissing as a possible basis for a more formal study of expressions of power, affection, and hostility through literature, history, and current events. (In fact, it is incorporated into another project described below.) We also would have liked to use the students' complaints about the school as the basis for studying schooling itself, how knowledge is constructed and distributed through particular power relations, using their own school as the basis for investigation. Throughout the year we tried to offer an alternative model of learning in which control was not strictly in the hands of the adult leaders but in part depended on the mutual trust established by the group. This proved challenging but rewarding. We tolerated a certain level of chaos, uncertainty, and disruption and often would manage to discuss the disruptive events. This helped us gain a clearer sense of what everyone was then willing or unwilling to do to work together.

THING ADDICTION

After we established a working arrangement we undertook the practice of problematizing everyday objects.[9] The purpose here was to consider our relation to things or commodities, when are they self-enhancing and when are they pushed and consumed as druglike entities to which we can become addicted and which supply us with an ineffective self. The group decided to look at designer sneakers. This was a significant topic; at that point in the development of the group the students were not willing to bring in their sneakers as we had suggested because they were not yet ready to trust the group by disclosing their personal choices. We decided to continue with the topic on a more abstract level and listed positive and negative qualities about sneakers. Some of the benefits were that they felt good, they made you look good, they helped you run and play basketball. The list of bad things included that they were expensive, they did not last long, they could be stolen, and their value depreciated immediately. As the exchange continued, we began to draw a circle of topics around a picture of sneakers on the board. These included where the sneakers are made and by whom, including Haiti and South Africa, who sets the price and profits from their sales, how the young men get their money from their parents to buy them, the response of friends to the sneakers one buys, the popular brands and whether they are in fact better than others, and the names of black males who appear in sneaker commercials (Spike Lee, Michael Jordan, David Robinson). This model represented how an embodied, personal issue like choosing and wearing sneakers is also an integral part of popular culture, dispersed through media images and consequently located in foreign countries as well as in neighborhood streets and on a youth's own body.

In the ensuing discussion we linked the different topics surrounding the sneakers and looked at the contradictory relations around black role models, profit, exploitation, athletics, self-image, family, and physical pleasure. Do profits from sneakers go to South Africa? Are black women workers who make them exploited? How does Spike Lee possibly feel about making sneaker commercials? We tried to tease out all the conflicting forces around buying and wearing sneakers which on the one hand contribute to enhancing one's sense of pride and power and which on the other exploit, manipulate, and pressure black males. We looked at commercials and the corporations which produce sneakers, questioning what we were not told. We role-played the various ways students dealt with their parents to get money for the more expensive sneakers and how they handled their peers around who wears the right sneakers. We considered whether sneakers are at all like drugs and the ways in which the word *addictive* applies to sneaker behavior and ways in which it does not: In what ways are the ads pushing a high which is short-lived? What are the feelings when you go without having the right sneakers? Throughout the discussion we introduced some of the words from the relational literacy list, including *manipulation, addiction,* and *anxiety* and applied them to topics as they came up.

By beginning with commodities (other examples are rap music and sports based on the discussion from the previous chapter, and clothes) students can get a feel for evaluating addictive qualities such as possessiveness, the need to control others, the investment in one fixed aspect of identity, and the denial of feelings and information. After looking at things, the curriculum can move on to looking at relational forms themselves, such as male/female relations, the family, school, and workplace, and explore self-enhancing and addictive aspects. The purpose is for students to actively theorize about their everyday relations by interrogating their own experience as well as some traditional canons, to create their own critical worldviews instead of being passive recipients of handed-down knowledge. But theory is not the end goal. One result of the project was that the next year the seventh graders took on the responsibility of acting as older brothers with boys in the second and third grades. They worked with them around school and personal interests with new awareness about the vulnerability of black males and some of the other issues we had discussed. They continued to meet with some of our staff who supervised them and encouraged them to keep examining and reconstructing their everyday relations as they took on new responsibilities.

VIDEO SELF-DISPERSAL/CONSTRUCTION

The other project we began to work on with the young black men was a video exchange with some white male counterparts in a school in Bensonhurst. These students were mostly of Italian heritage, and like many of the Haitian-American students, first-generation Americans. Instead of meeting during class time these young men volunteered to meet with a teacher after school. Both schools were respectively all black and all white, neither ethnic group had any significant encounters with the other in any part of their lives, and the reality was that neither was likely to find itself in the others' neighborhoods anytime soon (they were also likely to go to mostly segregated high schools). For these reasons a video exchange seemed to be a realistic way to connect them with one another. In each group students took turns working the camera and came up with questions which they asked of themselves and of the other group. I shuttled between the schools and brought each one the tapes. The project was far from realized because of time and logistical constraints but was an exciting chance to do some border crossing, postmodern style, for both students and adults.

The video exchange gave students some chance to explore and cross the boundary of different cultures. Students did share some things in common, such as having immigrant parents who were strict around the house and were seen as old-fashioned in other ways. Popular culture to some extent mediated racial and ethnic differences and served as a common ground for both groups. There were certain elements with which they were all familiar, including watching TV sitcoms like the "Simpsons" and "Fresh Prince." Some of the Italian-American males wore earrings, listened to rap music, and had personal graffiti tags (monikers), aspects of hip hop culture which had originated in African-American and Latino neighborhoods but which had crossed over into white neighborhoods through exposure by MTV and other media forms. They began to share views on girls, an interchange we adults were interested in furthering and in participating because of the blatant sexism among some members of both groups.

On the other hand, there were many rivers to cross; white students from the beginning were more fearful of the black students and were more cautious, defensive, and self-conscious about disclosing themselves. The discussion about music revealed cultural differences; black students had more developed tastes in styles and bands. We would have liked to get the exchange really rolling so that the young men could have formed a relationship in which they felt safe enough to ask frank questions about each other in order to acknowledge both similarities and differences. But in general, within the limitations of the project, students from both schools were refreshingly concrete in discussing their lives, preferring to discuss everyday things rather than issues like racism or stereotypes, as we adults had first thought. They served to remind the adults that it is on the level of everyday relations that people can define themselves, by exploring difference as well as connecting beyond it. The purpose of the exchange was to promote an alternative vision of possibility and community which challenged the dominant view of relations between people. At the same time it encouraged the interchange of different voices and tried to allow for both appreciation and questioning of difference. The exchange was the possible basis of a rich curriculum in which both African-Americans and Italian-Americans could come to look at similarities and differences in family and ethnic histories and how each dealt with oppressive forces from the dominant culture.

The postmodern irony, of course, was that these relations occurred not face to face but through the electronic medium. A plan for an actual meeting was never realized but may not have been necessary. The electronic medium itself is a powerful means of both personal and collective expression for youth. This is also evidenced in the movie *Pump Up the Volume* (1990). The hero, played by Christian Slater, is a new student at a high school who secretly broadcasts a popular and influential underground radio program from his room. He is adept at articulating some of the unspoken feelings of alienation and yearnings of many of the students and is instrumental in both affecting a suicide and in subverting the hypocritical practices of some of the adults in the school. Despite the melodramatic ending, the movie shows how media use can transform and free people in imaginative ways.

VIDEO AS BODY SIMULATION

Another kind of border crossing occurred when we were using the video camera with the young men from East Flatbush. One day after months of working together, two of them who were good comics spontaneously improvised a skit from the weekly TV program "In Living Color," a variety show written and produced by talented African-Americans which presents humorous parodies and musical numbers. The students did a send-up of one of the show's frequent skits, itself a send-up, of two gay critics reviewing a movie. The young men, in front of the camera and the rest of the group, sat on each other's laps and displayed blatant affections throughout the lengthy parody, in which they reviewed a book and movie they were studying in class. All of this took place in the sanctified classroom, which became liberated territory. When we played back the video, it was even funnier than the live performance. From what we knew of them, the young men were heterosexual thirteen- and fourteen-year-olds. Yet within a homophobic milieu (but mediated by the safety of simulated TV culture) these youth felt free to bodily express an alternative forbidden relationship.

To perform as stars in front of a video camera and creatively interpret a popular culture TV show allowed them to feel safe enough to explore crossing over a restrictive border and play out with their bodies a stigmatized relation in front of their peers. The students' sharing in this familiar piece of popular culture in turn allowed the adults to introduce the topic of homophobia and gendered behavior as something which could be critically discussed alongside the students' video clip. If addictive relations restrict people's self-expression, then expressing and discussing prejudice and fears as relational aspects is an essential part of prevention. The video camera and popular culture mediated the physical act of exploring selfhood. Both the young men's own subjectivity and the selfhood of the Other, in this case gays, were dispersed through the video. The transparency and fluidity of the electronic media allowed the educators to ask several questions: What is there in you that is also contained in the Other? Where does the young men's self end and the Other's begin?

KISSIN', DISSIN', AND . . . LISTEN!

Another project I initiated along with a colleague, Julia McEvoy, was a conference for high school students which we named Kissin', Dissin', and . . . Listen! The title was meant to signify that the conference would be a place where it was OK for students to talk about sex, relationships, and feelings like anger, and that it would also be about learning communication skills like listening and being assertive. We involved counselors and teachers from nine Brooklyn Catholic high schools in the planning. They agreed to pick ten sophomores from each school who were potential leaders to attend. The students represented a broad spectrum of ethnic groups. Our prevention program staff led most of the workshops, which were on such topics as helping a friend who is in trouble, how to talk to parents, exploring one's family ethnic identity, learning about what the opposite sex thinks, discussing the messages in popular music, analyzing the significance of clothing styles, and looking at the image of youth portrayed by the media. The leaders included activities, role-playing, and media in their presentations. The conference started off with a physical activity as an icebreaker and concluded with a speak-out. Almost all students participated with enthusiasm and said they learned new things about themselves and others.

Part of the purpose of the conference was to bridge the gap between the formal structure of the school and students' lives, including peer and sexual relations, involvement with popular culture, and other personal issues. We tried to convince the schools that these workshop topics were worth incorporating into the everyday curriculum. We invited any available teacher and guidance staff to the conference to meet together while the students were in their workshops and to discuss how they and the students could bring back some of the information and skills from the conference. We challenged the staff to make the study of the everyday experiences of students part of the schools' mission.

We were also committed to promoting real student involvement in planning and carrying out the conference. In the first year we made a long-term plan to have some of the same students help run the conference when they became seniors. By the third year the conference organizers had succeeded in involving the seniors in the planning of the conference in a number of ways, including running some activities, selecting the discussion topics, and coleading some of the workshops. In one school the original group of students continued meeting with a counselor for two more years, discussing and working on some of the issues they learned about at the conference. As a result of their experience in the conference, some African-American girls from one high school spontaneously contacted students, both white and black, from other schools after the 1992 Los Angeles riots and arranged a forum without the help or presence of any adults.

PARENT PROGRAM

Parent work is a common piece of both school- and community-based drug and alcohol abuse prevention programs. Parent training, support programs, and curricula appear to be part of a growth industry which has conflicting tendencies. Typical parent education curricula, for example, Dinkmeyer's and McKay's Systematic Training for Effective Parenting (STEP), Gordon's Parent Effectiveness Training (PET), Ginott's Parent Education, and Popkin's Active Parenting, are written by white, professional males, although it is mostly women who come out for parenting workshops.[10] In most cases the word *parent* is a code for *women*, although men especially could stand to benefit from parenting programs. For the most part the curricula reflect an enlightened middle-class liberalism and favor democratic rather than authoritarian parenting. They teach parents how to listen with empathy, share feelings (I-messages), avoid sarcasm, lecturing, or nagging, negotiate conflicts so that everyone wins, and hold family meetings. They suggest that parents encourage children instead of praise them and use natural and logical consequences in response to misbehavior instead of punishment. Besides teaching communication skills, parent programs may give information on drugs and alcohol use and its impact on the family as well as on childhood and adolescent development. They also promote lots of peer support and sharing among parents within the course.

The parenting curricula are useful to the extent that they encourage parents to challenge outmoded beliefs common to certain modernist families, such as the need to be in control at all times, to be perfect parents, and to meet disobedience with force. But in other ways the models perpetuate old patterns which are less helpful. The communication skills are middle class in origin and the method of teaching them is through abstract principles rather than through the use of actual, complex situations of the culture of everyday. The curricula tend not to acknowledge the explicit difficulties of working parents, recalcitrant or abusive fathers, parental ambivalence toward children, children with learning problems, ethnic and class differences, or living with in-laws upstairs (a common occurrence in Brooklyn). For example, some single mothers with whom I worked found empathic listening to one child a difficult task when other siblings were in the room who might undermine and otherwise affect the interchange. The PET and STEP trainings abstract the principle of empathic listening out of everyday contexts and then encourage the parents to reinsert the principle into their own lives. But the nature of the interaction is now radically different, and empathic listening per

se may not be suitable for the situation. It requires a more concrete discussion of the contradictory dynamics of the family system and the various goals of a parent, who must balance her own
needs along with those of her children. Another problem is the
real concern parents often express around how to protect their
children from the increased violence of the streets, the bullies,
drug dealers, child molesters, and reckless drivers who endanger
children's lives. In modernist urban culture many mothers would
stay home and there was an extensive network of neighbors and
extended family members who would watch out for all the children and report back to the parents when their children misbe-
haved. Today parents are more isolated and feel more helpless in
the face of these problems. Parent education now requires building in some neighborhood and political organizing and discussing
different strategies with children beyond the kinds of suburban
examples that appear in the typical parent curricula.[11]

Because of the radical transformation of communities, families, and the relationship between adults and children parents
today need support in helping their children deal with a different
world than the one of only twenty or thirty years ago. In workshops with parents I have them contrast modernist life, the way
most of us grew up, with the culture in which children must grow
up today. We look at the four areas discussed earlier, the workplace, the family, the school, and the state, and contrast the way it
was with now. In terms of parenting we examine outmoded, modernist rules such as, Do as I say, not as I do, Do it because I say so,
and the pressures to be perfect parents always in control of their
children. We contrast them with relations today, the changing
roles of women, the way the electronic media have undermined
traditional authority in the family and school, and the need to be
honest with children and negotiate at times instead of always trying to control through power.

I place parenting within postmodern relations of single, working, female-headed families, step-families, alcoholic and substance-abusing families, the loss of traditional authority, the loss
of informal community networks, and the lack of state support
for families and children. Without abdicating my role as an educator with certain skills and information, I encourage a shift from
looking to me for correct answers to problem posing and joint
problem solving. We acknowledge the need to deal with the pre-
mature and often unavoidable influences on young children of

popular culture, including TV, commercials, music, fashion, sex, drugs, and the streets. In many cases these forces now contribute to socializing children as much as parents do. This requires that parents talk with their children about the form and content of popular culture so that children can question what they see and hear. Our program has run a number of successful structured workshops in which a group of parents dialogue with their children on issues which are important to both parties. We also teach parents to become skilled group leaders who run their own parent support groups under supervision. A future project is for parents to develop their own curricular videos and cassettes on parenting in order to reach more isolated parents and to network across communities.

PLP/CUNY

One significant topic we discuss in parent support groups and workshops is the influence of the school on their children and how parents in turn can become more knowledgeable about educational evaluation and reform. One project in New York City, the Parent Leadership Project (PLP) of the City University of New York (CUNY) Substance Abuse Prevention Programs, concentrates explicitly on training parents to become active leaders who improve schools and develop substance abuse prevention approaches.[12] Parents help plan the program, which operates in a number of poor and working-class school districts and includes mostly Latina and African-American women.

The project trains parents to run effective meetings, speak in public, resolve conflicts, conduct community research, and reach out to other parents to get involved in their Parent Teacher Association and school issues. Parents also learn about the structure of the city public school system. The substance abuse prevention piece includes pharmacology, childhood development, and parent communication skills. As a consultant I co-led a workshop series (in broken Spanish) for a group of mothers on family systems issues and listening and assertive skills. Some parent groups from different school districts used their new skills to implement action projects such as a parent newletter, forums on substance abuse, and a substance abuse prevention fair. As happens in my program's parent group facilitator training, a number of women increased their self-confidence and began to speak up for themselves in a variety of settings. Parents learned that they could effect change with their school personnel by calling for a meeting and making their needs known, and their overall skills and involvement increased from the training.

COMMUNITY-BASED PREVENTION

Some of the current trends in community drug prevention are adaptive of the changing times. For example, the National Partnership Program of the Citizens Committee of New York, a national leader in community-based drug prevention work, assumes a flexible approach to prevention.[13] It works on a local level, begins with community residents' concerns, adapts professional models to the communities' needs, and tries to bring in all groups affected by drug abuse.

First, the program works on a local basis. It does not aim to immediately reduce all drug dealing within an entire city but targets specific neighborhoods. After it achieves this goal, it urges that other neighborhoods do the same, block by block. It also encourages building coalitions and networks to link up with other groups involved in similar projects.

Second, since community residents' priority is to get dealers out of their streets, parks, and buildings, organizers start with mobilizing the community around ridding itself of illegal drug dealers and working with law enforcement. To some extent this flies in the face of certain traditional class-based organizing of poor or working poor people because it starts with a law-and-order issue rather than a conflict model of besieged residents against an oppressive system. It takes the conservative idea of safety and security based on law enforcement as a serious principle and demands that the government in fact do what it says it is supposed to do, protect and serve all citizens.

Third, as community organizers committed to involving citizens on a grass-roots level program staff take traditional concepts from the medical model but use them to help community members assess their needs. They ask the residents themselves to evaluate the prevalent risk factors and high-risk groups they see in their neighborhood, rather than letting professionals come in and tell them. At first, residents tend to say that everyone is using illegal drugs and that the problem seems overwhelming. The organizers use the medical concept of *at risk* to help people pinpoint who is more likely to be involved in drug using and dealing in their neighborhood.

Last, the partnership program aims to bring in all relevant parties as collaborators, not antagonists, including the police, merchants, corporations, the media, government officials, health and mental health service providers, schools, and religious groups, to work with neighborhood residents. The approach somewhat aims to override the classic antagonisms between citizens and police in many inner-city neighborhoods and between working people and corporate and professional interests. Drug pushing has become the common problem. Because times have changed, grass-roots citizens are in need of allies. They also need different criteria to sort out who their allies are and to come up with unlikely ones from the standpoint of traditional organizing. For example, this currently means collaborating with certain branches of the federal government. The federal government agency, formerly the Office for Substance Abuse Prevention (OSAP) and now the Center for Substance Abuse Prevention (CSAP), takes a different tack than the conservative Office of Drug Control Policy and endorses a community-based approach which aims to strengthen the power of everyday citizens. Another example is that in some inner-city neighborhoods the organizers work with the police and sensitize them to residents' concerns. They train the police to work with block associations, tenant organizations, and neighborhood patrols to get their help in arresting pushers and driving them from the area. For example, in the North Flatbush section of Brooklyn, which is plagued with crack and drug-related crimes, one community patrol group, Umma, a volunteer organization of Muslim African-Americans, works closely with the police in observing and reporting troublesome incidents.[14] But the group does not work only on law enforcement. In addition, Umma sponsors community drug education meetings, jobs fairs, and youth activities, provides an escort service for school children and senior citizens, and coordinates a voter registration drive, among other projects.

Besides law enforcement, the National Partnership Program, like Umma, also aims to educate and mobilize communities to advocate for prevention and treatment issues such as after-school activities for youth, family and parenting support programs, and treatment for users. They train residents in skills essential to build community organizations: how to speak in public, how to put on a conference, how to run a meeting, how to build a network, how to do public relations, how to lobby and pressure municipal government. They are committed to developing community leaders who are from the neighborhood and, unlike some providers, do not count leaders to be the church pastor or the professional director of the local social service agency. Their goal is to help build sustained organizations with local organizers and leaders who develop effective programs tailored to the needs of their specific community. In some cases one national organizer acknowledged that to the extent they did not achieve this the community residents became dependent on the national organizers and/or resented their power.

Those professionals and citizens involved in front-line community substance abuse prevention work are at the center of turbulent cross-currents of new practices and ideas. They must grapple with a number of contradictory and competing trends which are not easily reconciled. For example, Is law enforcement the way to go when it may only serve to push dealers into other areas and to ignore the white-collar suppliers higher up? To what extent can community residents trust and work with the police? How does one begin to address the problem of alcohol abuse within families as a community drug abuse issue? What is the nature of drug and alcohol treatment, and what kind is most effective for different communities? What constitutes a community, and how is a community leader defined? How much reliance should be placed on professionals and other experts? How do people take power without becoming addicted to control? Given the way power is redistributed and accessed today, is community organizing even the most effective way people can affect public policy? These are political and social issues which require continued discussion and debate from all involved parties on an everyday level.

Community-Based Prevention for Youth

The Youth Force division of the New York City Citizens Committee has developed an innovative series of prevention programs in which young people are significant leaders.[15] One of these, the Posse for Change, consists of young organizers and peer counselors who recruit youth age fourteen and up who did or still deal drugs. They speak to the dealers about the pros and cons of dealing, of what it does to themselves and to other people in their community. The posse has drawn in ex-dealers who are worried about getting busted, shot, or going to jail. Those recruited join local posses and apply for small grants to develop alternative activities. They in turn reach out and organize others as well as offer and receive peer counseling.

Posse members regularly convene at one central site and develop citywide educational campaigns which use videos, publications, and media announcements that challenge youth around dealing and abusing drugs. They discuss common experiences such as how the career track of dealing leads to stress and despair: the initial advantages of money, recognition, and power are outweighed by the dangers of drug taking and violence, and the things they buy with money are not necessarily fulfilling. The members begin to look at themselves as "at risk" of addiction and emotional problems; that is, they appropriate a public health term and apply it to themselves. Although dealers at age fourteen and fifteen tend to avoid drugs, the stress of dealing is such that after the high of having money wears off many begin using the drugs themselves by eighteen. They learn that risk is heightened for those who come from families in which adults abuse alcohol and crack (COAs and COSAs). A common experience is that some of them have had to lock their own rooms to keep their abusing parents and their friends from stealing from them. This kind of awareness leads to discussing their own drug taking, including drinking. They ask each other when and how it affects others, their friends, younger siblings, and the other youth to whom they are reaching out. Posse members also examine the meaning of wealth: What is it that people really need and want? How much do you really need? They discuss violence and alternatives to carrying guns. They also argue about language, including the tendency to verbally abuse women.

One of the draws of drug dealing is entrepreneurship, the sense of ownership, independence, and importance the youth feel from making money. A key component of the Posse for Change program is a proposal which offers youth the alternative chance to establish youth-run business cooperatives in inner-city neighborhoods. The project, called Strictly Business, plans to encourage entrepreneurial activities as well as offer a way for youth to help develop their community. Youth are to receive intensive and follow-up training in how to run a business from local organizations, businesses, and banks. They will also be required to reinvest a certain percentage of their earnings back into the neighborhood, for instance, by funding programs or events, buying equipment for a local day care center, or beautifying neighborhood space.

The Posse for Change projects wrestle with the issue of how youth can meet their needs for self-recognition and dignity in a culture which values money above all else. It is clearly a sign of the times that alienated youth are turning to business opportunities as a progressive alternative to street dealing. Questions of the high failure rate of small businesses and the conflict between personal and corporate greed and community needs are issues over which youth as well as the larger society need to struggle. How do the entrepreneurial values of the Strictly Business project square with the values of social change and support through community organizing? That these issues are part of the state of the art of community alternatives to the drug trade again testifies to the reality of popular culture in which commodified relations are the dominant but contested grounds for constructing selves.

Postmodern drug and alcohol abuse prevention aims to challenge addictive processes which turn people into static, thing-like selves which can be manipulated and controlled. It stands instead for flexible, fluid beings who actively create culture and whose attributes are open-ended and relational. It aims to challenge addictive processes which turn knowledge into privileged, petrified facts. Instead it regards knowledge as something socially constructed and intimately bound up with relations of power. It sees drug and alcohol use as part of this culture and does not attempt the addictive task of eradication through the control of others and the denial of awareness. It regards abuse and addiction as contestable phenomena which are part of a larger tendency for people to lose their fluid, open-ended natures within cultural relations in which control over others and denial of awareness is paramount. Finally, it joins with those democratic movements which seek to make full use of people's creative and critical capacities found within everyday life. This means that people continually reconstrue the cultural meanings of terms such as *self* and *community* as the boundaries of these terms shift within postmodern culture. It also means that people wrestle with those conflicting forms within popular culture which can both enhance and restrict self-expression.

NOTES

1. Douglas Kellner, "Reading Images Critically: Toward a Postmodern Pedagogy," in Henry Giroux, ed., *Postmodernism, Feminism, and Cultural Politics: Redrawing Educational Boundaries*, Albany: SUNY Press, 1991, pp. 60–82.

2. Elaine Norman and Sandra Turner, "Report from the St. Moritz Conference on Adolescent Substance Abuse Prevention Strategies," New York: Fordham University Graduate School of Social Service, June 1991.

3. Henry A. Giroux and Peter L. McLaren, "Radical Pedagogy as Cultural Politics: Beyond the Discourse of Critique and Anti-Utopianism," in Donald Morton and Mas'ud Zavarzadeh, eds., *Theory/Pedagogy/Politics: Texts for Change*, Urbana and Chicago: University of Illinois Press, 1991, p. 162.

4. *Ibid.*, p. 166

5. Stanley Aronowitz, "Mass Culture and the Eclipse of Reason: The Implications for Pedagogy," in Donald Lazere, ed., *American Media and Mass Culture: Left Perspectives*, Berkeley: University of California Press, 1987, pp. 465–71.

6. Nina Wallerstein and Edward Bernstein, "Empowerment Education: Freire's Ideas Adapted to Health Education," *Health Education Quarterly, 15* (4), Winter, 1988, pp. 379–94; "Alcohol Substance Abuse Prevention Program," Hospital and Detention Center Youth Curriculum, Department of Family, Community, and Emergency Medicine, University of New Mexico School of Medicine, n.d.; Nina Wallerstein, "Powerlessness, Empowerment, and Health: Implications for Health Promotion Programs," *American Journal of Health Promotion, 6* (3), Jan.–Feb. 1992, pp. 197–205.

7. Arnold Wesker, *Words as Definitions of Experience*, with an Afterword by Richard Appignanesi, London: Writers and Readers, 1976, p. 17.

8. Kellner, *op. cit.*

9. Ira Shor, *Critical Teaching and Everyday Life*, Chicago: University of Chicago Press, 1987; "No More Teacher's Dirty Looks: Conceptual Teaching from the Bottom Up," in Theodore Mills and Bertell Ollman, eds., *Studies in Socialist Pedagogy*, New York: Monthly Review Press, 1978, pp. 177–95.

10. Don Dinkmeyer and Gary D. McKay, *The Parent's Handbook: Systematic Training for Effective Parenting (STEP)*, Circle Pines, MN: American Guidance Service, 1989; Haim G. Ginott, *Between Parent and Child*, New York: MacMillan, 1971; Thomas Gordon, *Parent Effectiveness Training*, New York: P. H. Wyden, 1976; Michael H. Popkin, *Active Parenting: Teaching Cooperation, Courage, and Responsibility*, New York: Harper and Row, 1986.

11. "New Rallying Cry: Parents Unite," *New York Times*, May 25, 1989, pp. C1, 10.

12. Parent Leadership Project, City University of New York Substance Abuse Prevention Programs, John Jay College of Criminal Justice, Final Reports, 1990, 1991.

13. Interview with Gillian Kaye, Consultant, Citizens' Committee, May 29, 1992; also see "Drugs: Neighborhoods Fight Back, A Report from the National Partnership Project," Citizens' Committee, 305 Seventh Avenue, New York, NY 10001 November, 1992

14. "Neighbors Uniting in New York Crime Patrol," *New York Times*, Oct. 1, 1990; UMMA flier, P.O. Box 471179, Brooklyn, NY 11247.

15. The following is based on interviews with Kim McGillicuddy, Youth Force Director, and Angel Cintron, Coordinator of the Strictly Business Project, Citizens's Committee of New York, June 15, 1992, and the following handouts: "Posse for Change," "Strictly Business: Program Outline," and "Strictly Business: A Youth Entrepreneurship Project to Compete with the Streets," n.d., Citizens's Committee, 305 Seventh Avenue, New York, NY 10001.

PART 4

Recovery

CHAPTER 8

Adult Children/Inner Child

The fathers have eaten of sour grapes, and the children's teeth are set on edge.

Jeremiah 31:29

I am not my parents!
Stuart Smalley

The addiction recovery movement has spread throughout American society in a short span of time. Members have adapted the twelve-step program from Alcoholics Anonymous and have applied recovery principles to a variety of self-proclaimed addictions. Besides alcoholism and substance abuse, these include gambling, getting into debt, shopping, sexual behavior, and eating, among others. Many join because they identify as members of an addicted or so-called dysfunctional family or relationship (codependency). On the basis of membership in an alcoholic family alone, millions of Americans qualify to attend. The movement seems to appeal most to baby boomers, that generation born after World War II who grew up in a modernist culture and many of whose norms and values are fast becoming obsolete.

The idea of recovery from old addictive patterns undertaken as a process with others is an appealing one. It shares common ground with postmodern cultural practices which dismantle outmoded social forms and narratives. Yet because the recovery movement itself is not self-critical, it tends to lapse into restrictive narratives which do not break free of addictive patterns. In the following account I share my experience with twelve-step groups. I also attempt to wrest from the recovery movement some principles and practices which can become part of a postmodern cultural politics which can take on addictive relations in both personal and political ways.

In the second part I consider the image of the inner child as a popular cultural icon which has been adopted by the recovery movement. To some extent the inner child image is a melding of child and adult. Its popularity arises today in part because modernist boundaries between childhood and adulthood have blurred and because postmodern culture allows for a multiplicity of constructed selves. On an unreflective level its prevalence within the culture represents a crisis in childrearing and the nature of adulthood as children assume adult roles and parents become like children. For example, images of child-women abound in fashion and movies as role-models for girls, eroticized waiflike women who are helpless, weak, and unthreatening to men.[1] The inner child is an ambiguous metaphor which at best signals the possibility of a just realignment of social relations within a liminal epoch in which childlike and adult practices are being radically redefined.

WATCH THAT STEP

A few years ago after a lousy end to an unhappy relationship I was feeling stuck in certain patterns of relating. I became curious about the twelve-step movement after speaking with friends who found it helpful and after attending a conference workshop on "codependents in the helping professions." As is my custom I began by first reading about the program before making a move. I regarded some of the popular literature with skepticism; much of the analysis seemed simplistic and apolitical, and besides, there was no alcohol or substance abuse in my family. Also, the recovery language and ideas seemed easy to parody. Sure enough, "Saturday Night Live" did a skit on "Dysfunctional Family Feud" and spoofed daily affirmations and cartoons began appearing all over on codependence and inner child images. The idea of terminal recovery seemed capable of becoming a terminal addiction itself. ("Saturday Night Live"'s Al Franken later created a character named Stuart Smalley who hosted an inspirational talk program as a skit on the show and wrote a book entitled, "I'm Good Enough, I'm Smart Enough, and Doggone It, People Like Me!"[2] Since then recovery slogans have not been the same, and they may never recover.)

Nevertheless, at the time I found sufficient similarity between some of my own issues and background and the kind of problems the recovery movement was addressing and had reached the point

© 1991 by John Callahan. Reprinted with permission.

where I was willing to attend some Alanon and Codependents Anonymous meetings. For example, besides exploring my family upbringing and certain interpersonal patterns I wanted to reexamine the reasons I chose and have remained in the helping profession. Although helping others had been a significant value in my family and one I still hold important, I felt the need to sort out helping and caring about others from trying to fix their problems in a controlling way which teaches them what is proper while affirming my own niceness.[3] I also wanted to see to what extent professional helping was a means of self-denial by which I avoided dealing with some of my own needs. A similar issue was to examine my political activity: To what extent was it a genuine desire and yearning to help bring about social justice and to make the world feel like a home, and to what extent was it my way of trying to impose a particular version of the Truth on people who did not see things the way I did? My experience in the human service field and on the left is that there are a significant number of us who as children were assigned or took on certain restrictive roles such as rescuer or hero within troublesome families and who display controlling and self-denying behavior which now may even prevent us from helping to bring about the kind of change we desire. Both the

"Typical Characteristics of a Co-Dependent" from Codependents Anonymous (CoDA) and the "Laundry List" from the Adult Children of Alcoholics (ACoA) include the trait of feeling overly responsible for others. One CoDA sheet says that part of a control pattern is the attempt to convince others of how they "truly" think and "should" feel, and the Laundry List describes the tendency to "love" people one can "pity" and "rescue."

But this dialectic between focusing on legitimate needs rather than denying them and trying to control others can in turn be interrogated from a complementary political standpoint. To fail to do so would be to reduce rightful social and political endeavors to psychological phenomena. Like others, I have never been taken with the slogan that you must first heal yourself before you can help change the world; I do not see the two as mutually exclusive or that one is privileged over the other.[4] A crucial question then is to what extent the recovery movement offers insights and practices which can inform and affect educators, human service workers, and political activists who do care about others and to what extent it could in turn benefit from a critical understanding of power relations in this society. To what extent are personal control issues and the denial of needs part of multiple power relations involving the control of others and nature? The tension between a narrow personal view and a broad social view of power issues of control and denial shows up in the ensuing account of my experience with the twelve-step movement. Later on I would like to point to some ways in which these aspects can come together.

The controversy about whether people ought to be going to meetings who are not substance addicts and/or who have not been involved with an addict is an ongoing one within the program and testifies to the movement's flexibility, or ambiguity, depending on your view toward it.[5] Some members might have felt I was one of those people who did not really belong and was diluting the program, and in fact I never fully felt the meetings were for me. However, the program tends to welcome anyone who identifies with its membership, and it attracts a variety of people who voluntarily seek self-help. This is because there are now many different kinds of meetings someone can attend which refer to diverse social behaviors in terms of addictions and because the program is often socially engaging and communal in ways that everyday life is not. I ended up going to Alanon and Codependents Anonymous meetings for about one year and

attended some meetings after that. I also became somewhat familiar with Adult Children of Alcoholics (ACoA) literature. These
and other groups are all based on the Alcoholics Anonymous
twelve-steps principles and practices. According to some program
literature, ACoA groups tend to be more open to people from any
self-defined troublesome family and its members are more
inclined toward learning from outside authorities such as nonpro-
gram therapists and popular authors on the recovery circuit.[6]

The twelve steps are as follows:

1. We admitted we were powerless over alcohol—that our
   lives had become unmanageable.
2. Came to believe that a Power greater than ourselves could
   restore us to sanity.
3. Made a decision to turn our will and our lives over to the
   care of God *as we understood Him.*
4. Made a searching and fearless moral inventory of ourselves.
5. Admitted to God, to ourselves, and to another human
   being the exact nature of our wrongs.
6. Were entirely ready to have God remove all these defects
   of character.
7. Humbly asked Him to remove our shortcomings.
8. Made a list of all persons we had harmed, and became
   willing to make amends to them all.
9. Made direct amends to such people whenever possible,
   except when to do so would injure them or others.
10. Continued to take personal inventory and when we were
    wrong promptly admitted it.
11. Sought through prayer and meditation to improve our
    conscious contact with God *as we understood Him*, pray-
    ing only for knowledge of His will for us and the power to
    carry that out.
12. Having had a spiritual awakening as the result of these
    steps, we tried to carry this message to alcoholics, and to
    practice these principles in all our affairs.

For a time I learned, to borrow one of the phrases stated at the
end of each meeting, to "take what you like and leave the rest,"

and found some of it helpful. To an extent the simplicity of some of the slogans was refreshing and helped me cut through certain obsessive tendencies toward making things needlessly complicated. I became more aware of when I was engaging in certain undesirable thoughts and behaviors, and the meetings provided me with ways to let go of them and change for the better. I found it freeing to hear different kinds of people speak about similar kinds of childhood experiences and troublesome family patterns and tell of their efforts to overcome them in the present. To experience people coming together and sharing honest, personal statements as part of a safe, social endeavor was quite powerful. However, for better or for worse, in the end I did not "work the program," that is, regularly attend meetings, follow the steps, and find a sponsor, for a number of reasons. Like some of my friends who are also wrestling with outmoded aspects of themselves but who cherish their critical faculties, I find the twelve-step movement to be an exceptional amalgam of concepts and social rituals which are nothing less than both brilliant and foolish, sanity-restoring and maddening.

Whether the reader is an advocate of the program or a skeptic will likely determine whether he or she thinks I am "in denial" about my addictive patterns. In terms of the program a person is either in recovery or in denial, that is, still in the disease. One contradiction for me is that this approach is itself an example of the "stinkin' thinkin'" of which the program is critical, a dualistic, either/or, attitude which does not allow for distinctions, differences, and nuances. It was this aspect of the program which itself seemed addictive to me, what Elayne Rapping calls a "totalizing discourse."[7] I participated in those parts of the program which I could interpret to myself as making sense, up to the point where I no longer could. In the end I found the culture of the meetings was such that I was unable to keep going and sustain my critical stance at the same time; I was either going to have to stop attending or join and give up certain things about myself, some of which I wanted to shed but others which were too important to me and for which I felt there was no room in the program.

NO SURRENDER

The Alcoholics Anonymous (AA) recovery process on which all twelve-step programs are based shares similarities with some forms of therapeutic treatment which also aim to resocialize people. For example, some psychotherapists suggest that there are three phases of the twelve-step program which correspond to psychoanalytic ego psychotherapy.[8] They are an initial phase of engagement, a middle phase of working on one's ego strengths, and a third phase of integration. According to the therapists, the initial phase of the steps focuses on an alliance not with a therapist but with the group and aims to instill hope in the addict. They suggest that for alcoholics the transfer from a grandiose self to an outside, higher power is the establishment of a new ego-ideal (steps 1, 2, and 3). The middle phase is when the person works through the change. Working the middle steps leads to a healthier dependency on and identification with the program's ideals. The ego becomes strengthened through self-reflection (steps 4 and 5) and by taking concrete steps toward restitution (steps 8 and 9). The final stage is a synthesis of higher functioning ego strengths. The ego is integrated by practicing the program principles every day (steps 10, 11, and 12). The result is supposed to be a more mature, integrated personality. Some ACoAs who work the steps and attend meetings speak in parallel terms about reparenting themselves and providing for their "inner child." This aspect of themselves at some point should become more integrated with their adult self, allowing them to have more grown-up, fulfilling relations with others.

I myself, however, was not even willing to give up control by working the first step ("We admitted we were powerless and that our lives had become unmanageable"). Now, as Ellen Herman points out, every political activist knows it is anathema to admit powerlessness when the very thing you want is more power for everyone.[9] From this perspective taking that first step places you on a slippery slope leading to the next two steps, believing that "a Power greater than ourselves could restore us to sanity" and deciding to "turn our will and our lives over to the care of God, *as we understood Him.*" The sexist language is the official wording, although some people read *Him* as *Her* or *God*. The God part, also known as a "Higher Power," is the sticking point for a lot of people. (There are at least two small, secular networks of self-help groups which do not refer to God, Women for Sobriety and Rational Recovery, based on Albert Ellis's rational-emotive therapy. Ellis's absolute faith in his own brand of rational thinking makes any group patterned after it suspect for me.)

But there is a dialectic at work here. The italicized part of the third step is the escape clause which allows you to define God/ Higher Power in a flexible way so that He/She/It becomes a kind of do-it-yourself concept. People can and do consider nature, or society, or even Gumby, the cartoon character, as able to be a Power greater than themselves. One politically active lesbian got around the repugnant, patriarchal God image by defining her higher power as Marx's theory of history, historical materialism.[10] There is no doctrine within the program which says you must regard the Higher Power in traditional terms. God has become deconstructed.

The compelling side of turning yourself over to a Higher Power as you define it is that there are indeed ideas and social and natural forces which are more powerful than yourself, that you cannot control everything about your life, let alone others', and that when you acknowledge this dialectical principle you can feel more powerful and free because it then allows you to determine what you can and cannot do instead of feeling responsible for everything. The meetings end with the dialectical Serenity Prayer in which you pray, or hope, for the sensible qualities of serenity to accept things you cannot change, courage to change the things you can, and wisdom to know the difference. Turning it over to a Higher Power doesn't mean giving up complete responsibilty because you are still responsible for those things you can change. Historical materialism is not such a far-fetched concept for a Higher Power after all, since it asserts the analogous dialectical statement that people do make history through choice but not exactly as they please, through broader conditions greater than their will alone and handed down from the past; that is, there are some things we can change and others we cannot, and we all need wisdom to figure out which is which.

With the popular deconstruction of God/Higher Power the twelve-step program takes on a postmodern dimension. The concept is ingeniously ambiguous: it can represent something which is both part of yourself (members refer to their higher power) and also beyond it. It becomes a sign for the self/Self which shimmers between a personal ideal self and a larger, Other Self, each one reflecting the other. This dialectical approach allows for the possibility of transcending the traditional dualism of spirituality whereby inner, psychological, spiritual things are contrasted with outer world, political materiality. Spirituality instead is something which infuses everyday life and assumes different forms at different times. For example, one feminist theorist, Starhawk, when asked whether the goddess symbol is something within or outside herself, says, "It all depends on how I feel. When I feel weak, she is someone who can help me and protect me. When I feel strong, she is the symbol of my own power. At other times I feel her as the natural energy in my body and the world."[11] Some feminists who theorize about knowledge argue that this is a legitimate kind of wisdom which is not sloppy thinking. Instead it speaks to a fluid, relational arrangement between subjectivity and otherness which allows for identity, difference, and interchange.

The problem for me with respect to the program, however, was and is the idea of *turning over* my will and life to a God or Higher Power, however defined, which is giving up too much. It is not as if there is never a willingness or need to surrender to something beyond myself, whether it be to love, to desire, or to creative, inchoate forces somewhere within the world, nature, or myself; as Bruce Springsteen sings (with no apparent apologies to Kierkegaard), sometimes "It takes a leap of faith to get things going / In your heart you must trust." But the language of the program does not speak to me or encourage me to express myself in a fully genuine way, with enriching, complex metaphors which allow for interpretations and subtle distinctions. One must basically give up all control because one's life is "unmanageable." In one meeting I shared that the Hebrew name I was given at birth is Jacob, who wrestled with God. I said that, to the extent I am willing to deal in images of a Higher Power at all, I find this to be more of an apt one for me because I am never quite willing to surrender my own powers but instead must engage with other forces, albeit higher or stronger ones at times, with my full critical abilities on hand. Of course, this interpretation can in turn be deconstructed from different perspectives: besides the infinite number of Biblical analyses someone in the program might suggest that it means I am still addicted to control, and that, after all, it is the very nature of my disease to equivocate between wanting to combat my isolation and wanting to stay within the familiarity of my pain. Although this may contain some truth, it is not the whole truth the way recovery language would have it.

How the dialectic of the self/other takes shape within the group may be the most significant factor in whether someone works the program in an effective way. At first glance the meetings appear to reflect the consummate American quality of alienated individualism. People come in on their own for self-help. Their identity and anonymity are respected, and everyone can speak a monologue for a certain amount of time aimed at no one in particular and focusing just on his or her self/higher self. But in fact the power of the group is essential in providing support, and it is through the group that people let go of their futile, individual attempts to control things that are out of their control. From a sociological perspective, then, the group itself becomes a form of the Higher Power. This is true to the extent that it offers support and wisdom as a healthier parent substitute for the destructive or inadequate parenting the members endured as children and which they have taken in. When people "turn it over" to their higher power, they are in effect speaking to the silent but present group, which becomes an accepting, nonjudgmental, positive, and healing parent or higher self. The self is dispersed within the other and the other in turn infuses the self. But to the extent the group itself does not serve as a power to the prospective member, as was my case, then he or she does not gain a sense of what a Higher Power is like within the particular form of the twelve-step program.

One of the leading proponents of the twelve-step program, Ann Wilson Schaef, might suggest that by rejecting the group I am in my disease because I was too judgmental. She thinks that what someone takes back from the group is "often more of an indication of one's willingness and openness rather than what is or is not happening at the meeting. Judgmentalism is a characteristic of the disease."[12] But the latter sentence exemplifies the very phenomenon it seeks to condemn. It is this kind of blanket statement which dismisses, that is, judges, another's experience by equating it with a pathology that reflects a kind of thinking most disturbing to me. It is similar to a therapist who brands a client with the pathological label *defensive* because the client does not agree with the therapist's judgment. Schaef's statement invalidates someone's negative judgements about a twelve-step group by saying that the fact of making a critical evaluation is by its very nature pathological. After all, Schaef believes, it is mostly your attitude rather than the ongoings of the group which determines whether you can recover or not; that is, you should suspend judgment, or evaluation, and keep working the program. Schaef does not bother to distinguish a legitimate judgment (that is, the kind she favors) from the symptom of judgmentalism which occurs when she disagrees with the judgment.

What is absent from Schaef's judgmental declaration of pathology is the nonaddictive awareness of the fluidity of terms such as *disease, addiction,* or *recovery.* Like Starhawk's sense of the goddess, they are not absolutes but are useful in certain contexts and at certain times and not others. Yes, sometimes we have to let go of things, but we also need the full wisdom of all our faculties to figure out the differences. Such crucial differences include the one between the overly rational obsessions of the controlling male ego and useful critical thought, and between psychological and political levels of analysis.

The social rituals and norms of the meetings can be liberating or restrictive. On the plus side people are entitled to make their statements anonymously without interruption or criticism and for this reason many find the meetings to be a safe place. No one has to attend or say a word; there is no authoritarian leader, brainwashing, or social coercion, and the suggestion that the movement is like a cult does not hold up.[13] In fact, there is a fair amount of democracy in that everyone has an equal chance to speak and a say in the housekeeping procedures of the group. No one actually labels you as being in denial because there is no "cross-talk," that is, no direct dialogue during the meetings, and you are free to work the program at your own pace. One of the positive informal norms is to avoid "taking other people's inventory," to not gossip or complain about or criticize someone else. When you speak you "keep the focus on yourself": your own feelings, thoughts, and experiences, not a raging diatribe against a parent or mate, not an obsessive second-guessing of what a lover is thinking, not a denying of yourself for the sake of another. This is not intended to be a selfish exercise but to counter the tendency for people to avoid dealing with their own issues. Many people who have grown up in alcoholic or similar families have had to deny what they see and hear with their own eyes and ears and have been told that their perceptions are not accurate; in order to survive they learned it was more functional to tend to others' perspectives and feelings and as a result have lost a sense of their own. The slogan that you can take what you like and leave the rest is not simply a way to minimize conflict, as one critic argues, but is another useful dialectical guideline which respects people's needs. The principle of "attraction rather than promotion" and publicity is in keeping with the laudable goal to place "principles above personalities." The idea is that people come to freely want to participate instead of being aggressively recruited or pressured into following the program or some charismatic leader. Members also give back to the program through service such as tending to the literature, making the coffee, chairing meetings, and other duties.

The groups are part of a fellowship in which people share phone numbers and are available to talk at all hours of the day to someone in need. The positive aspect of a shared language of addiction, or the shared situation of being a spouse, sibling, or child of an alcoholic or member of a similarly troublesome family is that it allows men and women and people from different backgrounds to speak the same language and dissolve class, gender, and race distinctions within the meeting. Although women predominate at Codependency and Alanon meetings, at some Codependents Anonymous meetings there were as many men as women. Men also said they feel overly responsible for others' feelings, fear rejection, tend to give up their needs in order to please the other, and often need to have everything perfect. True, the groups do not address gender and economic power imbalances, as feminist critics point out, but they serve as a kind of postmodern forum for bypassing differences in favor of a certain language of commonality which speaks to a number of people.[14]

On the down side I found there was a conformist norm of language in the meetings with which I was uncomfortable. At some chapters the practice at the beginning of each meeting is to say your name and add something like "and I am a grateful, recovering codependent" or whatever. When I was the only one who consistently refrained from this, on matters of principle, I often felt that I did not fit in to the group in a proper way. ("Aha, so you *are* codependent and in denial about it!" "No, I think there is a subtle form of group-think going on which I didn't like. That seems more like the opposite of codependency, actually.") Now it can be a freeing experience to admit something about yourself in a safe, semipublic setting; it is perhaps akin to the lost practice of acknowledging your sin or mistake to the *gemeinschaft*, which allows you to reconnect with it. But although I felt, and had no problem acknowledging, that some of my behaviors had so-called codependent qualities, I disliked using the disease language as well as saying I *am* a such and such which totally defined me. There never seemed to be a place to address these kinds of metaissues, not just the meaning of the statement but the practice of say-

ing or not saying it, within the rituals of the meeting. Another alienating experience occurred once at one chapter when we went around the room for part of the meeting and just read from a Melody Beattie book in which she interprets the twelve steps. I found this practice disturbing because coming from an intellectual tradition I wanted to interrogate and challenge the text and have a discussion about what we had just read. I felt straitjacketed and somewhat dishonest about participating, but I chose to read that one time in order to give the group a chance.

The language of sharing also assumes a norm which I found constraining. Although the rule of no cross-talk allows people a safe space to share or "turn it over" (put your thought or problem out to the group and in the hands of your Higher Power), it prevents dialogue and forfeits a place where statements can be questioned and clarified. Before I felt I could share, I felt I first had to find out what the norm of the group was. ("Aha! So you *are* codependent and in denial about it!" "No, I think just being sensitive and sensible.") I have heard honest, powerful, gut-wrenching, and insightful accounts at meetings which moved and inspired me; these were often the reason I would continue to go. At those times the meetings felt unlike anything in which I had ever participated, including political meetings. But more often the sharing tended to rely on certain slogans, clichés, and generalities. I found that most sharing was about some difficulty experienced during the week followed by a positive statement that showed the person was recovering. I learned later that one informal way to gauge whether a certain regular meeting was a good one was whether there was a lot of "recovery" being spoken.

As other critics have complained, the language spoken at meetings is devoid of any social or political analysis of a problem. For example, people would talk about their boss or about being out of a job without any anger toward the economy and the powers that be or about the fact that sometimes paid work itself is just rotten and unfair. There was no speaking about gender or class differences. Many feminists are critical of recovery groups because they do not deal with issues the women's movement has worked to address and feel the groups water down political issues into personal pablum instead of connecting personal pain with political action.

A major criticism is that to see codependency as a disease is yet another way to blame women, since many women are raised to emotionally care for others. Without a political analysis of power relations, women may then fault themselves. Again, there was no place to discuss the difference between healthy and unhealthy caring within society, for women or anyone else. Within a political climate which is hostile to women and contemptuous of caring this is a serious flaw. The irony is that the groups are a potential way for an increasing number of people to reach beyond themselves and accept others, although many also use them to remain self-involved. I myself never felt comfortable sharing some of my personal experiences, in part because I felt the meetings were not open to the political and theoretical categories and constructs I personally used to examine my life, including class and patriarchy. Perhaps this may say something about my lack of courage to speak in my own voice. But I also learned that you are not supposed to introduce any other philosophy other than that found in official program literature. It also may say more about American society rather than the twelve-step program per se. At a workshop a political activist once mentioned that she attended twelve-step meetings in Nicaragua and that people found no contradiction in speaking about their personal experience in politically conscious terms. But of course even there or elsewhere such a politicized language could become a ritualized constraint.

What many critics who are not that familiar with the program do not acknowledge is that the informal conversations which go on after the meetings are just as important as the meetings themselves. They serve to counter the lack of dialogue, critical discussion, and impersonal anonymity of the meetings. They give people the chance to directly discuss issues and raise questions with others about what they said during the meeting. It is here that people can connect and are free to argue political and social distinctions, although I did not find many people who were interested in doing so. For those who find the program helpful, the safety and acceptance of sharing during the anonymous part of the meeting is nicely balanced by the personal networking which goes on afterwards as well as during the week between meetings. But if you do not feel safe speaking the language of the movement during the meeting and are unable to connect with the regulars, many of whom know each other and so are certainly not anonymous, you are likely to feel discomfort and alienation on both ends.

The twelve steps which are adapted from AA are the heart of the Anonymous programs. A key point about them is that they offer a moral alternative to the problem of drinking; that is, recovery from alcoholism means a whole other way of living. They include distinctly moral directives and aim to resocialize the addict toward healthier behaviors. Although the twelve steps have helped many alcoholics, it is not known how many have been turned off by the program. Yet the steps have been adopted as part of recovery programs for every kind of addictive social behavior. As a social and cultural phenomenon, *recovery* has gone from a term used by alcoholics to a generic word seized by other people who are seeking a way to go beyond patterns of relating they learned as children which they now see as hampering their development.

It is arguable whether the twelve steps as they stand are the best model to apply to overcome compulsive patterns other than alcoholism. Proponents claim that splintering twelve-step programs into specialized groups (for example, gambling, sex addiction, incest survivors, codependents) allows more people to identify with others, gain self-insight, and find better ways to live to the extent they are motivated to do so. Critics counter that the abstinence model cannot be applied to food disorders or relationship issues and that to see everything as a disease promotes a victim mentality which tends to lead to further vulnerability and a perpetual dependence on the program.[15] My mixed experience appears to reflect this conflict. I found that some but not most of the model could be applied to relationship issues. Yet I felt there was much of value within the recovery movement which could benefit from a synergistic encounter with progressive movements.

TAKING IT ONE STEP FURTHER?

With the widespread use of the twelve-step program, as with any new form of social practice, such as psychoanalysis in the early twentieth century, there is a tension between a conservative and normative moment on the one hand and a progressive and transformative moment on the other which must be articulated. Perhaps it is not coincidental that therapists operating on the modernist principles of psychoanalytic ego psychology find compatibility between their form of psychotherapy and the process of the twelve-step group. Both to a degree abandon rational thought and place primary faith in the power of the therapist or group in order to re-gain ego strengths or sanity, respectively. People in recovery groups need to determine to what extent the alliance and realignment with the group is self-enhancing and to what extent it only seeks to adjust them to a puritanical, self-denying status quo.

The twelve-step model requires that a member initially set aside his or her critical capacities in the service of a higher authority. From a progressive modernist perspective, to give over your vulnerable self to the group principles because you have a permanent disease over which you declare your powerlessness is fraught with reactionary possibilities for anyone.[16] When the recovery principles are removed from the confines of a voluntary self-help movement and are commodified as part of a burgeoning and highly profitable treatment industry, the risks of authoritarian abuse increase.[17] Private thirty-day rehab facilities or recovery spas aggressively market recovery. They accept insurance for various medically defined addictions and take on employees sent by their companies.

One friend voluntarily spent a month in an elite, prestigious facility when she was in a vulnerable state and had a mixed experience. Although the staff helped her deal with her feelings and family relations, she also described how they often employed recovery principles in a rigid, puritanical way which clearly deemed certain of her behaviors to be addictive. To argue otherwise was to be in denial about her disease and to fall prey to overanalysis. They also pigeonholed some of her issues into reducible disease jargon which did not match the problems as she experienced them, and she found this to be alienating and unhelpful. In this instance recovery language ironically was used as a totalizing discourse to restrict voice, prevent dialogue, and deny difference in the service of conservative norms. For those whose jobs may or may not be waiting for them contingent on their presumed recovery, the program language and norms become a form of social control which allows little or no room for disagreement with those in power. Recovery becomes encoded as certain acceptable behaviors: hard work, obedience, and temperate forms of leisure.

But from the standpoint of postmodern culture, in terms of the fluid nature of the self the twelve-step model is more ambiguous and allows for flexible, creative constructs of self, other, and higher power. Within this kind of space there is a hint of possibility of a progressive practice which allows for an alternative to the rigidly dichotomous, either/or approach, that either you must abandon your addictive self and rational faculties to a higher authority or stay diseased. From this viewpoint the model is not simply an apolitical, psychologistic movement which washes over political problems, as some critics maintain.[18] This is a distinctly modernist critique which depends on a rationalist, individualistic analysis and a view of politics as usual, divorced from personal life. But if codependency is not just a feminist concern but also a "family, community and societal issue,"[19] then to declare American families and the society in general to be dysfunctional, a psychologism in modernist terms, can be stood on its head and made to carry political weight in postmodern culture. It shifts the ground of the meaning of politics to include a broad-based grass-roots movement expressed in personal terms. It critiques hierarchical, competitive, nondemocratic modernist structures in which control of others, denial of voice, and dishonest relations rule the day.

Critics note the popular phenomenon of people who declare their victimization, mourn their past, and pronounce their self-recovery from troubled childhoods and addictive patterns on media talk shows and at groups, conferences, and in other public spaces. Wendy Kaminer, for example, dismisses these as self-indulgent displays which dissolve into empty rituals.[20] Elayne Rapping even regards talk shows about compulsive disorders as a form of social control by which television denies any political understanding of these problems and focuses solely on the level of personal and familial cures.[21] But these confessional forms may also contain a piece of a new, incipient form of political expression. In this framework politics is no longer the control of others based on master narratives but is the practice of shedding controlling, dishonest selves in favor of creating fluid, nonaddictive relations which allow for compromise and shared power.

The contrast between a more self-disclosing form of politics and the traditional individualistic, self-denying kind showed up in the 1992 presidential campaign. During the Democratic convention candidates Bill Clinton and Al Gore acknowledged participating in family counseling and adopted a confessional tone which promoted self-realization and the triumph over addictive relations. Clinton, an adult child of an alcoholic, was more willing to discuss his past than former President Reagan, who had a similar background.[22] Clinton spoke of his family's other compulsions, including his mother's gambling and his brother's recovery from cocaine addiction, and Gore spoke of his involvement in family therapy after his son was injured and used the analogy of the dysfunctional family in his book on ecology. President Bush, however, was averse to any introspection, and his campaign spokeswoman countered that "real men don't get on the couch."[23]

It is no accident that Clinton and Gore used popular TV talk shows such as "Donahue" and "Arsenio Hall" which rely on a confessional form of relating that allows for the interchange of subjectivity between the viewer and the program guests. Conservative Republican speechwriter Peggy Noonan is skeptical of the Democrats' approach and picks up on the surface nature of a public self-disclosure made through the media. But she misses the broader significance of this postmodern relation created by the media and reverts to the dualistic private/public model in her analysis: "The real pain in a person's life is interior; the anguish unveiled in these speeches seems a surrogate for genuine pain, and the device seems not revelatory but deceptive."[24] But the question of "real" or "genuine" pain is now rendered irrelevant. The point is that public confessions made though the media dissolve the modernist duality between inner and outer life and demand a new alignment of the personal and the political. It is not surprising that Clinton has received more letters than any other president from citizens who write as if they know him on a personal basis.

Two family therapists, Michael White and David Epston, propose a framework that helps connect up the two different discourses, one which analyzes dominant forms of power and the other which describes how individuals experience a personal problem.[25] They base their analysis on Michel Foucault's argument that power and knowledge are inseparable. Foucault argues that power constitutes people's lives through normalizing truths or unitary knowledge, constructed ideas that are accorded a truth status. Foucault also describes techniques of power or social control which objectify people and which have established the growth of unitary knowledge; under certain conditions people come to use the techniques and normalizing judgments themselves to regulate their own behavior. White and Epston suggest that people experience a problem when the dominant truth narratives which they or other people use to describe their problem do not sufficiently represent their lived experience and when significant aspects of their experience contradict the dominant narrative. Their therapeutic aim is for the person to protest and challenge his or her subjugation to unitary knowledges and techniques of normalizing judgments, and they argue that helping people along in this process is a political activity.

From this framework, when people in voluntary recovery programs experience a problem with the rules of their family and the modernist world in which they grew up, they also politically challenge the normalizing, dominant truth narratives of modernist social relations which control others and deny experience. For many of us the normalizing truths about work, the family, school, and the state, the official versions of reality offered by the Boss, Dad, Teacher, and President, no longer account for our experiences. These normalizing truths can then be highlighted as things from which people are recovering. For many baby boomers the discrepancy between the childhood expectations about marriage, work, and upward mobility and the reality of postmodern life is one between outmoded dominant truths and their own experience, which can be articulated as a cultural politics. For example, the slogan in some recovery groups, "I am enough," can be read as a corrective to the imperatives of a consumerist and competitive culture which induce in many a profound sense of inadequacy. This feeling in turn drives much compulsive consumption and money chasing as a means to seek security. It also contributes to unrealistic expectations about partners in relationships, who are supposed to perfectly complete the missing aspects of yourself.

From the political side those doing political work may also learn to recover from controlling patterns of patronizing, manipulating, and deceiving others for the sake of power. This process further stands as a potential counterweight to rigid or authoritarian tendencies in the left, in particular, toward moral and ideological purity (political correctness).[26] Recovery within a political framework may also allow some women and men to overcome the niceness which impedes their ability to effectively organize around their own needs. I disagree with the argument that "It was never 'us' [the social movements of the 1960s] that was the problem," but instead the "damaged," "dysfunctional" society itself.[27] Although we do live in a damaged society, to say "never" lets the progressive movements off the hook altogether. After all its members grew up in that damaged dysfunctional society as well as everyone else.

In terms of a radical approach, then, there are significant aspects of the recovery movement which I think are useful for many people. Perhaps its best elements can be reworked within shifting contexts such as educational and political ones, perhaps a political party. In particular, to allow for a safe, community type of place where people can tell their stories, put forth their issues, take moral inventory of themselves with others, work on giving up their negative and controlling aspects, and provide restitution to others, when done freely and in a noncoercive, supportive context, can be restorative and allow people to recover from troublesome past patterns of relating. These practices when combined with the safe opportunity for dialogue, the exploration of difference, a rigorous analysis of power relations, and sensuous, body-centered, ritual celebrations of pleasure, desire, and humor may make for a powerful cultural politics in which people come together around a common vision of a greater good. Creative use of the electronic media can enhance this process through new forms of expression as well as allow different people to connect with one another.

A significant aspect of recovery is to tell your story in the presence of others. Alcoholics, children of alcoholics, and others in the recovery movement do grief-work. They mourn the early losses and disappointments in their lives in order to overcome the negative memories of their childhood and families. As they are eventually able to face their pain, they can retell their lives in new, alternative narratives which appropriate lost positive forms of knowledge, strengths, and skills from their backgrounds. These activities articulate with and complement certain practices advocated by some progressive educational theorists. Peter Park argues that the practice of participatory research, in which community members actively investigate and work to change a problem in their community, enables people uprooted from their traditions to remember their history and to "bring back suppressed traditional knowledge that can be re-used for creating a self-sufficient life."[28] Stanley Aronowitz and Henry A. Giroux take up Foucault's practice of "countermemory" as a pedagogical tool.[29] Students rewrite history through the power of their own voice. They retell their histories through new narratives which reject predetermined endings and speak to a positive alternative vision of the future. White and Epston similarly suggest "archeological endeavors" in which people can investigate their family and community archives to locate useful subjugated knowledge. They argue that the desirable goal of therapy is for people to generate alternative stories that incorporate essential and previously ignored aspects of lived experience.[30]

All these practices critique the use of dominant knowledge to control others. They encourage people to instead rediscover, create, and share knowledge through new narratives which speak to democratic and emancipatory relations. To some extent they are in accord with the multicultural movement's efforts to deconstruct dominant narratives and reconstruct lost cultural knowledge within new postmodern cultural relations. They also are in accord with the feminist movements' aim to discover and generate women's voices in fiction, autobiography, and "herstory." Feminist Gloria Steinem has proposed that people create a network of groups which discuss both personal and political needs, although it is not clear how the political issues get addressed.[31] The creative, critical elaboration of some recovery program principles along with postmodern education practices may serve as an antidote not only to addictive relations but to some of the controlling dominant narratives of substance abuse prevention because they begin with the critique of control itself.

The Left and the women's movement can acknowledge the legitimate appeal of those aspects of the recovery movement which speak to so many people. They also can critically engage and inform the recovery movement around an analysis of power on both personal and political levels. On an interpersonal scale progressives, by attending to theories of power, can help guard against the repressive potential of confessional practice in which the group denies difference. On a broader scale people can learn how they become saturated with certain normative truth narratives from the dominant culture which contribute to their sense of overdependency, perfectionism, and other restrictive feelings. In this way they can find a way to let go of limiting patterns and develop their own forms of mutually determined relations. The self may emerge as fluid, many-sided, and multivoiced as it is both shaped by and creates a democratic, nonaddictive culture which allows for both commonality and difference of expression.

CHILDCARE FOR THE INNER CHILD

Inner child images have become popular in recent years in part because of the writings of Alice Miller, followed by John Bradshaw and other professionals within the recovery movement. The inner child is an ambiguous metaphor. It may or may not literally represent parts or all of your actual childhood; if yours was marked by pain and unhappiness from incest or other traumas, it often is not helpful or even possible for you to recall it as a positive image. The point is then to learn to care for and nurture your inner child, especially if you had a painful past marked by unresolved feelings of hurt and anger. But invoking it can also justify self-indulgence and ceding to infantile desires. Performance artist Eric Bogosian parodies John Bradshaw's plea for people to get in touch with their inner child by playing an aggressive salesman/evangelist who exhorts people to minister to their "inner babies." He reminds the audience that babies live in "the now" and do not worry about the consequences of their actions; the ultimate inner baby experience is the happiness of shoplifting a candy bar behind the storekeeper's back.[32] The further irony of the current popularity of the inner child metaphor is that it occurs at a time when society is increasingly indifferent and hostile to the welfare of actual children.

In more earnest terms, as in Charles Whitfield's *Healing the Child Within*, the inner child metaphor can represent a freer, more playful, assertive, and trusting way of being in contrast to disturbed patterns governed by rigid rules, denial of experience, and dishonesty.[33] However, Whitfield adopts an essentialist view which assumes that there is literally a hidden true self covered by a false one and that our compulsive behaviors are the direct result of unresolved inner conflicts. Although this modernist take is intuitively appealing, it is inadequate and dualistic in nature. First, it does not address the postmodern problematic of distin-

Calvin and Hobbes   by Bill Watterson

CALVIN AND HOBBES copyright 1992 Watterson. Reprinted with permission of UNIVERSAL PRESS SYNDICATE. All rights reserved.

guishing a true self from a false one but instead assumes that there is one true, essential self which can be revealed once all the other inauthentic selves are stripped away. But people now experience many selves with varying degrees of truth within different relations, and the idea of uncovering a real self begs the question. Second, this analysis denies the compulsive nature of everyday cultural relations themselves in which the self is embedded. It is not just the self but the competitive, hierarchical social activities in which the self participates, such as working, shopping, and playing, which are compulsive forms in their own right. I would like to offer two readings of postmodern male inner child images which I think manage to avoid both the cynicism of those who would entirely dismiss the concept and the glib, overwrought positivism often found in the recovery and men's movements. In both versions the inner child, broadly interpreted, is more about a living relationship between people and less a symbol of inward self-involvement. The inner child within postmodern cuture can signify a multiplicity of selves as well as a standing relation to an Other which may be both alien and familiar to oneself.

Shepard Again

One of the more powerful images within the inner child genre, written before the recovery movement was popularized, is evoked in Sam Shepard's 1979 Pulitzer Prize-winning play, *Buried Child*.[34] Shepard again sheds light on the crazy, disturbing, but often hilarious patterns of a classic alcoholic family system with its secrets, denials, and control issues. By keeping the meaning of the buried child ambiguous, he heightens the visceral, liminal possibilities of its disclosure.

In this play the family has a shameful secret which no one is supposed to talk about, and the members are estranged from each other as if they were half-dead. The elderly patriarch, Dodge, is a sick, bitter alcoholic living in a farmhouse in Illinois. His wife, Halie, is in perpetual mourning for their dead son, Ansel. Ansel died long ago, but Halie still mourns him as the family hero who could have brought them honor and wealth. Halie says that "when Ansel died that left us all alone. Same as being alone. No different. Same as if they'd all died."[35] Their oldest son, Tilden, in his late forties, is emotionally damaged. He has returned to live with them because of his limited ability to function on his own.

Halie had put faith in Tilden as the hero, but he failed and had turned to Ansel. Their second son, Bradley, is also incapacitated, having lost a leg from an accident and requiring an artificial one. When he possesses the leg he becomes a bully, but when it is taken from him he is reduced to a whimpering child.

In Act 1 Dodge first alludes to the family secret, that his flesh and blood is buried in the backyard, as a way to get back at Halie after she has angered him. But it is Tilden who is most eager to uncover the secret. It has been raining all day, but Tilden has come in from the backyard with a load of corn which he proceeds to husk in the living room. His parents are alarmed that he keeps rooting about in the back, and they insist that there is no corn growing there. When Dodge orders Tilden to put the corn back where it came from, Tilden dumps it on Dodge's lap. Tilden says to his father, "You gotta talk or you'll die."[36] Tilden at one point asks Dodge for some of his whiskey, but Dodge angrily denies he has any. Halie soon leaves for lunch with the minister to discuss the idea of arranging for a monument to Ansel. When Dodge falls asleep, Tilden takes Dodge's whiskey from beneath the sofa and finishes it off. He then takes the cornhusks from the floor and buries his father with them.

Into this family enter Vince, Tilden's son, and his girlfriend from Los Angeles, Shelly, who are traveling cross-country. Vince is eager to become reacquainted with his kin after a six-year absence but is shocked when neither his grandfather nor his father recognize him. Dodge is focused on his anger toward Tilden for taking his whiskey. Tilden says that the family had a son once but they already buried him. In one hilarious scene a desperate Vince performs a series of tricks using his body to try to jog their memories of who he is, to no avail. He then volunteers to drive off to a liquor store in the rain for Dodge's whiskey as a way to try to regain his place in the family. Meanwhile, to calm herself Shelly offers to help Tilden cut the carrots he has brought into the living room from out back. Tilden then confides in Shelly the family secret that Dodge once had a baby but he killed it and buried it somewhere in the backyard.

In the last act it is morning, the rain has stopped, and neither Halie nor Vince has returned. Shelly says she feels like she is the only one alive in the house. Soon Halie returns with the minister; both do not know what to make of Shelly and at first ignore her. When they continue to deny her presence, Shelly tells them they are the strangers, not she. As the outsider she confronts them about the secretive way they deal with their affairs. To Halie's and Bradley's horror, Dodge decides to tell the secret to Shelly, a stranger. Halie warns Dodge that if he does, he will be as good as dead to her, to which Dodge replies that that would not be much of a change. Dodge then tells Shelly how Halie had a son, which may not have been his, and that in any event it was not supposed to happen at that time when they were well along in their life and the family and farm were successful. So Dodge killed it.

Suddenly Vince shows up drunk and is violently throwing liquor bottles out on the porch. The family calls out to him, but he is the one who now asks who they are. Halie, distraught, recalls to the minister that Vince was "the perfect baby" and that she thought how as a child he must have been a guardian angel who would one day watch over all of them. Halie and the helpless minister retreat upstairs as Vince cuts the porch screen and enters the house. Dodge offers Vince the entire house because he says he knows he is dying and declares his last will and testament as Vince inspects his inheritance. Shelly implores Vince to leave with her, but he tells her he will stay because "I've gotta carry on the line. I've gotta see to it that things keep rolling."[37] He tells her that last night in the car he studied his own reflection and saw a face "dead and alive at the same time," a face that kept changing into his father's face and into that of his grandfather and down the line, faces he had not seen before but still recognized.[38]

At the end Dodge has died unnoticed amidst the commotion. Halie can be heard speaking to him from upstairs. She acknowledges that Tilden was right about the corn and praises the bumper crop of vegetables she sees from the window, which she attributes to a "good hard rain. Takes everything straight down deep to the roots. The rest takes care of itself. You can't force a thing to grow. You can't interfere with it. It's all hidden. It's all unseen. You just gotta wait til it pops up out of the ground . . . "[39] In a wordplay on the *sun/son*, her last words of the play are, "I've never seen a crop like this in my whole life. Maybe it's the sun. Maybe that's it. Maybe it's the sun."[40] While she speaks, Tilden appears from the backyard, covered with mud, carrying the corpse of a small child wrapped in muddy, rotten cloth.

As an ambiguous image the buried child appears to represent something both "dead and alive at the same time." In one sense the buried child is only a grisly, literal corpse which represents the perpetual cycle of an alcoholic family and its disturbed patterns of death worship. The family is mired in death. Tilden was obsessed with finding the corpse; Halie mourned her dead son; Halie and Dodge treated each other as if they were dead anyway. Dodge killed the child in the first place because it imposed on their controlled, deathlike lives. The appearance of the corpse coincided with the death of Dodge, who was in turn replaced by Vince, who felt compelled to carry on the alcoholic line.

But in another sense the buried child image is optimistic. The rainfall and sun/son yield up the bounty of the fertile ground. The secret is able to come out in the open in both literal and figurative ways. The child could appear in part because Dodge discloses his secret to someone outside the family. Dodge is released from his deathlike existence, and his telling of the secret and his death allow for a kind of rebirth within the family. The prodigal sons, Tilden and his son Vince, have returned home to unbury the child and carry on the process of regeneration on some hopeful level. Tilden symbolically buries his sleeping father with husks from corn his parents had denied were from their own land.

In *Buried Child* the liminal power of the images of death, childhood, fertility, and regeneration is akin to that of the New Testament analogy of the corn of wheat: "if it dies it brings forth much fruit," that is, the old self needs to die in order to bring forth a new one. That analogy also relies on a burying of a seed in the ground which allows for a rebirth. However, Shepard is clear that this process of regeneration is not to be carried out within the confines of traditional religion. His minister is utterly inept, hypocritical, and spineless and is of no help to Halie, who keeps turning to him for guidance. In the end it is left uncertain whether the alcoholic family relations, the drunkenness, loyalty at all costs, lack of recognition among family members, family secrets and denials, and need to control others will be perpetuated in a hopeless natural cycle. Will Vince carry on the wounded alcoholic family relations or will he be able to unbury his own "child," the one Halie said was the "sweetest little boy," a "guardian angel,"[41] and be reborn as a guardian of his family and the land? To an extent it depends on some things beyond anyone's control; as Halie says, "You can't force a thing to grow." Shepard's portrayal of a family system with its own rituals resonates with many families and suggests the liminal possibilities of uncovering many kinds of buried children.

Definitely K-Mart: Rainman

In recent years Hollywood has been taken with the changing image of the postmodern self, a self with fluid boundaries which allows for an interchange with other selves. The industry has made a rash of movies in which people literally transcend bodily limits (*Heart Condition*, 1990; *Ghost Dad*, 1990; *Memoirs of an Invisible Man*, 1992), return as dead lovers (*Always*, 1989; *Dead Again*, 1991; *Ghost*, 1990; *Hello Again*, 1987; *Truly, Madly, Deeply*, 1992), or change gender and identities (*All of Me*, 1983 *Prelude to a Kiss*, 1992; and *Switch*, 1990). Part of this trend of presenting protean selves includes movies in which young males switch bodies with adults (*Big*, 1988; *18 Again*, 1988; *Like Father Like Son*, 1987; and *Vice Versa*, 1988). These movies play up the inner child image by exploiting the boyish nature of men and men's difficulties with the adult-child, father-son relationship, which affects men's relationships with women and their own children. In *Big* Tom Hanks plays a preadolescent boy in the body of a grown-up who succeeds at creating toys for children but has no idea how to deal with a woman colleague who is drawn to him. That he gets as far with her as he does is a commentary on the emotional level of some men as well as on what some women will accept from them. In Stephen Spielberg's *Hook* (1991), a less literal movie about an inner child, Peter Pan (Robin Williams) is an adult workaholic executive who has forgotten his childhood identity and is neglectful and critical of his children until he is forced to rescue them on a return trip to Never-Neverland. Spielberg allows for the adult to return to his childhood in order to become more grown-up, which in his terms means more childlike, playful, and humorous.

Rainman (1989) suggests an inner child image of a different sort. It involves an adult child of a rigid, perfectionistic father and a family that like Shepard's also shares a secret child hidden from everyone. The movie is about the transformation of a manipulative, workaholic yuppie into a more caring, emotionally connected person. In Los Angeles Charlie Babbitt (Tom Cruise) is a driven young man trying to make a quick buck by turning over imported sports cars bought with money he does not have. He manipulates his business partner and his girlfriend, Susanna (Valeria Golino), who complains that he is uncommunicative and never shares his feelings with her. Charlie is obsessed with trying to work out his deal and has a habit of repeating himself when he is anxious and upset.

When his wealthy father, from whom he was estranged, dies, Charlie flies with Susanna to Cincinnati to settle the estate. In their hotel room Charlie tells Susanna that his mother died when he was two and that nothing he ever did was good enough for his father. At sixteen after failing to please him with good grades Charlie had angrily taken his father's prize car for a ride without his permission. The father called the police and let his son remain in jail for two days. Charlie left home after that and never stayed in touch with him. At one point he tells Susanna about an imaginary childhood friend, Rainman, who would always come and save him when he got scared. At his meeting with the lawyer the next day Charlie is devastated to learn that the only thing of value his father has left him is the vintage car over which they had had the falling out; the $3 million estate is to be held in trust by a hospital for a benefactor he does not know.

Charlie is stunned to discover that he has an institutionalized older brother, Raymond (Dustin Hoffman), who is an autistic savant, and to whom the money is willed. Raymond has an exceptional memory and mathematical skills but is unable to express feelings and depends on rigid rituals and routines to get him through the day. He does not like to be touched or hugged. He has absorbed tastes from popular culture such as religiously watching TV shows like "Wheel of Fortune," wearing clothes from K-Mart, and repeating again and again the modulated voice of a disk jockey from a commercial rock station. Raymond can only regard statements in literal terms and cannot distinguish irony and humor. When he is anxious he repeats a comedy routine which relies on wordplay as if it were an actual riddle he is trying to solve. Charlie learns that his father even used to allow Raymond to drive his cherished car on the hospital driveway. Charlie is furious at his father for never telling him he had a brother and for leaving the money to Raymond. He abducts Raymond from the hospital and plans to fly him to Los Angeles and keep him until he gets his half of the estate.

But Raymond is too fearful to fly or even drive on interstates. Through a number of exasperating incidents which for the viewer are often touching and funny, Charlie must learn to accommodate Raymond's rigid needs for comfort and familiar rituals. Over time he learns to take care of Raymond's anxieties and accept his limitations. In one scene Charlie crams Raymond into a phone booth with him in order to keep him from wandering into trouble while Charlie is calling L.A. about his deal. Both are having a childish fit, Charlie because he has lost the deal and Raymond because he is feeling trapped, but Charlie gives in to his brother's anxiety. In a scene in a motel Charlie discovers that his brother was Rainman who used to sing to him and take care of him, until he accidentally scalded Charlie in the tub, which led to him being put away. In Las Vegas Charlie takes advantage of Raymond's memory by playing blackjack and uses him to earn back the money he lost. But he also gives to Raymond. At Raymond's insistence Charlie teaches him how to dance. He then lets Raymond drive the car on the hotel driveway, a request Raymond had been making from the beginning of the trip. Throughout the trip Charlie tries to get Raymond to go beyond taking things literally and to understand what a joke is.

Back in Los Angeles Raymond finds it too difficult to adjust to Charlie's apartment. At a medical hearing to determine Raymond's best interests Charlie tells the doctors he has come to care about his brother and realizes Raymond needs to return to the hospital in Cincinnati. He tells them he is no longer angry at his father and acknowledges some of his own responsibility in maintaining the estrangement. Toward the end Charlie tells Raymond he likes having him for a big brother and they gently touch. At the train station as Raymond is leaving his doctor asks him if he will be happy to get back into his comfortable clothes from K-Mart. Charlie prompts Raymond to tell the doctor, "K-Mart sucks." Charlie points out to Raymond that he made a joke, then assures him he will have time to watch his TV show on the train.

If we allow, without diminishing the personhood of Raymond, that Raymond was a kind of inner child or other side of Charlie, then we can see the story as a redemptive one for Charlie and to some extent for Raymond as well. Raymond represents many of Charlie's traits in a more childlike form. Raymond is saturated with the shallow images of popular culture, as Charlie is obsessed with fancy cars and making money. Charlie's anxious habit of repeating himself is taken to an extreme by his brother. Charlie's drivenness for money is also without humor, as Raymond is without irony. Charlie too has trouble expressing himself emotionally and getting close to another, as seen in his relationship with Susanna. Charlie must learn to parent Raymond in a way his father did not parent him. During the trip he learns to for-give, accept, and care for someone other than himself, in some sense his child-self. By allowing Raymond to drive the car he becomes a good parent to his own child, since his father refused to allow him to do so. By teaching him to dance and touch another he allows a way for Raymond, and thereby himself, to become closer to another person. By teaching Raymond irony and humor he is able to gain perspective on his own humorless com-pulsions. This latter success occurs within the grounds of post-modern culture. Raymond represents a casualty of one form of postmodern life in that he is saturated with tastes and language from popular culture, all literal surface devoid of any critical per-spective. His speech is akin to digital coding in which there is a one-to-one correspondence with word and meaning. Charlie must use different postmodern weapons of humor and ambiguity of meaning to shatter the one-dimensional nature of Raymond's and thereby his own values, which they have absorbed in their own way from popular culture. Raymond can then joke about K-Mart, and Charlie can let go of the need to compulsively hustle money.

Raymond was the Rainman whom Charlie believed would save him when he was a boy, and by caring in turn for Raymond as an adult Charlie has been saved by him in the end. That is, even as a boy Charlie invented his own parentlike guardian who would comfort him when he was anxious, and who it turns out was liter-ally based on a real person he did not remember, Raymond. Ray-mond himself benefits from Charlie's parenting in a limited way and becomes more flexible, humorous, and trusting of contact.

But Charlie has changed the most by becoming a good father to a childish part of himself which did not receive love. Charlie had to work through his childish anxieties, closed-off feelings, and compulsions which stemmed from a relationship with a harsh, perfectionistic, and secretive father whom he could never please. He manages to come to terms with his own traits, which Raymond reflects back to him in a childlike way. In the end he is able to let go of his demand for the inheritance, be more expres-sive with Susanna, and even forgive his own father. In *Rainman* the inner child is a living, childlike Other who reflects back to the adult his childhood needs to which he must attend. By nurturing him the adult is able to satisfy his inner child and take on more grown-up, less addictive forms of relating. Charlie recovers to some extent from certain competitive, controlling, and predatory patterns which characterize American culture and becomes a more flexible, loving being.

At its best the inner child then stands as a hopeful sign that adults can recover their spontaneous, childlike nature and sense of trust and no longer need to assume dominance over others or deny suppressed voices and perspectives. It means they can surrender the myth that adulthood is equated with constricted expressions of rationality and control and instead engage in freer, more mutually satisfying relations.

NOTES

1. Elizabeth Kaye, "So Weak, So Powerful," *New York Times*, June 6, 1993, section 9, pp. 1, 10.

2. Stuart Smalley (Al Franken), *I'm Good Enough, I'm Smart Enough, and Doggone It, People Like Me!* New York: Dell, 1992.

3. See David Treadway, "Codependency: Disease, Metaphor, or Fad?" *Family Therapy Networker,* Jan.–Feb. 1990, pp. 39–42.

4. Elayne Rapping, "Needed: A Radical Recovery," *Progressive*, Jan. 1993, pp. 32-34.

5. See Melinda Blau, "Recovery Fever," *New York*, Sept. 9, 1991, pp. 31-37.

6. C. C. Wilson, "ACA Comes of Age," Sept. 1989, Adult Children of Alcoholics handout.

7. Rapping, *op. cit.*

8. Elizabeth Spiegel and Elizabeth Mulder, "The Anonymous Program and Ego Functioning," *Issues in Ego Psychology,* 9 (1), 1986, pp. 34–42.

9. Ellen Herman, "The Twelve-Step Program: Cure or Cover?" *Utne Reader*, Nov.–Dec. 1988, pp. 52–63.

10. *Ibid.*

11. Starhawk, quoted in Carol P. Christ, "Why Women Need the Goddess: Phenomenological, Psychological, and Political Reflections," in Seja Gunew, ed., *A Reader in Feminist Knowledge*, New York: Routledge, 1991, p. 294; see also Janet Mittman, "Creativity, Postmodernism and Paradox: A Rationale for the Non-rational in Feminist Pedagogy," unpublished paper, School of Education, University of Massachusetts, 1992.

12. Ann Wilson Schaef, "Recovery as Process," *Utne Reader*, Nov.–Dec., 1988, p. 73.

13. Herman, *op. cit.*

14. Treadway, *op. cit.*

15. Blau, *op. cit.*

16. See Wendy Kaminer, *I'm Dysfunctional, You're Dysfunctional: The Recovery Movement and Other Self-Help Fashions*, Reading, MA: Addison-Wesley, 1992.

17. See "Chain of Mental Hospitals Faces Inquiry in 4 States," *New York Times*, Oct. 22, 1991, pp. A1, D4.

18. Kaminer, *op. cit.*, pp. 151–52.

19. Mary L. Bassett, Bank Street College of Education, quoted in "I Need You, You Need Me," *New York Times*, July 14, 1992, p. B3. Some critics see recovery from codependency as necessarily embracing Anglo-western values of individualism and self-centeredness. (See Margit Kellenbenz Epstein and Eugene K. Epstein, "Codependence as Social Narrative," *Readings: A Journal of Reviews and Commentary in Mental Health*, 5 (3), 1990, pp. 4–7; and Jaime Inclan and Miguel Hernandez, "Cross-Cultural Perspectives and Codependence: The Case of Poor Hispanics," *American Journal of Orthopsychiatry*, 62 (2), April 1992, pp. 245–55.) But learning to stop feeling responsible and guilty for another's feelings does not mean you then must be selfish or detached from family members but instead can mean you can have better relationships with others when possible.

20. Kaminer, *op. cit.*

21. Rapping, *op. cit.*

22. "'You Didn't Reveal Your Pain': Clinton Reflects on the Turmoil in his Childhood," *Newsweek*, March 30, 1992, p. 37; "O.K. on the Self-Realization, What about the Issues?" *New York Times*, July 27, 1992, pp. A1, A10.

23. "O.K. on the Self-Realization . . .," *ibid.*

24. *Ibid.*, p. A10.

25. Michael White and David Epston, *Narrative Means to Therapeutic Ends*, New York: Norton, 1990.

26. See Lawrence Grossberg, *We Gotta Get out of This Place: Popular Conservatism and Postmodern Culture*, New York: Routledge, 1992, pp. 385–96; and Barbara Epstein, "'Political Correctness' and Collective Powerlessness," *Socialist Review*, No. 91 (3, 4), 1991, pp. 13–35.

27. Rapping, *op. cit.*

28. Peter Park, "What Is Participatory Research? A Theoretical and Methodological Perspective," unpublished paper, School of Education, University of Massachusetts, May 1989.

29. Stanley Aronowitz and Henry A. Giroux, *Postmodern Education: Politics, Culture, and Social Criticism*, Minneapolis: University of Minnesota Press, 1991, pp. 124–28.

30. White and Epston, *op. cit.*

31. Gloria Steinem, *Revolution from Within: A Book of Self Esteem*, Boston: Little, Brown, 1991.

32. "Eric Bogosian Offers Parodies of Humanity's Dark Side," *New York Times*, July 20, 1992, p. B2.

33. Charles L. Whitfield, *Healing the Child Within: Discovery and Recovery for Adult Children of Dysfunctional Families*, Deerfield Beach: Health Communications, 1987.

34. Sam Shepard, *Seven Plays*, New York: Bantam, 1984.

35. *Ibid.*, p. 73.

36. *Ibid.*, p. 78.

37. *Ibid.*, p. 130.

38. *Ibid.*

39. *Ibid.*, p. 132.

40. *Ibid.*

41. *Ibid.*, p. 128.

EPILOGUE

At the heart of the cultural politics of addictive relations lies the longing for desire and democracy, the struggle to create full, satisfying relations for all. An ideal over which many have fought and died, the battle now occurs within a postmodern landscape in which the body disappears, people traffic in a jumble of cultural signs, and technology is the language of pain and passion.

What does a radical cultural politics of addiction look like with respect to policy, prevention, politics, and personal recovery?

The best preventive policy against addiction is a just, caring society which guarantees decent income, education, housing, health care, and recreation as a right to all. Power in the hands of drug companies and other corporations needs to be dispersed within new forms of democratic community which cherish the contributions of all citizens who share power and knowledge together. In the short term a substance abuse policy which aims to help those in need in the least harmful way may be the most effective.[1]

Prevention specialists such as educators and health and mental health professionals can critically investigate and challenge everyday addictive relations together with those whom we serve. We can explore and contest cultural forms which restrict us and challenge the denial of knowledge which limits our power. Prevention, treatment, and recovery then become inseparable from the effort to create a democratic society which celebrates difference within commonality.

The Left can stand as a prefigurative utopian form of everyday life which fuses desire and democracy. As a force of moral outrage against the injustices of addictive relations it can practice recovery from its dependency on one truth narrative, from the need to control others, and from the denial of its own sensuous pleasures.

Recovering adults can locate their personal development within new cultural political forms which challenge addictive relations within everyday institutions. They can realize how their addictions are part of broader cultural forms involving power relations and work to change them with others. They can allow for differences in readiness and ways to overcome addictions instead of promoting one single message to every one.

In the past the great teachers of the West proposed spiritual and political solutions to the problem of addictive relations, the suffering of the flesh, and its tendency to seek refuge in false fixes such as idolatry. Jesus embodied the moral principle of the Golden Rule within his own being; the word and the flesh were one. To the extent that people enter into a living relationship with the Universal Signifier, the principle lives as well. Yet history has shown that people continue to crucify the Word every day, and its message is far from universal.

In his early writings Marx prophesized that one day moral knowledge and material science will each be subsumed under the other. When the world creates communism, commodity addiction and alienated relations will disappear and there will be one science, one form of moral knowledge. Yet the kind of world which believes in progress toward one universal truth has vanished and along with it a viable language that allows for Science to serve as Universal Signifier.

Today there are still attempts to seek a universal expression of truth which literally embodies moral principle. The spiritual yearning for a total moral way of life which can speak to an addict's cells, that is, which binds together the word and the flesh through a Higher Power, lies behind the recovery movement's drive to solve the problem of addiction. In this sense disease is both a physical and spiritual problem, a personal and political malaise.

But now there is no hint of a viable Universal Signifier which can provide a cure. We live in a world where no one cultural sign can mean one thing to all. The world has fragmented into a billion microworlds even as it ensures that a fast food joint, a video store, and a cash machine will always be just around the corner anywhere on the planet. And yet addictive relations themselves, as failed forms of life, give testimony to the continued quest for universal, transcendental, or spiritual experience. We now must seek these through the changing images of ourselves which surface and vanish within videos, computer terminals, satellite dishes, and other fluid forms of social expression.[2]

In the excerpt from the poem at the front of this book Walt Whitman, the poet of desire and democracy, prefigures the postmodern condition of today. He acknowledges the dissolution of selves yet senses an almost ineffable connectedness between them which transcends time and space. Everyone is fragmented yet still somehow part of the overall pattern, and even images of the past and the future commingle in the present. Elsewhere in the poem Whitman addresses the reader with his awareness that he is being read at another time, yet he leaps out from the past to join the other in crossing over the water. It is fitting that this epiphany occurs as he is in motion, crossing over a fluid border, neither on one shore nor the other. It is the creative elaboration of this very act, the sensuous, temporal, routine crossing, that allows for the hint of universality, the awareness of the unspoken web which comes from all things at all times, which holds the poet up and connects him to everyone across time and space.

It is for us to effect this transcendence through our own everyday crossings and within our own temporal forms of relations, those which dissolve the self yet bind us together. The embodiment of transcendent power, or democratic desire, is found in temporal forms in which subject and the other conjoin through freely determined creative acts. In these acts of border crossing addictive relations dissolve. Control over others and denial of self-knowledge vanish in a moment of radical recovery, and self and community can appear in the form(s) of love.

NOTES

1. See Mark A. R. Kleiman, *Against Excess: Drug Policy for Results*, New York: Basic Books, 1992.
2. See Celeste Olalquiaga, *Megalopolis: Contemporary Cultural Sensibilities,* Minneapolis: University of Minnesota Press, 1992.

ABOUT THE AUTHOR

David Forbes, Ph.D., worked in a school-based drug and alcohol prevention program in Brooklyn, New York, for nine years. He studied at the University of Chicago, the New School for Social Research, and the University of California at Berkeley, where he earned his doctorate. He currently teaches at the Borough of Manhattan Community College and lives in Brooklyn.

INDEX